LINCOLN CHRISTIAN COLLEGE AND SEMINARY

P9-DFN-142

God's Call to
mission

LINCOLN CHRISTIAN COLLEGE AND SEMINARY

God's Call to

mission

DAVID W. SHENK
Foreword by Leighton Ford

HERALD PRESS
Scottdale, Pennsylvania
Waterloo, Ontario

Library of Congress Cataloging-in-Publication Data
Shenk, David W., 1937-
    God's call to mission / David W. Shenk : foreword by Leighton Ford.
      p. cm.
    Includes bibliographical references.
    ISBN 0-8361-3669-1 (alk. paper)
    1. Missions—Theory. 2. Christianity and culture.
    3. Christianity and other religions. 4. Mennonites—Missions.
    I. Title.
    BV2063.S49 1994
    266'.001—dc20
                                              94-402
                                               CIP

The paper used in this publication is recycled and meets the minimum requirements of American National Standard for Information Sciences—
Permanence of Paper for Printed Library Materials, ANSI Z39.48-1984.

All Bible quotations are used by permission, all rights reserved, and unless
otherwise indicated are from *The Holy Bible, New International Version*,
copyright © 1973, 1978, 1984 by International Bible Society. Used by
permission of Zondervan Publishing House.

GOD'S CALL TO MISSION
Copyright © 1994 by Herald Press, Scottdale, Pa. 15683
    Published simultaneously in Canada by Herald Press,
    Waterloo, Ont. N2L 6H7. All rights reserved
Library of Congress Catalog Number: 94-402
International Standard Book Number: 0-8361-3669-1
Printed in the United States of America
Book and cover design by Gwen M. Stamm

1 2 3 4 5 6 7 8 9 10 99 97 96 95 94

To
Dan

Daniel Ray Wenger joyfully embraced
God's call to mission
which included serving among suffering people
in Nicaragua
until December 30, 1989, when, at twenty-three years of age,
an auto accident
while accompanying youth for a weekend church retreat
opened the door of heaven,
where Dan joined those multitudes
who are cheering us onward in the way of Christ.

90807

Contents

Foreword

I MUST begin this foreword with a confession: I had not planned to write it!

When my longtime friend, Eugene Witmer, wrote asking if I would consider doing a foreword for the forthcoming book on missions by David Shenk, I was honored. But I immediately wrote back that, as much as I would like to do it, time would not permit.

Somehow this word did not reach the publishers, who sent me the proofs anyway. I thought I would just glance at the book. After all, a good friend had introduced it, and I have always respected Mennonite writings on evangelism and mission. After a few minutes of scanning, I was intrigued and read on. Now I am, obviously, writing the foreword—for a number of reasons.

First, *God's Call to Mission* is a work of love. David Shenk explains that he was born and grew up on a pioneer mission field in Africa, among people who had never heard of Jesus Christ. There in Africa he became, as he describes it, "a voluntary and joyful captive of Jesus Christ and his church."

Shenk also writes from the standpoint of one who spent his entire life involved in the mission of Christ—from his childhood in Africa to his time working with steel crews as a Pennsylvania student, from his work with young street people in New York to urban church planting in Kenya.

I like this book because it is "Bible-based," in the best sense of that term. Some books on mission take a few texts from the New Testament as a launching pad, then spend the rest of the time on pragmatics and planning. Shenk takes the whole Bible—Old and New Testament—as the mandate, the message, and the model of mission.

I also like the narrative format. The author helps us see how Bible truth affects very real people, like the textile salesman from China who sat next to Shenk and "had never met a Christian before."

I like this book because it is theological. That doesn't mean it's heavy. It means starting with God and opening up what God shows of himself. When David Shenk writes of the "foolish cross," he asks why almost all religions have sacrifices. He beautifully shows how the quest for reconciliation from which sacrifices spring was answered in Jesus, "the best heaven and earth could offer," God's Son, the sacrificial victim who breaks the cycle of hostility.

I also like this book because it is simple and clear. Shenk avoids missiological jargon. He writes in words that will be plain and compelling to lay readers as well as pastors. Yet the material is challenging—based as it is on the points of Manila Manifesto (issued by church leaders who met at the 1989 Lausanne Congress in Manila).

Most of all I like the fact that this book is Christ-centered. Applying the gospel to our age of technology, Shenk writes, "Our explorations of the universe have revealed that God is greater, more powerful than we have ever conceived . . . and the greatest surprise is that God loved us so much that he sent his one and only Son to walk among us on planet earth. . . . Jesus is the clarification event . . . any image or perception of God which is contrary to Jesus is false."

Perhaps these small tastings and samplings will move you to buy, read, learn, teach, and pass on this book.

I am glad my friend's letter stimulated my curiosity to open this book. I hope this foreword will inspire you to open it too.

—*Leighton Ford*
Charlotte, North Carolina

Author's Preface

DIVERSE STRANDS are woven into the tapestry of this book.

I was born and grew up in a pioneer mission in Tanzania, East Africa, mostly among peoples who had never heard of Jesus Christ.

It was in Tanzania, when I was still a child, that the Holy Spirit invited me to confess Jesus Christ as my Lord and Savior. I said "yes." I was baptized with others in a Swahili worship event in the Shirati congregation.

I have become a voluntary and joyful captive of Jesus Christ and his church. I am a sinner, not worthy to be his servant; yet he has forgiven and called me. In thankfulness and obedience I serve as a member of the church reaching out to the poor and oppressed, and I desire that as many people as possible experience the joy of being captured by Jesus Christ, in whom we experience salvation.

My engagement in mission has been incredibly rich. It has included going, as a child, with my brother to the home of a Tanzanian Zanaki blind man every Sunday and guiding him to church with his walking stick; as a youth working with construction and steel fabrication crews in Pennsylvania; as a young adult preaching and pastoring in the Blue Ridge Mountains of Virginia during my college days; working with young street people in New York City for two years as alternative service to participation in the military, while involved as a member of Fox Street Mennonite Church in the Bronx; teaching

North American high school students for two years; instructing Somali students for ten years on topics as varied as English gerunds and the mystery of atmospheric jet streams; urban church planting and university teaching in Nairobi, Kenya; writing books on church history, religion, and culture; serving as a visiting professor in religion at Franklin and Marshall College in the United States; pastoring and evangelistic outreach in Mountville, a suburban American community; and the joy of being husband to Grace and father of Karen, Doris, Jonathan, and Timothy. Such dimensions of my pilgrimage in mission have formed me.

In over thirty years of service with Eastern Mennonite Missions, I have shared with churches in mission in more than fifty countries in all continents. For over seven years as director of home missions, I witnessed the miracle of several score new church planting fellowships being created within about a dozen language groups in eastern United States cities and communities. As current director of the overseas department, I am engaged with churches and mission initiatives within some sixty language groups.

These communities of ministry and witness, whether in North America or overseas, are present among people of extraordinary cultural and economic diversity—the gentle rural folk of Kussoth, New York; the casino addicts of Atlantic City, New Jersey; the exuberant black working folk of New Haven, Connecticut; the affluent of ultramodern Singapore; the isolated riverside villagers in the jungle heartland of West Kalimantan; the secular former Marxists of Halle, eastern Germany; the meek K'ekchi' of Alta Verapaz in Guatemala. I am a debtor to the peoples and churches within diversities such as these.

For the past dozen years, Mountville Mennonite Church has been my primary church community. That congregation nurtures my relationship with Jesus Christ. The preaching of the Word and the worship builds my faith and deepens my commitment to the mission of Christ in our world. The congregation disciples me. It is a community of prayer and a fellowship in mission. In my travels within the global church, I am sent forth again and again from this congregation. I am their ambassador for global mission.

The Bible has formed me and so has our modern world. As a youth I developed the rhythm of reading through the Bible from Genesis to Revelation. Daily prayer and reflection on the Scriptures forms my perspectives on the meaning of life and nurtures my relationship with my heavenly Father. My Bible is in my right hand.

In my left hand I carry *Newsweek*. My shortwave radio is also a companion for a window on global events. Through wide reading and listening, I keep informed about our global village.

This book is the fabric from the threads of my experiences and observations as a servant of Christ and his church in local and global mission. Eastern Mennonite Missions has encouraged and supported this effort in recording aspects of the drama of the Holy Spirit and the church cooperating together in mission.

I often pray, "Lord, what a privilege it is that to me is this grace and calling given to be the servant of Christ and his church in mission!"

Several people have critiqued the manuscript. Others have offered counsel. They have included mission and service administrators, students, young adults, missiologists, pastors, parents, laborers, professionals, and friends.

Important in forming this book have been Roy H. Kreider, Raymond E. Reitz, Rhoda Kennel, Allen Brubaker, Janet H. Kreider, Barbara Witmer, Calvin E. Shenk, Lawrence Yoder, Jay C. Garber, Robert Brubaker, José A. Santiago, Mark Emerson, Wilbert R. Shenk, Paul M. Gingrich, Galen Burkholder, Glen J. Yoder, Willard Eberly, Paul M. Zehr, Jonathan Weaver Kreider, Janelle Guntz, Linda Herr Wheeler, Jeryl Hollinger, Leon J. Miller, Cara Longacre, Karen Shenk Zeager, John A. Lapp, Irwin Rempel, Norman G. Shenk, and Richard L. Landis. I thank them all.

—David W. Shenk
Salunga, Pennsylvania

Introduction

Tourists "go." So do missionaries. Tourists go to enjoy new peoples and places. They take pictures. No obligations. No commitments. The people and scenery are all so very interesting. That's the tourist approach to the global village. It's a cozy way to view the world. The tourist approach is comfortable; mission makes us uneasy.

Why?

We are often uncomfortable about mission because we do not want to be arrogant. Most of us have friends or neighbors who are devoutly committed to faiths different from the Christian gospel. Some of these acquaintances, who never participate in church, seem more whole than many of the Christians we know.

We live in a world in which there are many viewpoints and religions. The cornerstone of harmonious relations with others must be respect for everyone, including the religions they practice. We suspect that mission might be a way of imposing Christian convictions on others, of relating in disrespectful ways toward others. We do not want to be insensitive and arrogant.

Western culture urges us to avoid developing any deep convictions about truth. It is all right to have one's private values and beliefs, Western culture asserts, but the different faiths of others are equally valid. Buddha, Mohammed, Krishna, and Jesus each have much to offer. Jesus is Lord for the Christians. But Krishna is Lord for the Hare

Krishna. Modern society urges the Christian to accept that all religions within our world are true and good.

This book is not a defense of mission; in fact, it is a critique of insensitive mission. This is not an effort to prove the validity of mission. Rather, this book describes mission from the perspective of the Bible. This exploration hears the call for mission to engage cultures gently. It is a confession of faith in God's call to mission and a narrative of the church in mission.

This exploration of mission is a response to the counsel of Peter recorded in a letter he wrote to young churches. A close friend of Jesus, Peter urged Christians to follow the example of Jesus in their mission.

> Whoever would love life
>   and see good days
> must keep his tongue from evil
>   and his lips from deceitful speech. (1 Pet. 3:10)

> But in your hearts set apart Christ as Lord. Always be prepared to give an answer to everyone who asks you to give the reason for the hope that you have. But do this with gentleness and respect. (1 Pet. 3:15-16a)

Mission, Peter counsels, requires respect for the other person. It also requires integrity. There is no place for focus on the negative in the cultures of others. Mission is gentle, sensitive to the needs and perspectives of others. Mission serves others in the name of Christ. Mission shares, with those who will hear, a clear confession of faith in Jesus Christ who is Lord and Savior. Mission invites faith in Christ.

This exploration probes the twenty-one affirmations of the *Manila Manifesto* of the *Lausanne Covenant* on world evangelism (see Appendix 1). Five thousand Christians from 165 countries gathered in Manila in July 1989, to hear in a compelling way of God's call to mission. That global congregation covenanted together for a fresh commitment to global mission. The covenant is known as the *Manila Manifesto*.

Shortly after the Manila event, Eastern Mennonite Missions (EMM) developed an outline of mission commitments fundamentally informed by the *Manila Manifesto* and the Anabaptist heritage of the global Mennonite and Brethren in Christ family of denominations. This statement is called *God's Call to Mission*. It explores the biblical basis for mission as well as the modern context for mission.

This book is an amplification of that outline. The thirteen chapters are tailored for use as a weekly study for a three-month period. Pertinent questions at the conclusion of the chapters probe the issues. A note at the end of each chapter recommends Scripture readings.

The first five chapters explore biblical foundations for mission:

1. the creation, humankind turning away from God, the promise of Messiah, and the call of Abraham and Sarah for mission;

2. the call of Israel to become God's covenant people in mission;

3. the amazing mission of Jesus Christ;

4. the formation and mission of the church as a sign of the presence of the kingdom of God among the nations;

5. the plan of God to bring all things under the lordship of Jesus Christ.

The next two chapters survey our modern world:

6. the characteristics of the global community as the twentieth century becomes the twenty-first;

7. the presence and role of the church in the modern global community.

The next five chapters explore expressions of congregations and people in mission:

8. the confession that Jesus is Lord within a pluralistic world;

9. the four pillars of mission—prayer, plan, partner, and praise;

10. the calling forth and empowering of people from the congregation for mission;

11. the sharing of resources for mission;

12. the incarnation of the gospel within culture and ways the gospel relates to other faiths and religions.

The final chapter describes congregations in mission among the Quechua of Peru and ways the new Quechua congregations are also becoming involved in mission.

The text narrative is only lightly documented. A bibliography at the end includes texts referred to in the documentation and other relevant resources. Unless otherwise noted, all biblical references are from the *New International Version*. When the use of the name of a person might be inadvisable, a fictitious name is used.

This book is excellent casual reading. It is also written as a college-level text on world missions. Sunday school classes, Bible study groups, or small groups exploring modern world mission issues will be fascinated by *God's Call to Mission*. The exploration hears and addresses the issues raised by the tourist approach to the global village.

1

In the Beginning

"OH! I HAVE NEVER met a Christian before!" exclaimed my surprised seatmate on a Bucharest-to-Moscow flight.

My companion was in his mid-twenties, a textile sales-person from Beijing, China. The high-decibel vibrations of the turboprops made conversation difficult, especially when he was trying to decipher my American-accented English.

Yet he persisted. "Tell me all about the Christian faith. In our Chinese schools, we learn that all religions are only superstition. I am surprised that an educated person could be a Christian. Why are you a Christian?"

With my Bible open, Cui Kun from Beijing and I explored the Scriptures; we began with the first phrase in the Bible.

Cui Kun gazed at that verse, then in gentle reverence he commented, "Wow! In the beginning God!"

Cui Kun's astonished "Wow!" is heard wherever people discover the first verse in the Bible for the first time. It is a worldview blockbuster. That statement is completely astonishing when compared with all other ancient Middle Eastern worldviews. This is also true for all other worldviews, whether of modern secular people like Cui Kun or animists like Nyerere Itindi.

I Worshiped the Leopard!

"I worshiped the leopard before I heard the astonishing news, 'In the beginning, God,' " mused the aged Nyerere.

We were enjoying tea in Nyerere's neat courtyard, absorbing the sunset over Lake Victoria's Mara Bay. The delicious coolness of early evening within East Africa's high plateaus invited hot tea.

"The leopard was the god of my clan. Other clans had other gods. The gods competed with each other. Of course, a few among us spoke of a creator, but the creator had little influence over the matters which concerned us; he was too busy. We believed competing gods permeated all phenomena. We were afraid of these gods. Even our clan god, the leopard, often struck deep fear into our souls.

"Then Christian missionaries came with the Bible. We were amazed by the first sentence in that book. 'In the beginning God created the heavens and the earth.'

"God created the leopard! That discovery broke the uncanny power of the leopard over my life. Now I have no fear, only peace, for my Creator God loves me."

A Worldview Revolution

Anthropologists refer to Nyerere's traditional worldview as animism or dynamism. I prefer the word *ontocratic*. That is a worldview in which nature and divinity or the divinities are united, are one. Hinduism is the classic example of an ontocratic worldview; all phenomena are divinity. That is also pantheism.

The ontocratic worldview is the soil from which magic and the veneration of nature gods and spirits flourish. Magic is the notion that there is impersonal sacred or divine power permeating nature. Through magic people try to bend that power to suit their purposes. For example, one might sprinkle water on the ground to induce rain. People also offer sacrifices to the gods or spirits of rain in times of drought. Such beliefs permeate cultures everywhere, unless they have been influenced by biblical faith.

The nature gods entrap societies and cultures. For example, the gods are linked with the cycles of nature. Dying and rising gods cause the changes of the seasons. People and societies are also linked to the death and rising of the gods. In such societies human history is a meaningless cycle of life and death. There is no purpose or direction to life. The gods are capricious and often malicious. The fate of people is linked to the whims of the nature gods.

The first sentence in the Bible announces that the stranglehold of all nature gods is broken. It invites a radical break with the ontocratic worldview. Wherever people hear the astonishing proclamation, "In the beginning God created," they experience an invitation to accept a radical freedom from all the gods of nature.

We Don't Fear the Birds Anymore

"In what ways is the Bible good news among your people?" I asked a Dyak chief living in the heart of the jungles of West Kalimatan, Indonesia.

He stroked his amber beard as he contemplated his answer, "We aren't afraid of the birds anymore. Even when they squawk, we just keep on harvesting the rice. We pray and plan and ignore the birds. It's much easier being chief now that we have the Bible."

The Dyak have believed that the birds are the messengers of the gods and spirits. Whenever they squawked ominously, all work had to cease, and the people offered sacrifices to the divinities. Sometimes the gods demanded a human sacrifice, a handsome man from a neighboring village.

Imagine the Dyak astonishment and relief to hear the good news recorded in the first sentence in the Bible—"In the beginning God created"!

No wonder it is now easier to be a chief. God created the birds. They are not gods to be feared. And God is good.

Faith in God the Creator has broken the stranglehold of the birds; the power of the leopard and all other gods has been broken.

A Faith for Secular People?

Although Cui Kun from Beijing might not be aware of it, the first chapter of the Bible nurtured the perspectives which have made a technological-secular worldview possible. In fact, that might account for his fascination with the Bible. There is an uncanny suspicion all around the world these days that the Bible is the real source of the desirable qualities within secular Westernized cultures.

"I am a Muslim, but I want to be a secular man with faith in God. Islam cannot provide that kind of faith. Can it be that Christianity is the faith for a secular person?" Mohammed mused with me over a late night tea in our Mogadishu, Somalia, home. (Islam is the name of the religion and means the submission to God which is peace. Muslim refers to a believer who practices Islam.)

I probed Mohammed, "What leads you to ask that question?"

"Because the church is the community most concerned for the secular well-being of people. Of course, Christians believe in life after death, yet in this life now you really work for the uplift of people. In Somalia you have been the first to encourage formal education for women."

"Secular" comes from the Latin word *saecularis*, meaning "time." A secular person is one who believes that our time on earth is real. A secularist believes that life is not an illusion, as Hinduism suggests; it is not without hope, as in African traditional religion; it is not entrapped by the nature gods, as described by the ancient Greek poet Homer.

Is the Christian faith especially equipped to empower and enable people to work for human development within time? We observe that even the concept of forward-looking secular human development is absent in all societies until they have been exposed to the Bible or to cultures which have been nurtured by biblical faith (van Leewen, 411-421).

Some societies are attracted to the Christian faith especially because of the secular dimensions of the gospel. They want a faith for living in a secularizing world. That is one reason for the rapid growth of the church in Singapore during the last two decades.

"Why are so many people in Singapore becoming Christians?" I asked my host, Tan Kok Beng. "I understand that in the 1980s, the number of Christians grew from 10 to 22 percent of the population."

Tan Kok Beng responded forthrightly, "Because people are seeking a faith for modern times. Christianity is that faith. The Bible invites people to turn away from superstition, nature gods, or ancestral spirits. The Bible commands people to care for and develop the good earth."

That is a secular command! Perhaps my friend Mohammed rightly muses that Christianity is the right faith for a secular person.

Till the Earth and Trim the Trees!

In the first pages of the Bible, God forms a covenant with the first human family. They are invited into a right and joyful relationship with their Creator and are to work with God in making the earth better. How? Have children. Till the soil. Trim the trees. Name the animals.

Work is good. We are commanded to work for the development of the good earth! That is why Creation becomes "very good" only after people are created.

Several themes from the first chapter of the Bible are the seedbed of a secular-technological worldview.

1. God creates and sustains the good earth, but it is other than divinity. Theologians refer to this conviction as the transcendent worldview. No god will bite you for digging in the garden, for the earth is not a divinity.

2. God is good and not capricious; God has planned and organized creation excellently. For that reason the earth and all creation is good and understandable.

3. People are created in God's own image. We are capable of observing and understanding the astonishing complexities of creation. We are responsible to work with God in caring for and developing the good earth.

These three themes have permeated Western culture. All the leading conceptualizers of the European scientific revolution of the 1500s and 1600s accepted these convictions as foundational. That revolution would never have been possible without these biblical themes.

A Colossal Catastrophe!

Alas! Genesis 3 describes a colossal catastrophe. The parents of all humanity turned away from their Creator. They misused the precious gift of human choice and freedom. Rather than confess that their Creator was at the center of the universe, they sought to become that center. In defiance against God, they ate from the tree of the knowledge of good and evil.

Evil enters human experience through the window of human choice. God created people in his image. This means that people are able to make valid personal choices. God experiences great joy when we voluntarily accept his invitation to worship him and enjoy fellowship with him. However, he never violates our freedom to turn away from and ignore or defy him. He respects our freedom. Evil enters when we choose to misuse our freedom.

Whose Fault Is It?

We are responsible. That is disturbing.

Other religions and philosophies often deny the reality of evil. They squirm at any notion that evil enters human experience through voluntary choice. Most religions blame the gods or spirits for human suffering. Hinduism and Buddhism blame ignorance for our failures. So do most philosophies. Others blame environment or heredity or the subconscious libido for the undesirable things we might do. The philosophies and religions of humankind mostly dodge the issue of evil; they avoid considering the reality of evil and do not face human responsibility for evil.

The Genesis account does describe the devil appearing in the garden where Adam and Eve lived. He came in the guise of a serpent and with enticing words encouraged rebellion against God. The Bible describes the devil and hosts of spirit beings as also having the ability to choose between good and evil. They have chosen to be enemies of their Creator and seek to destroy all that is good. That is why the devil urged Adam and Eve to turn against their Creator.

While the Bible does not deny the influence of factors such as an unwholesome environment or the devil, the Bible insists that the core root of evil is personal choice. Persons are responsible for the evil they do. The first human parents turned away from God; they were responsible for their choice and the consequences.

Broken Relationships

The tragedy of turning away from God, the life-giver, permeates all societies. Adam and Eve turned from God; all people everywhere also experience the enticement and reality of turning from their Creator. All people taste the evil, the wickedness, the brokenness of those personal and collective choices.

Here are consequences of self-centered choices.

Instead of our work blessing the good earth with wholesome development, the earth is now cursed because of us. We ruin the good earth through ecological irresponsibility; it produces thorns and thistles.

How long has God been creating and preparing this planet so that people could exist and have a good place in which to live? Are the scientists correct when they consider a billion years? It's not just the time which amazes us; it is also the intricacies and complexities of creation. Even the slightest deviation would make life impossible. God has planned well and with care for the creation of people.

Now we have developed hydrogen bombs. In minutes we can destroy it all. Indeed the earth is cursed because of us! In our wickedness we have forced the good earth to bring forth thistles called nuclear bombs. We have created many other thistles as well, including plastic bags which never decompose!

Evil is present even within the most precious human relationships. Instead of bringing joy, our sexuality becomes exploitative and painful. The man dominates the woman. She acquiesces. Too often sexual mores and marriage institutions reflect that sad reality.

Children should be a blessing; yet too often inter-generational strife creates deep pain. Sibling rivalry brought murder right into the first human family. No wonder the mother and father of all humanity were ashamed; as they turned away from God, they felt guilt.

Hiding in the Bushes

Adam and Eve sewed together fig leaves to cover their shame; they hid behind the bushes hiding from their Creator.

"Where are you?" pleaded God as he sought Eve and Adam.

"Here we are, hiding behind this bush," Adam moaned.

What a tragedy! Eve and Adam, whimpering behind the bushes, trying to hide from the one who had created them and loved them. Yet God did not abandon them. He walked right into the garden where they lived.

And he called, confronted, and invited. "Adam and Eve, where are you?"

God Is the Missionary!

God seeking us is the drama of the Bible. This is mission. Although we turn away from God, he never turns away from us. The Bible describes God entering the garden of human community from generation to generation, inviting people to turn (repent) toward him, their Creator. God is the compassionate missionary.

On the very day of that first human rebellion, God pronounced judgment on the devil and made a promise to all people. He would intervene decisively to save people from evil. He would send the Messiah!

Facing the snakelike devil, God declared, "And I will put enmity between you and the woman, and between your offspring and hers; he will crush your head, and you will strike his heel," God declared as he faced the snakelike devil (Gen. 3:15).

This was the first promise concerning the Messiah. He would be born of the woman; he would be wounded; he would crush the power of evil. In various ways God kept renewing that promise century after century. "The Messiah will come," God guaranteed.

Christos is Greek for the Hebrew Messiah. The English term is

Christ. The name means the anointed one. In ancient times the Hebrews anointed their kings with oil. The Messiah is the one anointed by God to save people from evil and to rule the earth. This exploration uses both names: Messiah and Christ.

The Bible

The Bible is the drama of God fulfilling that promise to send the Messiah.

The first portion of the Bible, known as the Old Testament (Covenant), was written before the birth of the Messiah. A significant part of the Old Testament is the account of Abraham and the covenant people known as Israel. These people heard God's call and rather reluctantly became his covenant people. These Scriptures include the messages of prophets who called on people to repent, to make a U-turn away from self-centeredness toward God and the covenant.

For a thousand years, different prophets provided intriguing and rather bewildering etchings concerning the Messiah God would someday send. He would be from the people of Israel and of King David's family. He would be born of a virgin in Bethlehem in Judea. He would be from Nazareth in Galilee. He would come out of Egypt. He would be a righteous king who would rule forever, saving people from their sins. *And* he would be rejected by his own people and suffer and die with the wicked.

The second portion of the Bible is called the New Testament (Covenant) and was written after the birth of the Messiah.

The Bible is the account of God calling a people to serve him in mission among the nations. God's call for a people who are faithful in mission begins with Abraham and Sarah.

God Called Abraham and Sarah

Just as Eve and Adam are the parents of all people, so Abraham and Sarah many centuries later became the faith parents of people who accept God's invitation to turn toward him and become his chosen people to serve in mission.

If the first sentence in the Bible is a worldview blockbuster, God's call to Abraham and Sarah is a cultural and sociological blockbuster. They were a Mesopotamian family, living a good life in Haran (within the borders of modern Iraq). They were probably seminomadic, herding cattle for their livelihood.

Then God called, "Leave your country, your people, and your father's household, and go to the land I will show you!"

For the close-knit Middle Eastern families of four thousand years ago, the notion of leaving your extended family and wandering as pilgrims among strange lands and peoples was incomprehensible. Yet the call of God to Abraham and Sarah was an invitation into a voluntary covenant, with God and others, more precious and enduring than family ties.

Sarah and Abraham are a great divide in human history. They are the first missionaries! Their journey with God in mission reveals important qualities of all faithful mission. We observe their journey with care, for these first missionary parents have much to teach modern missionaries.

Their Mission Is a Blessing

God clinched the call with several promises. The most amazing was this: "All peoples on earth will be blessed through you" (Gen. 12:3).

Now that is not the way the gods of the religions operate. The ancient and modern gods of people empower their favorite clients with the ability to prosper, even at the expense of others. The gods of the nations give prosperity to their devotees; they never consider blessing others outside their respective realms.

Anyone who says "yes" to God, discovers that she is becoming a blessing to others. That is a miracle. Whenever we turn toward God, our lives begin to bless others. That is true even when we experience hardship in our obedience to God.

Their Mission Includes Failure

Hardship is exactly what Abraham and Sarah experienced. Soon after leaving Haran, they arrived in Canaan. Some of their new neighbors were not very hospitable. The rains failed, and there was famine. It wasn't easy leaving home only to discover trouble. Yet even within these troubles, Abraham and Sarah were becoming a blessing to others.

Abraham and Sarah were not ideal examples of godly people. Twice Abraham was deceptive about his wife, saying she was his sister. Sarah was a stunning beauty. He feared his unfamiliar neighbors might kill him to marry Sarah. Not only was he deceptive, he was ready to exchange his wife for his life!

The couple didn't have rock-solid faith in God. They doubted

God's ability to fulfill his promise of providing them with a son, for Sarah had always been barren, and she was past her menses.

Without any counsel from God, Abraham and Sarah schemed. Abraham had intercourse with Sarah's maid, Hagar. A son, Ishmael, was born. That decision led to a deep cleavage in the home of Abraham. Jealousy reigned. These character etchings reveal moral and faith failures.

Yet in the midst of their failures, God was at work. Abraham and Sarah reveal that it is the grace of God which enables a person or a people to be involved in mission. No one is righteous enough to deserve God's call; no one is good enough to have the privilege of participating in the mission of God.

The call of God is a gift of his grace. Sarah and Abraham responded to God's call in wonder and in faltering faith. Throughout the centuries others, whose lives also reveal faltering faith, have followed the example of Sarah and Abraham by gratefully saying "yes" to God.

Mission Stretches Us

Following the call of God means leaving the evil in our cultures and becoming a new kind of people who influence our societies in wholesome directions. For example, in Haran people often sacrificed their babies to the nature god, the moon. Sarah and Abraham abandoned such practices as they began their journey with God.

It is always that way. God's covenant people are a people of change; they seek to transform culture and societies in ways which enhance human well-being. They turn away from evil and destructive practices.

A good way to evaluate a culture is to ask how that culture cares for its children. Sarah and Abraham left a culture which sacrificed babies to the gods; they formed a culture in which children were precious.

Abraham and Sarah were stretched in other ways as well. God promised them a son. They waited twenty-five years! Genesis 12—21 describes the agony of that wait. Sarah was ninety and Abraham one hundred years old when the promised son was born.

They named him Isaac, meaning laughter. Sarah guessed that people would chuckle in wonder whenever they heard she had a baby at age ninety. A few thousand years later, we do still chuckle, thinking about aged Sarah holding newborn Isaac.

However, tension developed between Ishmael, Hagar's son, and

Isaac, Sarah's son. Muslims trace their spiritual and covenantal lineage to Abraham through Ishmael. Israel considers Isaac and his son, Jacob (Israel), patriarchs of their peoplehood. Even today Muslim and Jewish people live within the long shadow of the conflict between Isaac and Ishmael in Abraham's home.

Mission Is Being a Good Neighbor

God promised Sarah and Abraham ample land for them and their descendants right within Palestine. Yet Abraham was a stranger in this land of promise. He had no army. The peoples among whom he lived in Palestine were much stronger than he. Abraham could only receive land through faith in the promise of God.

And he did acquire land. God enabled him to gain acceptance of the peoples among whom he lived. Abraham cultivated that acceptance by being a good neighbor. When he needed a burial plot, he paid Ephron the Hittite a fair price for that spot of earth.

Abraham acquired a place in the land nonviolently; he earned the favor of the people. This has always been a core theme in biblical mission. God's people in mission are a blessing to their neighbors; they live generously; they live nonviolently. They earn a place among the peoples by being good neighbors.

Good neighborliness is a core dimension of fruitful mission. God's people in mission need to earn a welcome. When they do violence to a culture or a people, they are not a blessing and they certainly are not welcome.

Abraham and Sarah were vulnerable missionary pilgrims. Had the Canaanites turned against them, they would have died instantly. They were completely dependent on the call and promise of God and the goodwill of the people among whom they lived.

Sometimes the church in mission has ignored the Abraham-and-Sarah principle of being a blessing. An example is the manner in which the sword and the Bible were used together in the European domination of indigenous peoples in the Americas. The fusion of mission with imperial conquest in the Americas has been a disaster for the indigenous peoples. That kind of mission is not biblical; it is not a blessing.

Missionary Stauffer Meets Chief Nyatega

When in 1933 missionary Elam Stauffer arrived at Shirati on Lake Victoria's eastern shore in Tanganyika, he sought out the chief of the Luo clan who inhabited the region.

They enjoyed the appropriate formalities. Then Stauffer asked, "May we enjoy the blessing of living as guests in your land? We in turn will bless your people with the Word of God and with education and medical ministries."

"Welcome!" exclaimed Chief Nyatega. "And your home will be on Katuru Hill!"

From that seed on Katuru Hill, a church has grown which has spread across the nation. A hospital thrives on that hill, just as missionary Stauffer had promised.

All who say "yes" to God's call to mission discover that they are blessed and become a blessing to others.

* * *

This chapter has explored God's astonishing revelation concerning the human condition recorded in Genesis 1—3. These biblical truths are a gift of freedom from enslavement to nature and nature gods.

Sadly the first human parents chose to turn away from God; in various ways all people participate in that tragic choice. Evil enters our experience through those choices of rejecting our life-giving creator.

Yet God has not abandoned us. He comes into the garden of our lives inviting us to turn around and renew fellowship with him. He promised to send the Messiah who, although wounded, would crush evil.

God also called Abraham and Sarah as the faith parents of all who hear and obey the call of God for mission within our world. Those who walk in mission as Abraham and Sarah did become a blessing to others.

The next chapter explores God's call to mission of a people known as Israel. They became an amazing nation!

Reflection

1. In what ways is the first sentence in the Bible amazing to people with

(a) a secular-atheistic worldview?

(b) an ontocratic worldview?

2. How would you respond to Mohammed who asked, "Is Christianity the faith for a secular person?"

3. Reflect on Abraham and Sarah as the parents of the worldwide missionary movement. What can the modern church in mission learn from their experience?

4. Consider examples of the church in mission being a blessing. Consider examples in which mission has not been a blessing. What is at the root of the differences?

5. How could your congregation participate in extending blessing "to all nations"? Consider ways your church can receive the blessing of these same "nations."

6. In what ways is your congregation known in your community as a people who are a blessing to those not involved in your church family? How could your congregation become a greater blessing in your community? To what extent are members of your congregation a blessing in the workplace?

* * *

Suggested background Scriptures—Genesis 1—3; 12:1-3; 17:19-21; Ephesians 1:3-10; Colossians 1:19-20.

2

An Amazing Nation

"IT IS a miracle!" exclaimed two Romanian youth, Livia and Ioan. With tears of wonder they described two hundred thousand people kneeling, including even communists and atheists, joining with the Christians in prayer.

We were standing in Opera Square in the center of Timisoara, Romania. These youth, Livia and Ioan, were describing the December 1989 prayer vigils which preceded the overthrow of the communist regime of Nicolae Ceausescu.

The two youth spoke in careful English, "On the sixteenth of December, the Christians in the Reformed Church had an all-night prayer vigil because the communist authorities had demanded that their pastor leave the city. By the next day Christians from other churches joined the vigil.

"Soon the assembly had grown so large they had to move into Opera Square, the large open area in the city center. Then soldiers moved in and opened fire. Many were killed, even children running for safety. Trucks picked up the dead and buried them in a mass grave.

"Yet the killings did not stop the prayer vigil. The assembly kept growing. When word of the killings in Timisoara spread to other areas of Romania, other vigils formed in other cities. By December 22 the vigil at Opera Square had grown to 200,000 people. The soldiers moved in a second time with guns at the ready.

"The air was explosive. A pastor mounted a podium.

" 'I have a word from the Lord for the soldiers,' the pastor announced. 'Lay down your arms!'

"And they did.

"The pastor called on that throng of 200,000 to kneel in prayer. All knelt. Even the soldiers joined in prayer for reconciliation and the healing of the nation of Romania. Even the atheists prayed! Those who had persecuted Christians now knelt with us."

That was the same day that Nicolae Ceausescu fled from his palace in Bucharest where huge demonstrations engulfed the city. And it had all begun when a few Christians participated in an all-night prayer vigil in Timisoara.

A Free People

All across Eastern Europe and the former Soviet Union there are similar accounts of Christians in prayer forming the vanguard for the overthrow of the communist governments in that region of the world. The churches were uniquely equipped for this role; the churches were the groups that persisted as alternative-thought communities.

Other communities were seduced or co-opted by the communist ideology. Of course, some churches were also seduced. Yet it was the churches who stubbornly insisted that there was an authority who transcended the authority of the communist party—Jesus Christ. The churches were free communities. God gave them a freedom the communist governments could not rob.

God's call to mission is a call to live in freedom. No system or ideology has the authority to usurp the freedom God offers his people. Even torture and death cannot rob God's people of their freedom, for Jesus Christ frees his people from the fear of death.

In the previous chapter, we learned that a journey into freedom began when Abraham and Sarah obeyed God's call to leave the cultural and religious snares of their land and kinspeople. We discovered that God provided a place for Sarah and Abraham in the region of Canaan, present-day Palestine.

Israel Loses Freedom

The people of Israel, as well as Muslims and Christians, trace their spiritual origins to Abraham, who found land and a home in Palestine. This chapter explores the biblical account of Israel as a people called into freedom and mission.

The people of Israel trace their spiritual heritage to Abraham and Sarah through Isaac and his son, Jacob, from whom they get the name Israel. That was a nickname for Jacob, meaning one who strives with God and prevails. Because of famine in Canaan, Israel and his twelve sons with their families all moved to Egypt, where one of the sons, Joseph, had become the chief executive officer.

Two centuries later an Egyptian ruler known as Pharaoh enslaved the people of Israel. It was a horrible slavery; for a time Pharaoh commanded the drowning of all boy babies. God heard the cry of Israel and called one from among them, Moses, to lead these people into freedom.

Conflict with Pharaoh and the Gods

There followed a series of colossal confrontations with Pharaoh. The battle was between God the Creator of the universe and the nature gods whom the Egyptians worshiped. The conflict climaxed with ten different plagues against those who had enslaved Israel.

Each plague represented a confrontation against one of the nature gods of Egypt—bloody water, frogs, gnats, flies, plague on livestock, boils, hail, locusts, darkness. The last plague was the death of firstborn sons throughout Egypt.

However, any family who had sprinkled the blood of a sacrificial lamb on the lintel and posts of its door was spared death. Even today the people of Israel scattered throughout the world celebrate the Passover, remembering that awesome night when the angel of death passed over their homes.

Instantly the grieving Pharaoh determined to free all Israel. Six hundred thousand men, probably a total throng of two million, left Egypt. That is the night of their Exodus from slavery into freedom.

After an amazing crossing of the Red Sea and the drowning of Pharaoh and his army in the sea, the people of Israel arrived at Mount Sinai. To arrive at this mountain, they took a long southern detour through the desert on the way toward Canaan, the land God had promised for Abraham and his descendants forever. The awesome deliverance from slavery under Pharaoh and the formation of this free peoplehood is recorded in Exodus 1–18.

God Creates an Exodus for Oppressed People

Although God had promised Abraham and Sarah land, they had no army with which to acquire it. God, not their own power, provided a place for them.

This same theme of God acting on behalf of a powerless people is at the core of Israel's Exodus from Egypt. They did not fight for their freedom. God called them into freedom; they obeyed that call, and God himself acted. God fought for his people; they could not and did not fight for themselves.

That is the same theme Ioan and Livia described in Opera Square, Timisoara, Romania. In both ancient Egypt and modern Romania, the oppressed cried out to God, and he heard their prayer; he delivered them. Israel's deliverance from Egypt is a seed of hope for oppressed people everywhere. God himself joins their nonviolent struggle for freedom.

Of course, the people of God needed to move forward in obedience to his call; Israel had to respond to God's invitation to live as a free people. We will not always notice what God is up to, yet God is at work. In biblical times and within the history of Christian experience, we believe God is acting to free people from oppression.

An Exodus from Communism

The collapse of communist governments in eastern Europe and the former Soviet Union is a modern example of God working with oppressed people for their freedom.

For over seventy years the communist hammer and sickle flew above the Kremlin. The regime oppressed huge portions of the population; the evidence now suggests that Lenin and Stalin were responsible for the death of 60 million of their own people. Then on Christmas Day, 1991, the communist flag was lowered from the Kremlin.

"It is a miracle," exclaimed Peter Kuzmic of the former Yugoslavia in a 1991 consultation at the Overseas Missions Study Center in New Haven. "No human institution dare take credit for what has happened. God has heard the prayers and seen the suffering of his people. Across this whole region, the momentum for freedom commenced in prayer meetings. This is an act of God."

An Exodus from Apartheid

For many decades the Republic of South Africa has deprived black people of political rights through the instrument of racial classification and separation known as apartheid. This system has guaranteed special privilege to Caucasians.

"How do you account for the astonishing support in the whites-only referendum which President F. W. de Klerk received for negotiating the end of apartheid in South Africa?" I asked Bishop Graham Cyster of Cape Town.

"It's a miracle!" the bishop responded. "God has heard the cry of the oppressed."

Indeed God does create the Exodus again and again.

God's Treasure!

The Exodus freed Israel from slavery. It also provided Israel with special responsibilities. God offers people freedom and in response invites service for the well-being of others.

Israel was surprised by God's expectations. Imagine their amazement when God exclaimed, "Out of all nations you will be my treasured possession. Although the whole earth is mine, you will be for me a kingdom of priests and a holy nation" (Exod. 19:5-6).

This astonishing privilege and responsibility was anchored in a covenant established between God and Israel at Mount Sinai. God would faithfully care for his people; they needed to love and obey God with all their heart, soul, and mind. The soul of Israel's covenant with God is known as the *shema* (hear).

> Hear, oh Israel: The Lord our God, the Lord is one. Love the Lord your God with all your heart and with all your soul and with all your strength. (Deut. 6:4-5)

Over a millennium later, Jesus linked the *shema* with an obscure command in Leviticus: "Love your neighbor as your self" (Lev. 19:18). Jesus exclaimed that the whole teaching of biblical law and all the prophets rested on these two commandments: love God and love your neighbor. These two commandments define the center of the covenant.

A Different Nation

God is personal and righteous. His encounter with Israel at Mount Sinai involved a command to live righteously. The Ten Commandments (Exod. 20:1-17) are a description of the ethical dimensions of living as God's covenant people among the nations.

With that ethical foundation, for the next thousand years (as the biblical account records) an amazing pilgrimage of discovery and moral growth unfolded within these people. They really were God's chosen covenant people. God planned for them to become a light to the nations.

Let us explore dimensions of this covenant nation. These people were not bonded by ethnicity nor coerced into nationhood by an autocratic ruler. The sole basis of peoplehood was voluntary participation in the covenant. All were welcome.

Many participants in the covenant came from other nations: Moabites, Hittites, Canaanites, Midianites, Amalekites, and other nationalities are mentioned.

Notions such as "ethnic cleansing" or "ethnic purity" were incomprehensible for a peoplehood based on covenant. Genealogical descent from Abraham was irrelevant; it was the covenant which was the basis of the new peoplehood.

It was a voluntary covenant. People could also forsake and neglect the covenant. They could leave the covenant people. (This bold creation of a nation based on covenant rather than ethnicity or autocracy is the forerunner of modern constitutional democracies.)

The covenant was profoundly concerned for the well-being of the person. For example, within the covenant there was no place for a prison. Confining a person to prison was incomprehensible, for that would rob a person of freedom. Incorrigible persons were ostracized from society, but never imprisoned.

It was never permissible to inflict punishment on a person's body for a crime against property. Of course, if a person harmed another person, then the punishment was an eye for an eye and a tooth for a tooth. Fines were appropriate punishment for crimes against property. But the person created in God's image is too valuable to be physically harmed for the sake of property.

The integrity and dignity of the person herself could not be touched as punishment for a crime against mere property. The systems of punishment for wrongdoing were anchored in the conviction that God has created people in his very own image; we have dignity.

Shalom

Shalom (peace and well-being) best describes the ideal nature of this covenant people. The covenant invited them into relationships of peace with God, with their own selves, with others, and with creation.

God in their midst blessed them with *shalom* and invited them into lifestyle patterns which created and preserved it.

There was great concern for the poor, the widows, and the aliens. Special efforts were made to incorporate aliens into the covenant community. They were considered special guests.

Creditors were to forgive all debts in the year of Jubilee, which occurred every fifty years. Those who did lend money were not permitted to charge interest, which could drive the poor into deeper poverty. The rich were to avoid buying so much land and property that they left none for the poor.

Those who could afford an annual vacation were to give a third as much to the poor as they spent on their personal vacation! Any farmer who harvested crops was to leave some behind so the poor could glean what remained.

The covenant invited people to be clean, practice good eating habits, and have wholesome concern for good health. They bathed frequently. They were to keep yards and homes neat. A person who did not have a latrine was to bury body wastes. God should observe no uncleanness in the fields or homesteads.

The covenant people were to eat foods which nurtured good health. They were to rest every seventh day and enjoy the rewards of their hard work. People were encouraged to treat themselves generously on the annual tenting vacation (Feast of Tabernacles).

The covenant people were to care for the good earth and all creatures. Every seventh year they were to let the agricultural land rest. They were to treat animals kindly; if an ox was treading out corn, they were not to muzzle its mouth. The ox should be free to eat as much corn as it wished. If children were out hunting and found a mother bird with young in her nest, they dared not harm the mother bird, for then the helpless birdies would starve. God is concerned for the weak!

Shalom was God's intention for his covenant people. And God intended that all nations be attracted by this people living in *shalom*.

A Light to the Nations

Modern nations have been significantly influenced by the *shalom* themes within Israel's experience. The United Nations Declaration on Human Rights is largely based on the human rights concerns which emerged in Old Testament times. This includes the global conviction that the rights of people should be defended by governments.

Within Israel the king never had the final authority; it was God through his prophets who confronted unjust kings again and again. Our modern world accepts that governments should be judged by the criteria of justice and human rights. Democratic systems give people opportunity to vote out a government they believe unjust or inept. In most modern societies, the rich are taxed more heavily than the poor. Through welfare systems, modern governments attempt to take some wealth from the rich and share with the poor.

Modern societies find it unthinkable that a person be imprisoned for debt. Bankruptcy laws are an echo of the biblical conviction that all debts should be forgiven every fifty years. God's covenant with Israel has indeed been a light to the nations, as God promised (Isa. 49:6).

Don't Be Too Religious!

The covenant included religious rituals such as animal sacrifices. God revealed how the center of worship, the tabernacle, should be constructed. It was rich in symbolism. For example, a veil within the tabernacle separated the holy place from the holy of holies. A little box known as the ark of the covenant was placed in that holy of holies. Precious mementos of God's covenant with his people were kept safe in that ark, including the Ten Commandments inscribed on stone.

Although the priests at the tabernacle offered daily animal sacrifices as part of seeking forgiveness from God for the sins of the people, a veil separated the holy of holies from the rest of the tabernacle. This always reminded the people of separation between them and full fellowship with God due to their sin and God's righteousness. No religious ritual could remove that veil.

After the people settled in Canaan, they built an awesome temple in Jerusalem which replaced the tabernacle. As in the tabernacle, the priests put a curtain in the temple between the holy place and the holy of holies. When Solomon dedicated the temple after its construction, he sacrificed 22,000 cattle and 120,000 goats and sheep. God was not impressed. The curtain remained in the temple. Even 142,000 animals sacrificed for the sins of the people in a single day could not remove that curtain.

The prophets reminded the people that religious ritual and practice could not create a truly wholesome relationship between God and his covenant people. The prophets insisted that God was more concerned about righteousness than animal sacrifices and religious practices. Consequently during the thousand years the Old Testament was developing, the role of religious ritual became increasingly less important in the life of Israel.

A decrease in religious ritual is not typical of other religions. Quite the contrary, in most religions as the years go on rituals become more binding and complex.

Yet the core of biblical faith is not religion. The Bible invites people to turn toward God, rather than toward religious practices as such. For this reason biblical mission is not a commitment to the expansion of a religion; rather God invites people to repentance. Religious rituals often obscure the real issues. A religious person might feel no need for God, no inclination for repentance, no concern for the poor, no commitment to be a righteous person.

Rituals as Signs of Truth

Many years later when Jesus Christ was crucified on the outskirts of Jerusalem, the curtain in the temple tore in two from the top to the bottom. What a revelation! The tabernacle symbols were signs pointing toward Jesus Christ (Col. 2:17). Israel's animal sacrifices had always been only signs preparing people to understand Christ, the Lamb of God himself, who would one day give his life as the ultimate sacrifice for sin.

The sacrificial death of Christ guarantees that we are forgiven; no further animal sacrifices are needed. No wonder the veil in the temple was torn at the time of his sacrificial death! Now no veil separates God and his people. We are forgiven. We are invited into full and unrestricted fellowship with God through Jesus Christ.

Keep Your Tent Ready!

In the Sinai desert, Israel began the practice of gathering around the tabernacle (tent) for worship. A tent as a worship center is for a people on the move. As Abraham and Sarah had been called to leave their place in order to become a new peoplehood, so Israel also was to be a people on the move.

During their journeys God went before them in a cloudy pillar by day and a pillar of fire by night. Whenever the pillar of cloud or fire moved, they closed camp and moved on. The priests collapsed the tabernacle and went ahead of the people in the next phase of pilgrimage.

They were a free people, accountable only to God. Place could not capture them. Whenever God commanded "Move!" they obeyed. Even after they settled in Canaan and the surrounding grazing lands, permanency of place seemed to elude many of the covenant people. However, these moves into regions beyond Palestine often occurred because of God's judgment on them for disobedience.

Colossal calamities befell Israel, nestled in Palestine—the crossroads of Asia, Africa, and Europe. By the fifth century B.C., most Israelites had been taken into captivity into foreign lands. First Assyria and then Babylon overwhelmed the tiny nation. Most of the Israelites were removed from Palestine and resettled in the regions of Mesopotamia. Their enemies destroyed the temple and Jerusalem.

They became a people in diaspora, scattered among the nations of the earth. They formed fresh expressions of covenant communities from Spain to India and across North Africa. They were still a people on the move; they remembered their ancestors who had begun their covenant pilgrimage many centuries ago with their collapsible tabernacle.

Change Might Be Good

Biblical pilgrimage means a commitment to cultural or personal change for the good. Geographical change is only one dimension of pilgrimage (Jer. 29:4-8). A people in mission are always in pilgrimage. God's call to mission requires that we hold lightly our attraction to kinspeople, place, culture, tradition, or custom. God and his call are the center of life.

The scattering of God's people might be because of his specific call for a person or a people to move into a new location. Movement might also happen because of tragedy or relocation for economic reasons. We might even be forced to move as a consequence of personal failure.

Mission requires that, when leaving our many securities, we live in a manner which blesses others.

Going When God Calls

Often God calls people to become pilgrims in strange lands and cultures for the specific purpose of calling for repentance and faith in God.

"Clyde, I am calling you for mission in Africa," the Holy Spirit impressed upon the spirit of the young Pennsylvania farmer.

"Not me," the youth objected. "I am the only son of my father; he needs me as his farm assistant. Recently my father planted fruit trees just for me, because I enjoy orchard work."

The Holy Spirit persisted, gently yet firmly. Clyde lost thirty pounds as he struggled with the choice between the farm and the unknown of Africa. In the evenings he walked around the farm looking at the equipment, land, and cattle he enjoyed so much. He counted the cost. Death for missionaries in Africa was common in those days. He believed a decision for Africa would mean untimely death.

Finally he told his parents of the struggle. His father wept. His parents urged him to seek counsel from the pastors of their church.

"Son, let the Lord have his way," was the only counsel senior pastor Jacob Hess offered.

In 1936 Clyde Shenk and his bride, Alta Barge, sailed for East Africa. Alta's ministry was cut short because of an airplane crash. Clyde served forty years. Today the church districts they helped plant consist of some 12,000 members.

Take note! In all the districts where they served, African evangelists were pioneer partners. The missionaries only helped plant the seed of the gospel. Others embraced the gospel, accepted God's call to mission, and proclaimed the good news everywhere.

Just as God called Alta and Clyde, so he had also called Jonah of Israel in Old Testament times. This missionary drama can be read in a few minutes in the biblical book which is named after this reluctant missionary. God called Jonah to leave home and preach in Nineveh, among a people who were the enemies of Israel. Although Jonah resisted that call and consequently wound up in the stomach of a fish for three days, he finally did begin preaching in Nineveh.

"The judgment of God is at hand. In forty days Nineveh will be destroyed!" preached Jonah.

Nineveh repented. God changed his mind. Although Jonah was terribly agitated that God was so merciful, Nineveh was spared the judgment God had promised.

Beware of the Solomon Syndrome!

For nearly three years King Solomon of Israel could sleep with a different woman each night. That was how many wives and concubines he had. Most of his one thousand women were the daughters of kings; these women cemented political alliances with nations near and far. He used his position as the Lord's chosen king of Israel to use these women for his political ambitions. That is using God's covenant and blessing for self-aggrandizement and the exploitation of others.

Like Solomon, Israel too often used the covenant to secure privilege. Instead of living as a light and a blessing to the nations, the people turned the covenant into a political and religious institution. They acquired a king, thereby equating the covenant with the state. They substituted statehood for being God's people in mission.

They built a fabulous temple; the worship of the Lord became a religious cult. People from other nations who wished to worship at the temple had to surmount discouraging religious obstacles before they were worthy.

Israel's kings occasionally oppressed the poor. King Solomon used his position to load people with backbreaking taxes. He accumulated scandalous wealth; silver became like stones in Jerusalem. Other kings sought power from the nature gods. Some even sacrificed their children to these gods. Military defense became a fixation.

This was not what God intended when he called Israel to be his special treasure among all the nations. Instead of being a righteous, open, and generous people, Israel and her kings too often lived just like the nations around them. Wealth and power rather than mission informed their commitments.

Let us beware! The Bible does not describe wealth and power as proof of the blessing of God. The Bible is aware that sometimes wealth is acquired through unjust and exploitative means. Jesus does promise that God will bless his people with all they need—food and clothing.

If a person does acquire wealth, that can be acceptable—*if* it does not come through the exploitation of the good earth and other people. Sometimes people are able to acquire wealth through diligent work and integrity and just business practices. That is good. Such persons should give thanks to God for enabling them to acquire wealth. In that case the Lord invites the wealthy person to share her resources generously.

A biblical poet describes the righteous wealthy as one who "scatters abroad his gifts to the poor" (Ps. 112:9)!

Jesus said, "It is more blessed to give than to receive" (Acts 20:35).

Kill the Enemy?

The violence of Israel against her neighbors is one of the most perplexing issues in any reflection on Israel as a people of blessing and mission among the nations.

The accounts of Abraham and Sarah, as well as Israel's deliverance from Egypt, describe God acting on behalf of a vulnerable people. They were too weak ever to contemplate using violence to secure justice, land, or freedom. God fought for them. God judged those who oppressed them.

God promised that he would join in battle for Israel as they entered the Promised Land of Canaan (modern Palestine). The Bible describes the peoples of Canaan as wicked. Unless they repented, God's judgment awaited them. But judgment was God's responsibility; it was not Israel's duty.

God would act against the evil peoples of Canaan just as he had judged Pharaoh. God would send hornets ahead of them, who would encourage the people of Canaan to abandon the land voluntarily!

However, any Canaanites who repented were welcome into the covenant people. Such people were included within Israel and not destroyed. Rahab the harlot of Jericho was one such repentant Canaanite; she married Salmon of Israel and became the great-great-grandmother of King David.

God's national defense plan was the strangest strategy of any nation on earth. He commanded Israel never to depend on military power. They were prohibited from acquiring horses and chariots for war. They were to avoid taking a census of the men of military age, lest they began to trust in their manpower rather than in God.

If they ever had to fight, the newly married were excluded from battle, for it would be a tragedy if a man died before he had tasted the joys of marriage. At the time of battle, any who were fearful were free to abandon the army and return home.

The priests were to go ahead of this celebrating army of volunteers, singing praises to the Lord. God assured them that in any event it was likely that the enemy would have fled even before Israel arrived.

However, there is another side to the violence issue. Often Israel became embroiled in bloody conflicts. Often God himself seemed to command and bless these military convulsions.

Once they actually began settling in Canaan, Israel fought genocidal wars against the indigenous inhabitants. In some battles there were as many as one hundred thousand casualties. Israel also fought terrible civil wars. These were not skirmishes but genocidal wars. Israel developed a huge army; King Solomon had 1,400 chariots and 12,000 horses.

How should we interpret this violent edge in Israel's history? The Old Testament prophets struggled with the issues. So do modern believers. The spirituality of modern Israel is significantly influenced by the violent dimension of their Old Testament history. Churches often use this same Old Testament history to justify the militarization of their societies.

Christ Is the Center

The interpretation of the Old Testament in modern times is urgent. As of this writing, a peace accord between Israel and Palestinians headed by Yasser Arafat appears to have emerged. For generations, however, Palestinians have died and lost land, often at the hands of ones using the Old Testament to justify their actions.

A Palestinian Christian in Bethlehem lamented, "We Palestinians don't want anything to do with the Old Testament. Israel uses that book to kill us!"

The spiritual roots of this Arab Christian are the apostolic church which was formed at Pentecost.

How could I respond? Gently I observed, "Jesus said that he is a greater one than Moses. Jesus has the last word. Would it be helpful to read the Old Testament, interpreting it through Jesus the Christ?"

My Palestinian host was amazed. "Is it all right to critique the Old Testament in the light of Jesus?" he asked.

"Jesus gives us that authority," I assured him.

This approach to biblical interpretation is called a Christ-centered hermeneutic. Just as Christian interpretation of the Bible should be Christ-centered, so the mission of the church is also anchored in Christ. That is the exploration of the next chapter.

We shall discover that Christ does much more than help to interpret the Old Testament in a way that critiques excessive violence. Christ also frees people to love their enemies. In his crucifixion and resurrection, Christ breaks the cycle of violence and provides life-giving empowerment to love the enemy, live in peace, and seek reconciliation.

* * *

This chapter describes Israel as a people called by God to be a light and blessing among the nations. The exploration reveals revolutionary characteristics of this new covenant people. Many aspects of modern concerns for human rights derive from Israel of the Old Testament.

On the other hand, Israel has often betrayed her calling. The people of Israel experienced tension between their desire for security as a nation-state and the more demanding requirements of being a people in mission among the nations. It surprised them to discover that they could fulfill their mission anywhere, even when scattered among the nations with no state or political identity.

The people of Israel recognized that they were a preparation among the nations for the coming Messiah. The next chapter describes the Messiah as the great surprise. Even Israel was astonished.

Reflection

1. In what ways does Israel's Exodus from slavery under Pharaoh provide encouragement and guidance for modern quests for freedom from oppression?

2. Discern ways in which Israel has been a light to the nations.

3. What are some differences between a covenant people and (a) a nation-state, or (b) an ethnic group.

4. Reflect on ways in which ancient Israel or the modern church have not functioned in a manner which is a blessing to the nations.

5. How should Christians interpret the Old Testament? How do you feel about a Christ-centered hermeneutic?

* * *

Suggested background Scriptures—Exodus 1—20; 26:31-37; 33—34, Deuteronomy 32—33, Isaiah 6:1-4; 49:6, Jonah, Colossians 2:17.

3

The Great Surprise

"GOD IS LOVE! 1 John 4:8," chant the children in a million Christian Sunday school classes and a thousand languages as they learn their Bible verses.

Other global religions and philosophies have not imagined such a notion. "God is love" is an astonishing statement unparalleled in the religions and philosophies of humankind. Yet that is not the core of the gospel. The gospel is not an unprecedented philosophy or religious speculation. The gospel is much more than surprising theological insights. The gospel is an event.

"God so loved the world that he gave his one and only Son" (John 3:16)! That is the total surprise which is the Christian gospel. The word *gospel* means good news. God so loved us that he acted. History will never be the same. God sent his Son!

The Written Accounts

The written accounts of Jesus of Nazareth record two occasions when people heard the voice of God from heaven proclaim that Jesus is his Son: "You are my Son, whom I love" (Luke 3:22) and "This is my Son, whom I have chosen" (9:35). This man from Nazareth of Galilee in Palestine whom God named "my Son" was the greatest surprise people anywhere have experienced.

It is important to know whether the accounts of Jesus' life are reliable. That is a critical issue in these modern times, when our scientific worldview demands reliable evidence for everything we believe. The issue was equally significant for the early church.

After Jesus' death and resurrection, legends began circulating. The church sought trustworthy accounts. The medical doctor, Luke, summarized this concern for authentic reporting in his opening statement of the account of Jesus' life.

> Therefore, since I myself have carefully investigated everything from the beginning, it seemed good also to me to write an orderly account for you, most excellent Theophilus, so that you may know with certainty of the things you have been taught. (Luke 1:3-4)

The apostles were the early leaders of the church. Most had been disciples of Jesus during his three-year public ministry. The church determined to include in the New Testament only accounts written by apostles or persons closely associated with the apostles. The church objected to legendary material which would bring a separation between the Jesus of Scriptures and the historical Jesus of Nazareth.

The church was grateful that disciples close to Jesus kept some kind of diary of his teaching and ministry. Scholars refer to this "source" as *Quelle* (a German term) or "Q." Although modern scholars do not possess this document, there is evidence of a common written source which forms a basis for the Gospels of Matthew and Luke.

Shortly after Jesus' resurrection, others began a more systematic record of his life and teachings. Four accounts of the life of Jesus, known as the Gospels, are included in the New Testament: Matthew, Mark, Luke, and John.

The New Testament also includes the Acts, a history of the early church. Then there are letters written to people or churches by apostolic persons. These documents also provide valuable accounts concerning Jesus which further attest to the accuracy of the Gospel documents. In its missionary work, the church has always needed reliable accounts of Jesus, as well as of the counsel and teachings of the early church.

Are the Gospel Accounts Trustworthy?

Modern scholarship is increasingly impressed with the trustworthiness of these Gospel accounts. There are fundamental reasons for this confidence. We will mention only three.

First, the accounts describe unseemly behavior by the apostles. While working with Jesus, his disciples got into childish squabbles. Peter denied Jesus. Before any of the men knew it, the women discovered that Jesus had risen from the dead. The apostles acted in a cowardly manner during the arrest and crucifixion of Jesus. Paul and his best friend, Barnabas, had a sharp dispute, which somewhat crippled Paul's ministry for a time. The accounts include humiliating realism. If the writers wanted to alter the facts, they would not have recorded these personal failures.

Second, the documents are accurate in areas where details can be examined through external archaeological, historical, or textual evidence. For example, Luke often mentions interesting historical or cultural details—and always gets it right.

Look at this Lukan statement!

> In the fifteenth year of the reign of Tiberius Caesar—when Pontius Pilate was governor of Judea, Herod tetrarch of Galilee, his brother Philip tetrarch of Iturea and Traconitus, and Lysanias tetrarch of Abiline—during the high priesthood of Annas and Caiphas, the word of God came. (Luke 3:1-2)

Here is one more Lukan coup. The Romans placed one proconsul (governor) in charge of each province. Alas, for many years it seemed that Luke had struck out on that one. He wrote of proconsuls in his description of the riot in Ephesus, when the throngs tried to kill Paul. Roman provinces had only one, not several, proconsuls.

However, archaeological evidence has now demonstrated that at the time of that riot there were actually two proconsuls in Ephesus. There was a brief overlap between an incoming proconsul and the one ending his term. Scholars are impressed that Luke was indeed an accurate observer.

Third, studies in the Hebrew or Aramaic sources of the Gospels are important. Early church traditions note that Peter spoke Aramaic and needed a Greek interpreter. Mark was Peter's interpreter. The traditions also suggest that Peter was a principal source for Mark's gospel. Yet scholars have mused over why the Greek in the Gospel of Mark does not flow smoothly.

Under the leadership of professor David Flusser, Jewish biblical scholars at the Hebrew University in Jerusalem believe they have cracked the mystery. As an experiment these scholars have flipped the Greek words in Mark directly into Aramaic. What a discovery they have made. The result is smooth idiomatic Aramaic.

Their conclusion: originally Mark was written in Aramaic, the mother tongue of Jesus. Those who translated into Greek changed every Aramaic word directly into Greek so no meaning would be lost. That is the reason for the rough Greek.

This discovery is especially important because it provides scholars with an Aramaic account of the life of Jesus. It also reveals that the early church carefully worked at accurate preservation of early accounts of the life of Jesus (Lindsey).

The Church Needs Reliable Accounts

If New Testament writers accurately recorded minute details, surely they were even more concerned to report reliably the life and ministry of Jesus and the experiences of the early church. Yet why should that be a concern for Christians? Why should it matter whether the accounts of Jesus are authentic?

For Hindus, it makes no real difference whether Krishna ever lived. The accounts or legends of his life are valuable only as myths. The myths have nothing to do with historical accuracy.

Even Muslims do not view their primary scriptures, the Koran, from a historical perspective. They believe the Koran came from heaven; it supersedes or transcends history. Muslim scholars do not study the Koran from the perspectives of historical analysis.

Buddha was a philosopher and teacher. Although his story is interesting, that is irrelevant to the meaning of Buddhism.

Christian faith is different. Christians are historians; they are deeply interested in questions of reliable documents. It has always been so.

Remember—the soul of the gospel is that God sent his Son. Jesus of Nazareth is that Son. He is a real man living in real history. If God sent his Son into our world, then it is important indeed that we have in our hands authentic accounts of that greatest surprise which has ever entered human history.

Revelation Events and Response

In fact, the whole Bible is mostly a history book. Biblical faith insists that history is real; God acts in history. The center of biblical revelation is the salvation acts of God in history. The Spirit of God inspired the biblical prophets and poets to interpret and expound on those salvation events. That is why the core of the Bible is the descriptions of God's saving acts within human history. The faith perspectives of biblical writers are included within the written accounts. The event and the faith response interact.

The accounts of the resurrection of Jesus show the interaction of event and faith. When Jesus arose, women disciples of Jesus saw the angel who rolled the stone away from the tomb where Jesus was buried. The guards at the tomb also saw the angel, and they were terrified.

With great joy the women hurried into Jerusalem to tell the disciples the astonishing good news that Jesus had risen from the dead. On their way, the resurrected Jesus met them. Imagine! They told the disciples of seeing both an angel and Jesus.

In contrast, the frightened guards ran into Jerusalem to tell the authorities the terrible news that an angel had appeared and rolled the stone away from the tomb. Instantly the authorities developed an account which fit neatly into their worldview—the disciples had stolen the body of Jesus.

So two dramatically different descriptions of the same event spread like wildfire through the land. The faith response was great joy that Jesus had risen from the dead. The nonbelieving response was that the disciples had stolen his body from the tomb.

The event was of such a nature that the only possible response was belief or nonbelief. But belief or nonbelief in the resurrection of Jesus is a profoundly personal response, which represents a huge divide in ones ultimate commitments. Those opposite responses are the core issues of the meaning of life and destiny.

The Gospel accounts of the resurrection reveal that the church did not try to develop watertight evidence supporting the resurrection. There are several problems in putting all the accounts together. The early church was aware of these problems, yet the church never convened a committee to iron out the problems and get the sequence just right. They knew that those who choose not to believe would never be persuaded by systematic evidence presented by an investigation committee.

Nevertheless, from the perspective of modern scholarship, the problems actually strengthen confidence in the reliability of the accounts. Why? Scholars use the analogy of evidence in a courtroom. If witnesses in court agree totally on all details, the jury will suspect there has been collusion among the witnesses. Minor divergencies among the witnesses actually strengthen the case in court. The same is true of these biblical accounts. The problems strengthen confidence in the reliability of the accounts.

Nevertheless, there is always a division between a faith and a nonfaith response to the acts of God. These opposite responses interpret the same events very differently. Nonbelievers cannot accept the biblical accounts of the resurrection. In the apostolic era and today nonbelievers never consider the possibility of the resurrection of Jesus. They just know it can only be fabrication or illusion.

Believers, on the other hand, rejoice in the resurrection of Jesus. They elaborate and expound on the wonder and meaning of that event. Just as did the New Testament writers, so we also interact with the resurrection event, providing our personal and collective interpretations of its meaning.

The revelation event and the faith response are always in conversation and mutual interpretation. On the one hand, the revelation event invites faith; on the other hand, our faith response also affects our understanding of the revelation event.

That is also true of the people of faith who recorded the biblical accounts. The Bible declares that writers "spoke from God as they were carried along by the Holy Spirit" (2 Peter 1:21). They were not just writing about God's acts in history and doctrine. They were also communicating faith.

We now explore the greatest revelation event of all, this man from Nazareth whom God named "my beloved Son." We probe the meaning of four names for Jesus—Messiah; Emmanuel; Son of man; Lamb of God.

Messiah

Rejoice greatly, O Daughter of Zion!
  Shout, daughter of Jerusalem!
See, your king comes to you,
  righteous and having salvation,
gentle and riding on a donkey
  on a colt, the foal of a donkey. . . .
  He will proclaim peace to the nations.
His rule will extend from sea to sea
  and from the River to the ends of the earth. (Zech. 9:9-10)

The prophet Zechariah proclaimed this prophecy concerning the Messiah toward the end of the Old Testament era. Five centuries later Jesus of Nazareth rode into Jerusalem on the foal of a donkey. Jubilant children sang,

Hosanna to the son of David!
Blessed is he who comes in the name

of the Lord!
Hosanna in the highest! (Matt. 21:9)

Surely the children had no idea that the Messiah would ride a foal. They didn't have a clue that the one riding the donkey was the King who would proclaim "peace to the nations" and whose rule would extend to the "ends of the earth." They sang because they loved Jesus, and he loved them.

Nevertheless, the religious experts knew Zechariah's prophecy well. They were livid. Jesus was making a clear statement by riding that foal. He was announcing with a clarity which could not be mistaken: I am the Messiah whom God has promised, and my rule shall extend to the ends of the earth. I am the King and Lord who has come to proclaim peace to the nations.

The authorities of Israel could not tolerate the presumption of Jesus. They demanded that he silence the children. Jesus would not. "If they keep quiet, the stones will cry out!" Jesus responded.

With a boldness the authorities could not imagine, Jesus entered the temple and threw out the merchants who were selling animals, birds, or grain for worshipers needing to make sacrifices to God. He overturned the merchants' tables, proclaiming that they had made the house of God a den of thieves. With a whip he chased the cattle from the temple area.

That was too much. The authorities planned Jesus' arrest. There were many reasons for their anger. By cleansing the temple, Jesus had gone too far; he must die. Within several days he was crucified on a cross between two thieves. The three crosses were placed on a knoll called Golgotha on the outskirts of Jerusalem.

"Do you really believe that Jesus the Messiah was crucified?" asked Abdul Rauf of the Islamic Center in Washington, D.C. We were participating in a dialogue between Christian and Muslim theologians.

"Yes," we confessed.

Perplexity etching his face, Rauf continued, "That seems to suggest that the Messiah is vulnerable. If God is sovereign, the cross cannot happen."

We continued, "That is the soul of the gospel. God is vulnerable. He chose to break the back of our rebellion through the suffering love of Messiah revealed in that cross. A clenched fist is for striking. Folded arms are for indifference. Open arms are for vulnerability and embracing.

"In the outstretched arms of Jesus hanging on that cross we experience the extent to which God loves us. Those open arms reveal that God is seeking us and inviting us into his embrace. He is not indifferent to us; he chooses not to strike us. In the Messiah crucified we discover that God is love."

The cross is not futile. Love is stronger than hate. Evil powers plotted and crucified the Messiah. Just as God had proclaimed at the very beginning of human history, the forces of evil did indeed "strike his heel."

However, after three days in the grave, Jesus rose from the dead. His resurrection is the guarantee that the powers of evil have been unmasked and their authority broken. In his crucifixion and resurrection, Jesus has "crushed [the] head" of evil (Gen. 3:15). He has overcome evil and death. He is risen from the dead.

For the next forty days, after his resurrection, Jesus appeared occasionally to his disciples; about a dozen appearances are recorded in the Gospels and the letters to the churches. His resurrection is confirmation that he is Lord indeed.

"God has made this Jesus, whom you crucified, both Lord and Christ." Peter proclaimed in the first Christian sermon; that was at the feast of Pentecost on the birthday of the church (Acts 2:36).

If Jesus is Lord, then human destiny is in good hands. Jesus of Nazareth is the Messiah anointed by the Spirit of God,

> to preach good news to the poor,
> . . . freedom for the prisoners
> and recovery of sight for the blind,
> to release the oppressed,
> to proclaim the year of the Lord's favor.
> (Luke 4:18-19)

That is the way Jesus lived.

It is for this reason that of all the people who have ever lived, there is no one we would rather confess as Lord than Jesus.

Jesus' resurrection is also a guarantee from God that all people will someday rise from the dead. And Jesus promised that he will return again at the climax and consummation of history. He will return as Lord of all; God has given judgment into his hands. He will bring to fulfillment the kingdom of God. There will be a new heaven and a new earth.

This is the Christian hope—the hope that in God's own time the kingdom of God will triumph. This gives courage even when every-thing seems wrong.

Emmanuel

The first sentence in the Bible declares, "In the beginning God cre-ated the heavens and the earth." That is not difficult to believe. Surely there must be an architect who planned and formed the universe.

Advanced telescope technology, such as the Keck telescope in Ha-waii, or the Hubble telescope mounted on a satellite above the earth's atmosphere, are revealing unbelievable grandeur and complexity. Our own Milky Way galaxy comprises about 3 billion stars. Light moves quite rapidly, 186,000 miles per second. That's six times around the earth each second. At that speed it takes one hundred thousand years for light to transverse our galaxy. Our galaxy is enor-mous. Yet the Milky Way is only one galaxy among thousands. These other galaxy systems are evenly spaced in patterns, four hundred milllion light years apart!

The energy in the universe is also astonishing. For example, there are mysterious jets of gaseous matter which travel at more than one thousand miles per second and extend trillions of miles. These jets pack more energy than the Milky Way produces in one hundred thou-sand years (*Newsweek*, June 3, 1991, 47-52).

Scientists probing with their telescopes, computers, and electron microscopes discern the exquisite design, pattern, power, organiza-tion, and complexity of the universe—extending from the enormous galaxies to the minutest quark.

The slightest deviation from the complex and interwoven patterns within the universe would make human life impossible. Take carbon nuclei, for example, which are foundational to life. The formation of the carbon nucleus requires a tricky simultaneous high speed encoun-ter of three separate helium nuclei. This can only happen deep inside stars, where the complex conditions are just right for the production of carbon.

The formation of carbon nuclei is just one tiny window into a uni-verse delicately right for the creation and sustenance of human life. Even infinitesimal deviations would make life impossible (Davies, 199).

The discoveries of science surprise us with the intricacy, organiza-tion, and complexity of creation. Our explorations of the universe have revealed that God is greater and more powerful than we ever conceived. Even a few years ago we never imagined galaxies neatly spaced at 400 million light year intervals. We are tiny!

Yet the gospel is news so amazing its wonder can never be exaggerated. The greatest surprise is that God loved us so much he sent his one and only Son to walk among us on planet earth. And that Son is called Emmanuel, which means "God with us."

Jesus as Emmanuel clarifies who God is. Without that clarification, we are inclined to develop warped views of God. Psychologists and anthropologists have demonstrated that the gods of the religions are mostly an invention or projection of culture. Warlike cultures worship warrior gods. Peaceful cultures believe their deity is peaceful. It is for that reason that psychoanalyst Sigmund Freud believed God is an illusion.

The Bible also warns against any illusionary god. The prophet Jeremiah wrote,

> For the customs of the peoples are worthless;
>   they cut a tree out of the forest,
>   and a craftsman shapes it with his chisel.
> They adorn it with silver and gold;
>   they fasten it with hammer and nails
>   so it will not totter.
> Like a scarecrow in a melon patch,
>   their idols cannot speak;
> they must be carried because they cannot walk.
> Do not fear them;
>   they can do no harm
> nor can they do any good. (Jeremiah 10:3-5)

The gods of culture never call for repentance. The gods a society creates simply affirm the values of that society. For example, in Hinduism caste is identified as the god Brahman. In that case Brahman will never critique the caste system. There is no repentance, no turning away from the spirit of caste. The divinity of caste will never call on Hindus to transform caste, for god and caste are the same.

Any god who is the creation of people is a false god, an illusion, just as Freud said. Repentance means turning away from these false gods to worship the God who created us. This God is not an illusion. Whenever he meets us, we experience the call to make a U-turn toward God and away from the gods of our culture.

Yet how can we know God? How can we be confident that our perceptions of our Creator are not distorted by our culture?

Jesus is the great clarification event. He is the full, in-history revelation of God. "He is the image of the invisible God" (Col. 1:15). "For God was pleased to have all his fullness dwell in him" (Col. 1:19). For this reason, any turning toward God means turning toward Jesus.

Jesus proclaimed, "Anyone who has seen me has seen the Father" (John 14:9)!

This means that any image or perception of God which is contrary to Jesus is false. That is good news! In fact, if God isn't like Jesus, most of us would just as soon ignore him. But if God is like Jesus, then with confidence and joy we can give our total loyalty to our Father and Creator.*

* * *

Son of Adam

Luke records seventy-five generations in the genealogy of Jesus. King David of Israel is in the middle of it all; Adam is at the beginning. Luke is making a point in that genealogy—Jesus is the son of Adam. He is an authentic human being. The Bible describes Jesus as the "new Adam."

When Adam and Eve turned away from God, evil entered human experience. All people are touched by evil. Each of us is deeply aware that we are not as fully human as we want to be or as we should be. We are sinful.

Yet when we read the accounts of Jesus, there is a gentle awareness within our spirits that we are meeting the most genuine person we have encountered. He is the quality of person I know I should be.

---

*It should be noted that referring to God as Father in no sense suggests that God is more masculine than feminine. Both man and woman are created in the image of God; both feminine and masculine qualities describe God. However, although some would argue otherwise, I believe that to refer to God as both male and female erodes the core biblical conviction that God is that "other" and transcendent one who meets us in personal encounter.

In many cultures God as mother suggests pantheism and earth worship. Such worldviews encourage fertility cults which erode the dignity of women. As participants in both local and global mission, I believe it is wise to refer to God in ways which are in harmony with the practices of the universal church.

For these reasons I choose to use the name for God which Jesus used—our Father (Abba) who is in heaven. Our Abba is the transcendent one who encounters us and loves us.

He is fully human. He is the new Adam. He is the person who reveals winsome righteousness which is free of the taint of evil.

Nevertheless, Jesus walked life's journey just as we do. Although not born into a desperately poor home, he became a refugee in his infancy. It is likely that he was a carpenter and stonecutter in early life.

It seems that his mother, Mary, became a widow responsible for a fairly large family. Jesus as the oldest had considerable responsibility for his mother and siblings. There are indications that the home was marred by sibling tensions.

During his three years of public ministry, Jesus once commented that even the foxes had a place to sleep, but he as the Son of man had nowhere to lay his head. He spoke openly of his dread of crucifixion. Walking life's path does involve suffering. Jesus also tasted suffering. He is a son of Adam and Eve; we also are daughters and sons of the first human parents. We can identify with Jesus; he identifies with us.

Lamb of God

"Look, the Lamb of God, who takes away the sin of the world!" exclaimed John the Baptist on the first day of Jesus' public ministry, when introducing him to the crowds being baptized at the Jordan River (John 1:29).

The previous chapter described the Passover night in Egypt when the firstborn in Israel was saved from death through the sacrifice of a one-year-old lamb. It might seem strange that God would require the sacrifice of a lamb, with the blood from that lamb sprinkled on the lintels and doorposts, in order to pass over the homes of Israel when the angel of death destroyed all other firstborns in the land. We recognize that there must be a deeper meaning to that sacrificial Passover lamb than the Exodus account reveals.

Christians believe that the lamb slain as a sacrifice on Passover night was a sign pointing to the Lamb of God, who some thirteen hundred years later gave his life as the sacrifice for the sins of the world. On the night Jesus was betrayed, he ate his last Passover meal with his disciples. They celebrated that feast of remembering the deliverance from Egypt, just as Jewish people have always done.

Then at the conclusion of that Passover, Jesus took a cup of wine and shared a sip of it with his disciples saying, "This is my blood of the covenant, which is poured out for many for the forgiveness of sins" (Matt. 26:28).

For this reason Christians celebrate the communion together with broken bread and wine, remembering that Jesus the Lamb of God was crucified and gave his life as the sacrifice for our sin. Just as the blood of those Passover lambs sprinkled on the lintels and doorposts several thousand years ago in Egypt saved the firstborn from death, we also receive forgiveness and salvation from death through Christ whom the Scriptures proclaim to be the Lamb of God.

"No thought has ever entered my mind more wonderful than this: Jesus has died for my sins; he has taken my place," explained the aged African bishop Zedekia Kisare, as I sat in his courtyard awaiting a goat feast.

A few months later about twenty Christians and that many Muslims were participating in an evening dialogue in the Front Street Mosque in Philadelphia. The Muslims had just completed many prayer *rakas* that evening.

"Tonight we have said twenty extra prayers, for we have sinned. We hope that our extra prayers will outweigh our sins in the balance scales of good and evil. Yet we never know if we have said enough prayers. Each person must bear the punishment for his sin alone."

"What you have said is true," one of us commented. "Each person must bear the punishment for his own sins. Yet there is one exception. A person is free if the judge himself enters the judgment hall and standing by the guilty one proclaims, 'I will take your place!'

"The witness of the gospel is that Jesus the Messiah has taken our place in the judgment hall.

"One of the names of Jesus the Messiah is Lamb of God. As you know, in religions everywhere people offer animal sacrifices; usually they are hoping to find forgiveness for their sins.

"Although in modern times people might consider those animal sacrifices as meaningless, those sacrifices have always been important signs, preparing people to understand why Jesus was crucified on the cross. He is the Lamb of God who gave his life as the final and ultimate sacrifice for our sins."

The mosque was completely silent. The Holy Spirit was speaking.

After a long and pensive moment, the imam interrupted, "Too deep for tonight!"

We agreed to commence the conversation another day.

Joy that our sins are forgiven is a central theme when Christians meet together for worship. Christians never really get over the wonder of it all. Jesus is the Lamb of God. He took our place in the courtroom of life. No matter how evil a person might be, Jesus has taken his place in the judgment hall. We are free. We are forgiven.

* * *

This chapter describes that greatest of all events, that God sent his one and only Son into our world.

That event is so significant that it is important for the church in mission to be confident that the accounts are reliable. There is ample reason for such confidence. The New Testament includes both the account of the Christ event and the faith response and interpretation of that event through the inspiration of the Holy Spirit.

In their faith response believers discover Jesus as Messiah, Emmanuel, Son of man, and Lamb of God. There are other discoveries as well, but these four names for Jesus reveal in a special way the wonder of the gospel.

The next chapter describes the Christian hope. That hope is present within the church and provides encouragement in mission even when life is very difficult.

Reflection

1. Describe the surprising aspects of the four names of Jesus.

2. Give reasons for Christian interest in the reliability of the Gospel accounts. Reflect on the evidence for believing that the accounts are trustworthy.

3. How do you respond to the statement that the gospel is not speculation, that it is an event?

3. What difference does Jesus make in your life? In your congregation? In your community? In the world?

4. What are the core reasons for the great divide between faith and nonfaith in the resurrection of Jesus?

* * *

Suggested background Scriptures—Luke 10:1-24; John 1:12, 18; 3:16; 17:22-23; 20:21; Acts 4:12; 1 Corinthians 3:16; 2 Corinthians 6:16; 13:14; Ephesians 1:3-14; 2:19-22; 5:8; Philippians 2:10-11; Colossians 1:15, 19; Hebrews 9:1-24; Revelation 1:4-7.

4

The End Is Here

"Jesus will destroy all pigs and all the crosses when he returns to earth at the end of history," our Muslim host explained.

About 30 Christians and Muslims were sharing in an evening of dialogue in the Albanian Mosque in Philadelphia. Our theme was the final judgment. Muslims believe that God rescued Jesus from crucifixion and took him to heaven bodily, without having tasted death. Islamic tradition predicts that Jesus will return to prepare the world for the final judgment by destroying crosses, killing pigs (which Muslims consider unclean), and converting the world to Islam.

"What is your Christian belief concerning the climax of history?" the imam invited.

"The Bible describes the crucified Messiah, who has risen from the dead, returning to earth," we responded. "At that time there will be a universal resurrection of all the dead. The Messiah will preside at the final judgment. The kingdom of God will be fulfilled. There will be a new creation."

"What are you doing about that hope?" our hosts inquired.

Churches as Surprises

"Come to our churches and see," we invited. "The kingdom of God is already beginning. We are experiencing shalom (peace) in our congregations. For example, Christian farmers should take good care of their cows and cultivate their land in ways which preserve the earth.

"Of course, we experience sin within our faith communities. Yet you will be surprised to notice that the new creation is already beginning. Come and see shalom!"

Recall that *shalom* is a Hebrew term meaning peace and well-being. The presence of the kingdom of God is the fulfillment of shalom. God invites every local congregation to be a surprising expression of shalom.

That is why we invited our Muslim friends to visit with us. We wanted them to experience those precious indications of the presence of the kingdom of God in our midst.

They did come! Several carloads of Muslim friends drove sixty miles out of town to visit our churches for a weekend. They wanted to see the kingdom of God beginning.

The presence of the kingdom is always a surprise, because that presence is so different from the expectations of people. Yet God calls the church to be just that kind of a surprising people. The church is called to be a people in whom the surprising Spirit of Jesus is present. This chapter explores some dimensions of the church as a community of surprises.

The End Invites Hope

Theologians refer to the church as the eschatological community. *Eschaton* is a Greek word meaning "the end." The church is the community in which the end is already beginning; the end is here. What is that end? It is the fulfillment of the kingdom of God, the presence of shalom.

We recall God's promise to Eve and Adam that a son would someday crush the head of evil (Gen. 3:15). Later God made a similar promise to Abraham. His offspring would bless all nations (Gen. 22:18). The people of the covenant known as Israel were a beginning and a preparation for the fulfillment of these promises.

This gave the hope which permeates the Old Testament. Even in disastrous circumstances, the prophets of God invited hope. The Messiah would come. Israel was the people who were called to be a light to the nations as they prepared the earth for the advent of the Messiah.

The New Testament is the description of the Messiah who is the presence of God's reign in human history. He has overcome evil and death.

"Do not be afraid. I am the First and the Last. I am the Living One; I was dead, and behold I am alive for ever and ever! And I hold the keys of death and Hades," exclaimed the risen Jesus when he met John, who was in detention on the Island of Patmos (Rev. 1:17-18).

If we want to know what the new creation will be like at the climax of history, we should read the Gospel accounts of the life and teachings of Jesus. In Jesus of Nazareth the end has appeared. And he has promised to return again at the end of history to bring that end to complete fulfillment. At that time every knee will bow and every tongue confess that Jesus is Lord (Phil. 2:9-11). The new creation, which is already beginning, will be fulfilled at the *eschaton*, the final climax of history.

A Fellowship of Joy and Hope

The church exists in the confidence that the end of history has already begun within its own experience. The faithful church is in tune with that end. Like a powerful magnet, the end of history is pulling the church toward the *eschaton*, the fulfillment of the kingdom of God. It is not surprising that whenever the church is faithful to its mission, it becomes an energetic and potent community of change. It nudges and urges movement in the direction of shalom.

The Republic of South Africa was crackling with strife in 1989. Four North Americans—Lawrence and Nereida Chiles and my wife, Grace, and I—joined our South African hosts, Graham and Dorcas Cyster, for evening worship in the home of Fani and Ella Norxawana in the huge shantytown of Khayelitsha on the edge of Capetown.

Khayelitsha reveals the evil apartheid has been. Tens of thousands of blacks had been dumped into this community as areas of the Cape region were cleansed of black people to make room for white-only communities.

Two dozen people crowded the tiny Norxawana living-dining room. We heard the Word of the Lord and sang and prayed together. Then Fani led a concluding song as he and the congregation danced before the Lord in exuberant joy.

"Look, Jesus is coming. He is right around the corner," they sang as they danced. This was an expression of the hope and joy of a congregation who have tasted deep injustice.

The congregation was electric with hope.

As we left the meeting, I observed, "Christ has already freed these people. Apartheid is doomed. Shalom is at hand."

A Sign Showing the Direction

It is God who is pulling history toward the end when the kingdom of God, which has already begun, will be fulfilled. There is no impersonal law of nature or history compelling the world forward as the communists teach. God is acting in history. He is drawing history toward the end.

The church is the community called by God to be a sign pointing society in the direction in which history is going. No other communities are aware that Jesus is Lord and that a day is coming when every being in heaven and earth will acknowledge him as Lord.

Only the church knows this mystery of God's grand design for history. The unlocking of the mystery of history gives the church hope, patience, and endurance. The faithful church exists with a forward-looking dynamism which is unique and remarkable.

Who Knows the Mystery of the End?

What is the meaning of history? If you asked the head of General Motors where history is heading, he might respond that free enterprise is the wave of the future. Most North Americans seem confident that their way of life is what history is about. The Marxists are certain we are all heading toward a communist utopia. Hindus believe history is a tragic, meaningless, cyclical accident. Muslims believe that an expanding Islamic political order will someday bring peace on earth.

Yet present among the nations, cultures, several thousand language groups, the economic systems, and religions of the global village are a people to whom God has revealed the amazing mystery: Jesus possesses the keys of history. These people are the church.

The Powers in Heaven and Earth

The church is commissioned by God to reveal that mystery to the principalities and powers, both in the heavens and on earth (Eph. 3:10). Even the demons and angels are astonished by the wonder of it all. So are the powers on earth. Can it be true that Jesus of Nazareth, crucified by Pontius Pilate, possesses the keys of history?

"I was a young pastor, only twenty-six, when the Romanian communist authorities allowed me to baptize only nine people in a baptismal group of thirty-two," explained pastor Joseph Stifanutsi of Braila, in southeastern Romania. "After prayer with the congregation, I baptized the whole group."

"That action could have meant death for you?" I asked.

"Yes, of course. In fact, the security forces called me in and accused me of insubordination. For months they tried to brainwash me. They put me in detention and threatened me. Once they tried to kill me by driving a truck into my car."

"How did you respond to their accusations of insubordination to government authority? We Christians do believe that governments are ordained by God, and we should obey the civil authorities."

Joseph continued, "I told them that I am not insubordinate. I am subordinate to Jesus Christ and the church. I am the servant of Jesus who is Lord of the universe and Lord of Romania too. My life belongs to Jesus Christ; therefore, death is no problem to me."

Intrigued, I probed further. "The communists didn't have a clue concerning God's grand plan for history. You must have astonished them."

"Yes, they were surprised! They were amazed I insisted that a Palestinian Jewish peasant who lived nearly two thousand years ago is Lord of history and is bringing history to a wonderful and right conclusion. They thought I was crazy. Although it was foolishness to them, I knew that this Jesus crucified and risen was and is the power of God for salvation."

The faithful church reveals the mystery of the end of history to human authorities like governments; it also reveals the secret of God's plan to the spirits and demons.

Powers Such as Witches

"We are not afraid of owls that hoot at night, black animals that scoot across our path, guns, or witches," explained Luis Alfredo, a K'ekchi' pastor in the highlands of Guatemala. "Jesus Christ has broken the power of these omens of death!"

"Tell me about the witches," I prodded.

"The witches are empowered by the devil and demons. Before we knew about Jesus Christ, they had power over our whole region of Guatemala. However, wherever people believe in Christ, the witches become impotent. All the witches have fled into a distant town. We have commissioned an evangelist to preach there as well; Christ will break the power of the witches in this last stronghold of the demons."

What a fascinating responsibility the church has! This is the community to whom the end has been revealed; the church knows that a day is coming when every knee in heaven and earth will bow before Jesus, the Christ. God has commissioned the church to reveal that mystery to the powers in heaven and earth, to the evil spirits who empower witches, to the angels who are messengers of God, and to the incredulous human institutions as well.

Preaching the Gospel to All Nations

"And this gospel of the kingdom will be preached in the whole world as a testimony to all nations, and then the end will come," Jesus announced shortly before his crucifixion (Matt. 24:14).

Jesus linked the end of history to mission among all nations (*ethnos*). In the Greek language the term *ethnos* is translated as nations. *Ethnos* does not mean nation-states; it does mean people groups.

God's plan is that every people group have the opportunity to believe in Jesus the Christ. God commissions the church to move across cultural and language barriers into communities where people have not yet heard the gospel. His plan is for the church to carry the gospel from group to group until every tribe and nation has heard of Jesus Christ.

"Then the end will come," Jesus has promised.

As the eschatological community, the church has the astonishing responsibility of cooperating with the Holy Spirit in preparing the whole earth for the second coming of Jesus Christ. Preaching the gospel to all nations is at the core of that responsibility.

Through life and witness, the church demonstrates that Jesus is Lord now and forever. God calls the church to express that witness among all authorities, powers, and nations.

Trinity Means Mission

We have discovered that the church is the eschatological community. Theologians also refer to the church as a trinitarian community. That comes from the term *Trinity*, for the church experiences God as Father, Son, and Holy Spirit.

Trinity and *eschaton* belong together. We experience God reaching out to us in mission as Trinity; we experience his mission within history as the beginning of the *eschaton*. Mission is empowered through our trinitarian experience of God; mission is encouraged by our hope that the kingdom of God will be fulfilled.

We now explore ways in which the church's experience of God as Trinity empowers mission.

The North African theologian Quintus Septimius Florens Tertullian (d. 230?) introduced the term *Trinity* into Christian conversation.

Although Christians find *Trinity* helpful in expressing their experience of God as Father, Son, and Holy Spirit, others outside the church often find the term less helpful. To Muslims and Jews, the term seems polytheistic.

"Why are you teaching people in our community that there are three gods?" exploded Lugman. He was standing at the front door of our home in Eastleigh, Nairobi, Kenya, shaking with rage. He had just left the noon prayers at the mosque across the street from our home.

"I don't believe in three gods!" I responded emphatically. "Why are you accusing me in this way?"

"The Trinity!" he exclaimed. "That is what I am talking about."

"Oh, the Trinity," I responded. "Trinity means that you and I should love each other!"

"What?" Lugman was amazed.

"Yes, Trinity means that we should love each other. God experiences perfect loving communion within himself. In Jesus the Messiah, God has revealed his love fully. God invites us to participate in the same love for God and for one another which we observe in the Messiah. God has sent his Spirit into the world, and he wants us to invite him into our lives so that he might empower us to love one another as God does within himself. So Trinity really means that you and I should love one another."

"How amazing!" Lugman surprised me. "If loving one another as God loves is the meaning of Trinity, then Trinity is very good."

After that conversation Lugman always addressed me as "brother." He was no longer an antagonist.

In biblical revelation we meet God as Creator, Savior, and Presence. Let us reflect on this three-dimensional experience of God.

We meet God as Creator. We are astonished to learn that our Creator invites us to experience him as our Abba, Papa, Father.

We meet God as Savior. In Jesus of Nazareth, God enters human history. He walks with us within the sinfulness, tragedies, and joys of life. He gives his life as the sacrifice for our sin. God has named the Savior "my beloved Son."

We meet God as Holy Spirit. He is always present with us. He reveals the truth and convicts us of our sin. He empowers us for joyful and righteous living.

We experience God as Father, Son, and Holy Spirit.

God is personal; he is love. Personal love means fellowship within God; it also means inviting others to share in the same love God experiences in himself. God so loved that he sent his Son, that we also might participate in the fellowship with God and with one another that God enjoys within himself.

God as Trinity reaches out to us in invitation. God does not remain in lonely, self-contained unity. He has created the universe and all people. God sent his Son. He also sends his Spirit. He invites us into the same love he experiences within himself; that is the soul of mission. We therefore also must send and be sent (John 17:20-26).

Father, Son, and Holy Spirit are at the core of the Christian understanding of mission.

Jesus proclaimed, "All authority in heaven and on earth has been given to me. Therefore go and make disciples of all nations, baptizing them in the name of the Father and of the Son and of the Holy Spirit" (Matt. 28:18-19).

Mission atrophies when the church neglects the full-orbed revelation of God as Father and Son and Holy Spirit.

A primary emphasis on Father nurtures universalism; that is the notion that everyone is included in the family of God regardless of a person's commitments. There is no invitation to repentance. God becomes everything we wish.

A primary focus on Son nurtures humanism. Jesus becomes only a splendid example. People should also strive for goodness and in that way become daughters and sons of God. In time humanisms create discouragement; we don't measure up to our ideals.

A focus mostly on the Holy Spirit produces excesses and an unhealthy quest for personal power. Sometimes a Spirit-only emphasis also becomes a universalism, for people perceive that the Holy Spirit is working everywhere with no necessary relationship to Jesus.

No wonder Jesus stressed that his disciples shall baptize believers in the name of the "Father and the Son and the Holy Spirit." That commitment is the basis for empowered, balanced, and fruitful mission.

The church as the eschatological community prepares the world for the conclusion of history by going and making "disciples of all nations." The church as the trinitarian community baptizes those who believe in the name of the Father and the Son and the Holy Spirit.

The Birthday of the Church

God created the church as the eschatological community in mission at the time of the Jewish feast of Pentecost, about fifty days after the crucifixion and resurrection of Jesus. This birthday event is a revelation of ways the church is the community in which the end is here.

We will explore this surprising event and what it means for the church in these modern times. This should become quite practical. This is a description of the beginning of the church, which includes your local congregation.

Forty days after his resurrection, Jesus ascended into the heavens. Just before his ascension, Jesus commanded his disciples to preach the gospel among all peoples. First, however, they were to wait in Jerusalem until they received the Holy Spirit. So 120 people gathered in Jerusalem for a ten-day prayer retreat.

On Pentecost the Holy Spirit came upon them with the sound of a mighty wind and with tongues of fire which rested on each worshiper. They began to praise the Lord mightily. Hundreds and then thousands came running to the house to see and hear what was happening. The crowds came from at least a dozen different countries. They spoke many languages.

At this moment when the church was born, God performed a special miracle. Each person heard the disciples praising God in his own mother tongue. They were "utterly amazed" (Acts 2:7).

Take note; people are often astonished by the ministries of the church. They appreciate the compassion of the church as it cleans up after Hurricane Hugo in North Carolina or rebuilds medical centers in Armenia after an earthquake. Mother Teresa's ministry to orphans earned her a Nobel Prize for peace.

Yet being amazed about the church is quite different from becoming a believer and a participant. Something much more radical than amazed crowds happened at the Pentecost birthday of the church. Multitudes repented! They became members of a new and miraculous creation, the community of shalom established by Jesus Christ.

The U-Turn

"Repent and be baptized, every one of you in the name of Jesus Christ so that your sins may be forgiven. And you will receive the gift of the Holy Spirit," preached Peter at the climax of his sermon on the day of Pentecost (Acts 2:38). Repentance is the only way to enter the community in which the end is here. It is a U-turn away from a self-centered focus to face Jesus.

In Hong Kong a park perches atop a hill just off Waterloo Road in central Kowloon, in the heart of this dynamic metropolis. The hill is opposite the YMCA where I often stay when in town. I like to rise before sunup and climb that hill for a morning jog on the plateau above the city. Several score people are always there. Most are exercising, doing gentle Chinese shadowboxing. Their faces are alight, for they are facing east, where the sky is aglow with the increasing light of dawn.

The joggers prancing around the park are not always facing the dawning sun. When they face west, their faces are dull like the dark shadows of the city. Only faces turned toward the east glow. On that plateau in the heart of Hong Kong, all those facing darkness in the west must make a U-turn if they wish to face the source of the dawning light.

The metaphor of the dawn on the hill in Hong Kong might unlock the meaning of repentance (Newbigin, 21). We are invited to make a U-turn away from the darkness of the unlighted city toward the dawning light of a new day. Soon the source of the dawn's light will arise above us and scatter all darkness from the city.

Jesus Christ is that light. We see the dawn of Christ's imminent appearing, and we live in the expectation that he will soon return, scattering all darkness forever. God calls us to make a U-turn away from the darkness toward the one who is "the true light that gives light to [all]" (John 1:9).

Repentance is urgent. The kingdom of God is at hand. The true light is appearing. We urge people to turn from darkness to light.

Meeting in the Name of Jesus

"For where two or three come together in my name, there am I with them," Jesus promised (Matt. 18:20).

A new creation happens as people meet Jesus by gathering in his name. The Holy Spirit is also called the Spirit of Jesus. As people turn toward Jesus, as they gather in his name, the resurrected Jesus does indeed stand among them. Jesus meets with the worshipers.

They experience conviction concerning sin, the forgiveness of sin, joy, love, peace, empowerment for righteous living, guidance, answers to prayer, and fellowship with God and one another. They experience assurance that they are indeed sons and daughters in the family of God. As Christians sincerely gather in the name of Jesus again and again, they become more and more like Jesus.

Three Character Traits

We shall observe three character traits of the church as the global community of the *eschaton* in whom the Spirit of Jesus is present: (1) a patient and suffering community; (2) a people empowered by the Spirit of God; and (3) a community of reconciliation which provides good seasoning in societies, like salt seasons food.

First, the church is a suffering community. Christians do not always experience martyrdom. Yet in every generation of church history, somewhere within the global church, Christians have died for their faith. Why is suffering a characteristic of the church?

Human societies and institutions do not enjoy critique. Each nation and institution wants to function as final authority for its people. However, although Jesus of Nazareth lived within Israel as a genuine Jew, he was a stranger. Whenever his family, hometown, religious community, economic system, political institution, or a person were contrary to the mind of God, Jesus was disturbing.

"I must be about my Father's business," Jesus firmly rebuked his family, when they challenged his loyalties (Luke 2:49, KJV).

Jesus obeyed God. That meant he could not also run a popularity contest. He warned that all who follow him will also discover that they are moving in directions which are not popular.

Within days of the Pentecost birthday of the church, the authorities responsible for the operations of the Jewish temple commanded Peter and John to stop preaching about Jesus.

"Judge for yourselves whether it is right in God's sight to obey you rather than God!" replied Peter and John, who were unlearned peasant fishermen from Galilee (Acts 4:19).

Imagine the astonishment and perplexity of the sophisticated temple authorities when rebuked by uneducated fishermen. Yet faithful Christians are always perplexing; their focus is different from the world systems.

Faithful Christians can expect suffering because they face a different direction from the mainstream of their culture. The high school senior mocked by his peers because he refuses to lose his virginity; the honest business partner edged out of her position by colleagues who insist on using distorted advertisements; the factory worker fired because she objects to working on an assembly line producing trigger mechanisms for cluster bombs—all can expect suffering. In both subtle and sometimes confrontational ways, the faithful Christian in every society always goes against the stream of culture and peers.

"My fiancée was a student here in the University of Gorky," a Russian electronics technician explained. "When the university administrators discovered she was a Christian, they called her in for questioning. They gave an ultimatum: Christ or the university.

" 'I can never deny Jesus,' she responded.

"That was it. She was expelled. Her professional goals were destroyed."

Let us remember, however, that suffering is often healthy for the church. In fact the Christian faith needs opposition in order to thrive. But don't worry about that. Any faithful Christian will experience opposition, no matter where she lives.

Yet some Christians in some settings experience more than opposition. They experience severe persecution. This was true of many believers in communist societies. Nevertheless, even in those circumstances, some believers survived with precious testimonies of faith.

"Communism was very good for us," a young Romanian mother confided. She brushed a tear aside as she continued simply, "It taught us to love Jesus!"

Second, the church is an empowered community. The church is not a humanist organization. This community of believers who gather in the name of Jesus are empowered by the Holy Spirit to live righteously.

The Holy Spirit is at work within the church. People who have lived evil or self-righteously are converted; they become new creations. People who have been self-centered and self-sufficient discover a new center for their lives—Jesus Christ. The Scriptures describe this empowerment, this new creation, as the fruit of the Spirit: love, joy, peace, patience, kindness, goodness, faithfulness, gentleness, and self-control (Gal. 5:22).

The empowered church serves our world as Jesus served. In one of Jesus' resurrection appearances among his disciples, he completely astonished them with a commission and a promise.

> Go into all the world and preach the good news to all creation. Whoever believes and is baptized will be saved, but whoever does not believe will be condemned. And these signs will accompany those who believe: In my name they will drive out demons; they will speak in new tongues; they will pick up snakes with their hands; and when they drink deadly poison, it will not hurt them at all; they will place their hands on sick people, and they will get well. (Mark 16:15, 18)

Ibraihim Shafi was the first Christian among his people, a nomadic clan in northeastern Kenya. Someone had given him a Bible; that is how he learned of Jesus Christ and believed. He was empowered by the Holy Spirit and boldly invited his community to believe in Jesus Christ. Leaders in the community were livid. They plotted to kill him.

Late at night three hired thugs with spears crept toward Ibraihim's hut of woven grass mats. Suddenly, brilliant light burst from the sky and surrounded the hut. The thugs fell dazed. When they recovered, they ran to town and reported what had happened.

"Tonight," they announced, "God sent his angel from heaven to protect Ibraihim. We should respect that man!"

Of course, God does not always send his angels to protect believers. Sometimes the witness of the church is expressed most effectively through martyrs. Yet whether in life or in death, the faithful church is empowered by the Holy Spirit for fruitful mission.

Third, the church is a fellowship of reconciliation. The global village of humankind observes the constant strife between Catholics and Protestants in Northern Ireland, or the horrendous destruction in Lebanon created by the war between Christians and Muslims as well as between Christian factions and Muslim factions. We also notice that within Christian congregations there is occasional strife. Yet both Christians and non-Christians recognize that divisiveness and strife within the community of Christian faith is contrary to the Spirit of Jesus Christ.

"Be the church!" our world implores.

"Middle East Christians are the glue that hold this region together," explained King Hussein of Jordan to a global church leader in a conversation on October 16, 1986.

Professor Raymond Bakke, director of International Urban Associates, Chicago, was astonished. Yet close observation of the Middle East reveals that the Christians are a unique community of reconciliation within that volatile region.

A special Christian gift is that the churches in the Middle East are small and vulnerable. The political insignificance of the church within most countries in that region enables the Christians to salt rather than steer events. The church in such settings can influence but not direct the affairs of the larger society.

"We are one of the few inter-clan fellowships in the city of Mogadishu," explained several disciples of Jesus the Messiah. Their city and Somali nation had suffered through two years of clan against clan strife.

"Although we come from clans who have been at war with one another, when one of the brothers suffers, we do what we can to help," they explained.

A brother added, "A year ago one of the brothers was wounded. He is of a clan at war with my people. I walked right across the city to find him. However, when I got to the battle lines, the soldiers would not let me pass. Yet they understood well that I truly love my brother. We are a people of reconciliation."

They are so few, I thought. *Yet these disciples of the Messiah are a tiny mustard seed of reconciliation. They are the unobtrusive presence of the kingdom of God in a society which yearns for healing and forgiveness.*

Whenever the church does function as a reconciliation community, it is salt within any society.

In January 1992, Kalanjin clansmen attacked Luo farming communities in the Songhor community of Kenya. The attackers set fire to hundreds of acres of sugarcane; they burned homes and looted wildly. Many died in the conflagration.

Clyde Agola, a youth living in Songhor, described the healing ministry of the church after the disaster. "The churches collected money. Even churches in other lands who had never before heard of the church in Songhor sent money. We used the cash to buy blankets and food. Then in an orderly way, the church distributed the food and blankets to the homeless and hungry.

"The Luo Christians also delivered food and blankets to Kalanjin who had suffered in the clash. They did this, even though everyone in our region knows that the Kalanjin started the skirmish. That act of love and reconciliation is amazing. The church has really helped bring healing between the Kalenjin and the Luo."

* * *

This chapter describes the church as the eschatological community. Christians believe that Jesus Christ will return at the end of history to bring about a new creation when the kingdom of God is fulfilled. However, that wonderful end is already beginning within the church. The church urges people to repent for the kingdom of God is here.

The full-orbed and empowered mission of the church is a response to the experience of God as Trinity. It is for this reason that the missionary commission, as recorded in Matthew, commands the disciples to baptize all nations in the name of the Father, Son, and Holy Spirit.

The church in mission experiences suffering, is empowered by the Holy Spirit, and as a community of reconciliation brings healing to the nations.

The next chapter describes God's global plan. God is the model missionary, and he has surprising hopes and plans for our world.

Reflection

1. Reflect on ways in which the church experiences hope because of the end (Eph. 1:18-23).

2. In what ways does your own congregation reveal the surprising presence of the kingdom of God? Describe evidence of shalom in your church. Reflect on possible absence of shalom. What is at the root of the absence of well-being?

3. Reflect on ways in which your church is revealing to the authorities and powers God's mystery concerning his plans for the destiny of human history (Eph. 3:7-13).

4. Comment on this statement: Whenever a Christian community neglects Father, Son, or Holy Spirit, the mission of that church is distorted and wanes (Matt. 28:18-20).

5. In what ways have you observed the church as a suffering community, as a Spirit-empowered community, and as a community of reconciliation and salt?

* * *

Suggested background Scriptures—Isaiah 53:1-12; Matthew 5:13-16; 16:21, 24; 17:12; Mark 8:31-38; Acts 1—2; 9:16; Romans 8:16-17; 2 Corinthians 11:21-29; 17:3; Galatians 3:26-28; Ephesians 1:15-23; 2—3; Philippians 2:10-11; Hebrews 2:14-15; 12:2; 1 Peter 2:21; 4:12-19.

5

The Global Plan

"I ONCE HAD an awesome religious experience!" exclaimed the British businessperson who had joined me for a late night dinner in the Hargeisa Hotel, Somaliland, in the deserts of northeastern Africa. "I had a mystical experience gazing at Michelangelo's murals in the dome of Saint Peter's Basilica in Rome."

"So you are a believer?" I inquired.

"Not really," the Englishman responded. "The experience at Saint Peter's was inspiring, but I have never worshiped with Christians or any other believers. I am just going through life as best I can, and I admit that's not much to brag about."

The Englishman had a religious experience standing in a cathedral. Others are touched by similar experiences of mystical awe in other settings.

"The Himalaya Mountains are the best place in the world to experience spiritual vibrations," reverently counseled the pious swami in the Hindu temple in Nairobi, Kenya. "The spirituality of those mountains is indescribable."

"Are you and your community living righteously?" I asked.

"Frankly, that is an irrelevant question," the Indian swami countered. "Spirituality is a state of mind, not of conduct. I tell you absolutely that the best place to acquire that state of mind is in the Himalaya Mountains, which are filled with spiritual vibrations."

Religious Experiences

What is the attitude of the Bible toward the kinds of experiences which the English businessperson and the Indian swami described? The Bible is not impressed, unless religious experiences nurture within the person a thirst to know God their Creator. Otherwise such experiences are meaningless.

The Bible invites people to meet God. Yet even that meeting is meaningless, unless the person makes a U-turn toward the Lord. The Bible refers to that U-turn as repentance; that is the only kind of faith commitment the Bible considers authentic.

The unforgettable religious experiences described by the Indian swami and the English businessperson were only that: religious experiences. These experiences had taken these two very different men nowhere. They basked in the memories of respective experiences in Saint Peter's Basilica and the Himalayan forests, but that is all there was to it.

These religious experiences had not inspired them to live righteously or invest their lives in serving others. The spiritual insights had not introduced a fresh plan or a new humanizing direction into their lives. The experiences were a precious memory—yet the memory did not inspire day-by-day joy and love and compassion. There was no encounter requiring a change of direction toward ultimate goals.

As I waited with 300 other passengers in the New Delhi departure lounge for a late-night flight, I prayed, "Lord, if there is someone here tonight with whom I should share Jesus, arrange the seating so it will happen."

In a flash I noticed a woman at the far edge of the lounge. It turned out she was indeed my seat companion. I knew this was God's appointment. We talked all night.

She told me, "After the crash of my marriage, I set out on a quest for an authentic religious experience. I have been in India for one year, living in a Hindu ashram."

This very sad woman continued, "My swami has helped me acquire high mystical states of spirituality through yoga, drugs, meditation, and intimate sex. His spirituality is wonderful; he has a profound philosophy. I have learned to lose myself in the sea of universal mind."

"And now where are you headed? In what direction is your life turning?" I asked.

With deep sadness etching her face, she responded, "I have no idea. I have learned that life has no meaning."

"But that is not God's plan for you," I promised. "The Bible provides a blueprint, a plan, a focus for your life."

She perked up. "What is God's plan?" she asked.

The Global Plan

This chapter explores that question. The Bible describes God's global plan. It is also the map which shows the way God's plan is unfolding. Have you ever tried driving through a strange region without a road map? It is confusing and frustrating.

Life is also a journey. Each phase of life is new territory we have never traveled before. We need a plan and a map. The Bible provides both God's good plan for us and the map which reveals the way toward its fulfillment.

Philosophy also seeks truth. Philosophers such as the Greek Plato (d. 347 B.C.) spoke of the ideal good. That good is the principle within the universe which determines human destiny. Through intuition and rational thought, people can discern that ideal good and conform to it.

Communist philosophy rooted in Marxism also affirms that there is a universal, ideal good which determines the direction of history. Other philosophers such as Confucius of ancient China or Buddha of India have sought universal principles as well.

However, the Bible does not primarily seek universal principles. Philosophies seek to discover notions of universal truth through the abilities of human intuition or intellect. But you cannot study biblical philosophy. This is because the Bible is primarily a history, not a philosophy. It is an account of God's acts in history as he works to bring about his plan for the well-being of people and the whole earth. The Bible is an invitation to repent, not a blueprint for right meditation or an exposition on philosophical thought. It is an account of people's response to God and his plan.

Just a History Book!

Ibraihim Abdi Mohammed was a devout Muslim. One evening he joined me for a cup of tea and conversation in our living room.

Then he surprised me by saying, "Please give me a Bible."

I gave him a Bible. He wrapped it reverently in brown paper. With a tinge of excitement, he slipped away into the night.

The next evening Ibraihim returned, carrying the brown paper-wrapped Bible. He was dejected. "You Christians have hopelessly corrupted the Bible," he complained, returning the book to me.

"Why do you say that?" I asked, perplexed.

"You have mixed history and the Word of God all together. Muslims have never disrespected God's Word in that way. The Koran is the true Word of God; it contains no history."

I replied, "Ibraihim, I am delighted that you have noticed that the Bible is primarily a history book. The Bible is history because God reveals himself by what he *does*, especially in history. In the Bible we discover that God loves us so much that he has chosen personally to enter human history.

"The Spirit of God inspired and enabled the prophets to record and interpret the acts of God so that we can know God. The Bible is also an account of the human response to God. That includes accounts of people rejecting God."

Ibraihim was not impressed. He left the Bible with me.

The issue which divided us is this question: How much does God care for us? Does he care only enough to give guidance for life's journey? Or does God become personally involved within our history? Does God love us enough to send his one and only Son, who is the Word of God in human form?

John describes Jesus as the living Word of God "which we have heard, which we have seen with our eyes, which we have looked at and our hands have touched" (1 John 1:1).

Incarnation

Theologians refer to biblical revelation as incarnational. This means that revelation is expressed in human form.

Jesus Christ is the one in whom "the Word became flesh and lived for a while among us" (John 1:14). The Word of God was revealed in a Palestinian Jewish peasant born in Bethlehem. He is the incarnation, the in-human-form of God's full and definitive self-revelation.

However, it is important to recognize that all biblical revelation has an in-human-form, an incarnational dimension. The personality of the prophet of God is included in all the biblical accounts. The revelation acts of God happen within real human history, actual human culture, and specific societies. All biblical revelation is expressed in human categories and through human personalities.

For example, in an earlier chapter we have described Luke's amazing inclination to include historical and cultural details in his writings. Mark was less inclined to give attention to political and cultural details. His writings are packed with action. The different personalities of Luke and Mark are revealed in the Scriptures they recorded.

The Holy Spirit spoke through the personalities of the writers of Scripture; all revelation has happened within the particular historical and cultural context in which the writers of Scripture lived.

The Bible states,

> All Scripture is God-breathed, and is useful for teaching, rebuking, correcting and training in righteousness, so that the man of God may be thoroughly equipped for every good work. (2 Tim. 3:16)

Elsewhere we read,

> Above all, you must understand that no prophecy of Scripture came about by the prophet's own interpretation. For prophecy never had its origin in the will of man, but men spoke from God as they were carried along by the Holy Spirit. (2 Peter 1:20-21)

God used people as his instruments of revelation. And his acts of revelation are specific. They have happened within history and within culture. Revelation is incarnational.

Two Thousand Translations!

The conviction that biblical revelation has incarnational qualities is what compels Christians to translate the Bible into languages everywhere. A basic human right is the right of all people to receive God's Word in the language and cultural forms of their family. The gospel needs to become incarnated within each culture; the Bible should be clothed in the "at home" culture of every person on earth.

Translation of portions of the Bible began even before Jesus was born. The Old Testament was first recorded in Hebrew; that was the mother tongue of Israel. In the centuries just before the birth of Christ, the people of Israel who migrated to Egypt translated the Old Testament into Greek, which was widely spoken throughout the Middle East region.

The New Testament texts were written in Greek, so people in the Mediterranean region could receive the gospel in the common language of the area. Soon Christians produced other translations of the Bible. Within only a few centuries of the birthday of the church, the translations of the Bible included Syriac in Syria, Geez in Ethiopia, three different Egyptian translations of the three main dialects in that country, and Latin.

Even in far-off central Euro-Asia, the Goths were receiving the Bible in their own language. Ulfilas, grandson of a slave, reduced the language of the Goths into writing, for they had never written their language. Then Ulfilas translated the Bible into the language of the people who had enslaved his grandfather. He also taught them literacy so they could read God's own Word in their mother tongue.

However, one part of the Bible Ulfilas did not translate. The Goths were fighters. For that reason he avoided translating 1 and 2 Kings, which describe the wars of Israel, lest those portions inspire the Goths to continue warfare.

Ulfilas is the forerunner of the modern global network of Bible translators, who must place the language of people into written form before they can begin translating the Bible. The modern Summer Institute of Linguistics (SIL) is that kind of an organization. Governments often seek its services in researching unwritten languages of remote tribal groups and placing those languages in written form. These contracts include an understanding that SIL will translate and publish the Bible in the languages of these peoples.

Today portions of the Bible have been translated into over 2,000 languages. Over 98 percent of the people on earth have at least a portion of the Bible in their native tongue. For hundreds of tribal groups, the Bible is the first book available in their mother tongue. The desire to read the Bible is often the most compelling reason for an isolated people's quest for literacy.

However, there are still several thousand language groups who have no portion of the Scriptures. Although these are mostly small tribes, the Christian conviction is that even the smallest groups should enjoy the blessing of having the Word of God incarnated in their own language and culture.

Faithful Wycliffe workers have translated the Bible into the Cusco dialect of the Quechua Indians of the high Andes of Peru. I met with the first Quechua believers in the town of Lucre in a prayer meeting. Fifty were present. It was a cold, damp night. The meeting lasted three hours.

The Bible was at the center of the meeting. Women and men, youth, and even children read aloud from God's Word written in their mother tongue. Imagine the delight of a people learning to read for the first time. Imagine their surpassing joy when the first book they acquire is God's Word written in the same language their mothers and fathers used at home.

Islam does not have the advantage of mother-tongue scriptures in its worldwide missionary efforts. Muslims believe the Koran came down from God; it is an Arabic Koran. In recent years Muslims have placed a few interpretations of the Koran into languages other than Arabic. But these are only interpretations.

The Koran is only God's word in its heavenly Arabic form. Therefore all converts to Islam need to learn Arabic. Otherwise they will never be able really to hear God's word. In a similar manner the ritual prayers required of all Muslims can be expressed only in Arabic.

The phenomenon of an Arabic Koran makes it difficult for the Muslim nation to resist the temptations of cultural imperialism. Those who know Arabic best hold the religious and cultural trump cards, so to speak.

This is not an academic issue. It is serious and is real. For example, to my knowledge every Muslim theologian in Africa is calling for a de-Africanization of Islam. For Islam to be pure, it must be divested of traditional African culture. Of course, that ideal is impossible.

Empowerment

In contrast, African Christian theologians call for the Africanization of Christianity and the church. That is because incarnation is the very essence of the Christian understanding of revelation.

The translation of the Bible into the language of a people is an important step toward enabling the gospel to be incarnated in the local culture. The Bible in their own language empowers a people to think critically about their own culture as well as the culture of the missionary. The Bible in one's own language is a powerful force for liberation.

Missionaries are not always enthusiastic about the liberation and empowerment of people. Notions of liberation were especially dangerous ideas whenever mission and imperialism went together. In those circumstances, translating the Bible in the local language could be dangerous for the imperialists.

The liberation themes of the Bible are expressed in many ways. Indigenous Christian music is often a significant expression of the empowerment and liberation created through the message of the Scriptures. Contemporary Swahili Christian songs written in East Africa today usually include a biblical narrative. Then the songs apply the message to modern society.

Critique of Culture

The song often becomes a word of prophetic judgment. It might critique Western culture in which the gospel was clothed when it came into tropical Africa a century ago. It might critique traditional customs. The incarnation of the gospel in African culture enables and empowers society to critique both the arrogance of the missionary culture and that of African society.

The critique might be surprising to the missionaries. That is what happened among the Chagga living in the lush slopes of snowcapped Mount Kilimanjaro.

German Lutheran missionaries among the Chagga translated the Bible into the local language. These latter-nineteenth-century missionaries believed the gospel prepared people for heaven but had nothing to do with culture. Although they translated the Bible into the Chagga language, they did not comprehend the power of the gospel incarnated in a culture to change that culture.

During the missionaries' home leave, they wrote a book describing their missiology—a gospel which takes people to heaven but says nothing about culture. But, alas, they had left the Chagga Bibles in Tanganyika.

While the missionaries were away, the Chagga read about Jesus. They saw him as the one who could cleanse their culture of evil. So they held a covenant assembly and spoke openly about evils in their culture—female circumcision, polygyny, witchcraft, wife beating, dirty homes and trash in yards, and alcoholism. They made a covenant to lay aside evil practices. They invited Jesus to become incarnated within their culture and cleanse their community of evil.

What a surprise that was for the missionaries! Yet they were wise to avoid imposing their own critique on Chagga culture. It was the Chagga themselves who saw Jesus as the one who could liberate.

Jesus' liberation cuts two ways. The incarnation of the gospel in a culture not only liberates from evils in the culture but also from evils or imperialisms outside the culture. Whenever the gospel is genuinely received and incarnated, it empowers a people to resist any form of alien cultural influence which does not fit the local idiom, including inappropriate influence from the missionary.

Sometimes missionaries are bewildered. They don't know how to respond to the firm critique of their missionary culture from the newly developing church. Here is an example of an empowered church confronting a well-meaning missionary.

"Now we shall vote to choose the chairman of your church," the

North American missionary bishop announced when an African church chairman was needed. "First I will teach you Robert's Rules of Order, then I shall accept nominations."

The newly Christian Hamitic camel nomads were amazed. They couldn't find Robert's Rules anywhere in the Bible.

Finally a young man rose and said, "In our culture we don't choose leaders that way."

"All right," the bishop conceded. "Choose the chairperson in your way."

Instantly everyone began speaking in rapid-fire babble. Voices got higher and louder. Everyone was shouting. Hands were waving. Some stood and seemed to be shouting in anger. For two minutes there was bedlam. Then all was quiet. Everyone sat down.

The young man rose and said simply, "We believe God has chosen Abdullahi as our chairperson."

Everyone nodded in assent. The good bishop didn't have a clue how the choice was made. Yet he did know that the gospel was becoming incarnated with this culture. Although this wasn't his way of choosing leaders, it was their way.

The gospel had empowered them to resist alien patterns in their decision processes, even if those foreign influences were encouraged by the very bishop who had helped bring them the gospel. They sought to embrace Jesus Christ, not the culture of the missionaries.

The Plan and Map

At the beginning of this chapter we described the Bible as containing the plan and map for human destiny. What do people discover about human destiny when they receive the Bible? What is the plan? What is the map?

This is God's astonishing plan for human history and for all creation.

> For God was pleased to have all his fullness dwell in him [Jesus Christ], and through him to reconcile to himself all things, whether things on earth or things in heaven, by making peace through his blood, shed on the cross. (Col. 1:19-20)

This miracle of reconciliation is for everyone. That is what I heard from Romanian pastors in the wake of four decades of communist repression.

"What did you say to the people when it seemed violence would destroy your city?" I asked pastor Joseph Stefanutsi of Braila, Romania.

The pastor was describing the volatile events in his town surrounding the 1989 collapse of the communist regime in Romania. At the height of the crisis, when multitudes were in the square, the desperate town officials invited the pastor to address the angry crowd.

Joseph informed me, "I told them God sent Jesus Christ, his Son, to die for our sins. In him we have reconciliation with God and with one another. I invited everyone to turn to Jesus and experience reconciliation."

Joseph is right. God's plan is to reconcile all things in heaven and earth through Jesus crucified. That is the mystery of God's plan. In the apparent failure and foolishness and weakness of the crucified Jesus, God plans to bring about a cosmic reconciliation.

The Foolish Cross

Animal or human sacrifices are an enigma of traditional religions. Most anthropologists are inclined to ignore this universal phenomenon. Yet it is always there. In ancient and modern times, traditional tribal religions practice sacrifices. Even the universal religion of Islam has an annual day of sacrifices, when millions of Muslim families around the world slay animals. What is the mystery of truth hidden in this universal practice?

The French anthropologist René Girard has probed this mystery. He believes the origin of these sacrifices is the quest for reconciliation.

When there is hostility between protagonists, it is almost impossible to stop the cycle of vengeance. The principle of a life for a life becomes an endless cycle of a life for a life for a life for a life for a life for a life for. . . . The vengeance cycle may abate for awhile, only to be revived later. The only solution is the sacrifice of an innocent victim (Girard, 1-67).

The sacrifice for reconciliation must be the very best the enemies seeking peace can offer. If human, the sacrifice is often a virgin girl. The protagonists will project their hostility onto the innocent animal or human, which does not take vengeance. The sacrifice absorbs the hatred and violence. It takes no vengeance; it simply dies. By absorbing the hatred and violence, the sacrificial victim breaks the cycle of hostility.

That is exactly what Jesus has done. He is the best heaven or earth could offer. He is God's one and only Son. He is the ideal human. No other has ever lived with the authenticity, love, and power of Jesus. He is the innocent sacrificial victim who stands between all protagonists.

The protagonists crucify him—colonial Romans and colonized Jews, men and women, religious zealots and the nonreligious, the rich and poor, the slave and free, even the criminals and the prosecutors are there. He absorbs the hostility of all and forgives.

Jesus takes no vengeance. The innocent one dies. He breaks the cycle of violence and vengeance.

"Father, forgive them," he cries out from the cross as he dies.

This Jesus crucified is the fulfillment of the quest, which permeates religions everywhere, for a perfect sacrificial victim who can break the cycle of hostility, alienation, or violence.

Most churches celebrate communion regularly. The believers break bread together. They remember the sacrificed body of Christ which was broken on the cross by his enemies. They share a cup of wine. That reminds Christians that the hostility of people against Christ caused bleeding from beatings, nails in his hands, a crown of thorns beaten into his head, and a spear thrust into his side. The bread and wine of communion are a regular reminder that Jesus Christ was crucified; in his sacrificial death we experience reconciliation with God and with one another.

In times of war it is often especially difficult to live in reconciliation. That is what thousands of Christians discovered during the war for independence in Kenya. During the 1950s the Mau Mau war burned in the highlands.

Nevertheless, sisters and brothers within the East Africa Revival Fellowship chose the weapons of love rather than violence. Hundreds died as martyrs.

"A white government officer offered me a gun to protect myself," explained Heshbon Mwangi. "I refused that gun."

A deep scar etched his face, the consequence of lacerations when Mau Mau had attacked him at the school where he taught. They had slashed him, stomped on him, and thought he had died.

"Why didn't you take the gun?" I prodded gently.

Heshbon explained, "In our traditional religion, we used to slay a sacrificial animal for reconciliation. After enemies had been sprinkled with the blood of that sacrifice, they could never fight again, for the ancestors themselves had established that peace. The sacrifice of Christ on the cross is far more excellent than all our traditional sacrifices."

Heshbon paused and then continued in a spirit of confidence and peace, "I have drunk the wine of the covenant of the blood of the

Lamb of God. How could I ever kill anyone for whom Christ has died?"

No wonder Christians greet one another at the communion service with the words, "The peace of God be with you."

A Special Gift; A Vital Choice

God's plan is that all things in heaven and earth experience reconciliation through Jesus Christ crucified. And that reconciliation begins with the person. God invites each person to repent and experience reconciliation, peace with God and with others. That is a miracle. It is shalom.

Jesus referred to God-created reconciliation as a new birth. It is a gift of God, the creation of the Spirit of God within all who repent.

We cannot invent the new birth or create authentic reconciliation. It is a gift to be received—or rejected. It is a gift to be cherished and nurtured. God offers the gift of reconciliation, but he never compels us to accept it. He respects our freedom to reject his gift.

The choice is between alienation and reconciliation. Those who reject God's invitation to reconciliation experience deepening alienation. Jesus warned that there will be a final judgment at the conclusion of history. The eternal consequences of our choices will be fully evident on that judgment day. Yet the consequences of our choices are already bearing fruit within this life. We observe everywhere the bitter fruit of alienation; hints of hell are already with us.

The alternative to alienation is the joy of reconciliation. The new birth and reconciliation is the creation of the Spirit of God, who forms within the believer the same spirit of forgiveness and love for one's enemies which Jesus expressed on the cross. God's reconciliation plan is a gift of grace. Again and again the church has the privilege of expressing that reconciliation gift in difficult circumstances, including love for the enemy.

Love for the Enemy

The two incidents that follow describe reaching out in reconciling love to enemies.

A missionary was brutally stabbed and killed. The assassin also stabbed the victim's wife repeatedly. She was still in the hospital, hovering between life and death, when the trial of the assassin began. She wrote a letter to the judge and the court.

"I forgive the assassin. I press no charges," she wrote.

The court was astonished. Never had the judge or the people in that court encountered that kind of forgiveness.

A pastor was in prison for his faith for four years and four months. For twenty-two months he was in a room about four yards square with more than thirty men. The room was so crowded they had to sleep like sardines, lying on the floor side by side on their sides, head to foot and foot to head. The guard was obnoxious and cruel.

Many months after the pastor was released, he learned that the guard was in prison. The pastor visited that cruel man every week, taking a basket of fruit and other delicacies.

"Why do you do this?" asked the bewildered prisoner. "I treated you so cruelly."

"I am coming each week because God loves you. By God's grace, I forgave you already when I was in the prison cell."

Helping People Find the Way

The mission of the church is to be a community of reconciliation among the nations. They are already experiencing the reconciliation created in Christ crucified. They are a forgiven and a forgiving people.

For faithful Christians, the cycle of vengeance and violence has ceased. The church is a new creation among the nations, a community of reconciliation, a visual revelation of God's global and universal plan to reconcile to Christ all things in heaven and earth.

The faithful church is participating in God's grand global plan. It also possesses the map, showing both the nature of the plan and the way to participate in it. The map is the Bible. Yet the faithful church is also the map, because the faithful church lives in continuity with its Scriptures.

We invite people to receive the biblical message. We also invite them to observe the faithful church. Without the church, people might consider the Bible irrelevant and see the invitation to live in reconciliation as nonsense.

Living in God's Global Plan

We learn what it means to be reconciled to God and others in the experience of community. In other words, a believer in Christ must become a covenant member of a church. In the church we learn reconciliation. How will we learn the art of reconciliation if we practice our faith alone?

Who will teach us reconciliation if we relate only to friends or fellowship only with those with whom we agree? The church is not a community of friends, a club of buddies. It is open to whoever will come. People I would not normally choose as friends become covenant members of my congregation. The diversities within the church enable us to learn reconciliation.

We discover that believers in Christ must be servants. Just as Christ humbled himself and served others, so his disciples need to learn the art of servanthood. There should be no scrambling to climb the power structures in the church. Rather, believers should seek to minister to one another and serve in love.

The church is both a global and local community. Not all members of the family for whom we share responsibility are in the local church. Our neighbor might include someone suffering hunger in Timbuktu or Ougadugu. Christians seek to serve their brothers and sisters in need, not just in the local congregation, but wherever they might be.

The biblical map also reveals that the people of God shall be a community of prayer. Through prayer, believers cultivate a joyful and fulfilling relationship with God. Prayer is also interceding for the fulfillment of God's kingdom.

"May your kingdom come! May your will be done on earth as in heaven!" That is praying for the most authentic and dramatic revolution. It is praying for shalom on earth.

The church has the special privilege of serving as priests who pray for the healing of the nations. Christians minister to the whole world through prayer. They yearn for God's kingdom to happen on earth just as in heaven.

The church is a people of joy. Joyful song and worship embrace the congregation as it gathers in Jesus' name.

"What singing!" I exclaimed at the conclusion of an evening worship in a K'ekchi' Indian congregation in the mountains of Guatemala. "How those little children sang! Even the weatherworn faces of the old crinkled in joyful song. What an evening!"

"Yes," a missionary companion reflected pensively. "In traditional K'ekchi' culture, there is no song. When they believe in Jesus Christ, they ask the Holy Spirit to teach them to sing. Singing is the special gift of the Holy Spirit within this culture. The Holy Spirit fills them with joy and with song!"

These people had begun participating in God's reconciliation plan. No wonder they had walked miles through mud and rain to enjoy an evening of praise and song with members of the family of God who were visiting from other lands. Because of Jesus Christ, they knew they belonged in God's family. They knew that the purpose of living is to glorify God and enjoy him now and forever.

That is the reason for their exuberant singing!

* * *

This chapter discerns that the Bible is not impressed with mere religious experiences. The Bible invites a joyful relationship with God which cultivates righteousness and service for others. The biblical message provides God's plan and map for authentic life direction.

That plan is much more than written instructions. God himself has chosen to enter human history; theologians call this incarnation. God loves us so much that he meets us within our circumstances, and supremely so in Jesus Christ.

For this reason Christians in faithful mission have always sought to translate God's Word into local languages, with the goal that all peoples have opportunity to receive the gospel in their own idiom. When the biblical message is received and incarnated within a culture, the people experience liberation and empowerment.

God's plan and invitation for each person and all creation is reconciliation through Jesus Christ. Although the world considers the crucifixion of Jesus foolish and weak, we discover in his suffering death and resurrection a miraculous reconciliation and healing. That is shalom. The faithful church expresses that miracle.

The following chapter, "The Global Village," explores the context of mission. In what kind of a world does the church express the miracle of reconciliation and shalom?

Reflection

1. From a biblical perspective, how should a person evaluate a mystical religious experience?

2. Why would it be impossible to teach a course on biblical philosophy?

3. What is God's global plan? Why does the world consider that plan foolish?

4. Reflect on ways you observe God working to fulfill his plan.

5. In what ways does your congregation experience empowerment and liberation because of the message of the Bible? In what ways does that message liberate you?

6. Describe your congregation as a people in whom the gospel is

being incarnated. What difference does that surprising miracle make within your congregation? How does your congregation express that miracle in the world around you?

* * *

Suggested background Scriptures—Isaiah 6:1-6; John 13; Acts 2:1-47; 3; 1 Corinthians 1:18—2:5; Ephesians 2:11-22; 3:9-12; Philippians 4:10-13; Colossians 1:15-23; Hebrews 9:23-28; 1 Peter 2:5.

6

The Global Village

DARK MONDAY, October 19, 1987, was a thunderbolt in Hong Kong. The American Wall Street stock market crashed; a trillion dollars in assets evaporated in a day.

The morning after the crash I visited an isolated theological school on Cheung Chau Island in Hong Kong Harbor. At noon the students delayed their lunch to crowd around the television in the lounge. Even the walkway and yard were filled with students peering through the lounge windows at that TV screen.

"Why are the students so interested in the television program?" I inquired of the principal.

"Your president will be speaking shortly. Our economic destiny is in his hands!"

I was astonished. Hong Kong is on the opposite side of the earth from Wall Street. These students were destined for vocations as pastors. Yet they believed President Reagan would significantly affect their future well-being.

The Well-Being of the Global Village

We live in one global village. That village is the context in which we express God's call to mission. What are the modern features of that global village as the twentieth century yields to the twenty-first?

Every night 100 million teenagers sleep in homeless conditions.

Every day forty thousand babies die of malnutrition or avoidable illnesses.

Every day people contribute to the destruction of another animal or plant species; one species a day disappears from the earth.

Every day the global community of nations spend U.S. $1,500,000,000 in arms. (Following the collapse of the Soviet Union, there has been a reduction in global expenditures for arms among the great powers. Smaller nations have increased military expenditures, partly because industries manufacturing arms seek new markets for weapons.)

Every day thirty wars rage among the nations.

Every day the United States government borrows $1 billion in new money; this is like a sponge soaking up capital from around the world.

Every day the debt of the poor nations increases by $250 million. Much of this is interest on old debts which cannot be collected. So the interest is added to the old debt burden which had reached U.S. $1,500,000,000,000 by the close of the decade of the 1980s.

Every day the rich nations receive U.S. $150 million from the poor nations. (For a more thorough discussion of the global crisis, a useful statement is *Justice, Peace and the Integrity of Creation*, the World Assembly of the Christian Churches, Seoul, Korea, March 5-13, 1990.)

The global village is not healthy.

Population Growth

Our global village is changing. One of the most obvious changes is that there are more and more people. At the time of Christ there were about 140 million people on earth. By the beginning of the twentieth century, the global population had increased by somewhat over a billion people; that's nineteen hundred years for the population to increase by a little over a billion people. But hold on!

The twentieth century has been a population growth blockbuster. By the close of the century, the global population will have increased by five billion people. We entered the century with about one and one-third billion people on earth and will exit the century with about six and one-third billion. Whereas it took nineteen hundred years for the global population to increase by about a billion people, in modern times the population has increased by five billion in only one century.

Why this astonishing growth in the number of people? Technology is one core reason. Let me illustrate. My earliest recollections are of my mother sharing medicines for the children of Zanaki mothers in Tanganyika. They came with ill children to the back stoop of our home. I heard those mothers tell my mother of heartbreak.

"This is my sixth baby. All the others have died. I want this baby to live so very much. Please help me."

The killer of babies in that society was diet, dysentery, and malaria. As Mother dispensed the medicines for dysentery, she also gave simple lessons on diet.

"Don't feed your infant gruel," she counseled. "Your own milk is the best possible food for your baby."

Recently I returned to the place of my childhood among the Zanaki. The church was filled with children. A clinic stands beside the church, continuing the tradition of dispensing modern medicines and counsel which my mother had begun fifty years before. There is a population explosion within the whole region. The fertile countryside is filled with homesteads. The babies don't die anymore.

Medical Technology

However, high-tech medical care is beyond the reach of these people. For example, with the exception of South Africa, there is no medical facility in the whole continent which can perform cardiac surgery on infants. The extremely expensive notion which permeates the North American medical system—that life must be preserved regardless of the medical cost or quality of life—is a luxury which the Zanaki have no privilege of debating. They do not dream of nearly a trillion-dollar annual high-tech medical industry, which Americans have come to consider as their right. All these Zanaki people seek, and all they can afford, is basic care such as quinine for malaria or Kaopectate for diarrhea.

Yet a medical clinic and public health counseling has revolutionized the demography of the whole region. The population of the Zanaki has quadrupled in half a century! The church with her ministries of compassion expressed in the form of modern medical care is a primary contributor to this population explosion.

The peoples of the region rejoice, for children are welcomed as a blessing. The land is not yet full. Some day thoughts of population growth restraint might be welcome, but hardly at this time. For now, there is joy in the land; the babies live and do not die.

Food Production

The same spirit of scientific enquiry which has developed medical technology has revolutionized agricultural production.

"There it is!" exclaimed my Filipino companions on a recent drive through the rice fields of Laguna Province near metropolitan Manila. "There on your right is where experiments in genetic engineering of rice created the new strands known as miracle rice."

That miracle has turned some chronically hungry regions of the world into rice-exporting communities. Even Bangladesh can occasionally export rice, after raising enough to feed over 100 million people crowded into a region slightly smaller than the state of Florida. Other forms of genetics are developing arid-lands grains which might greatly alleviate the cycles of famine in Sehelian Africa.

As the twentieth century ends, scientific technology applied to agriculture contributes to the astonishing fact that global food stocks have kept pace with global population growth. There are 100 million more people each year.

This is not to suggest that there is no hunger; a fifth of the world do not have adequate food. In some regions excessive population growth is causing serious difficulties. Some countries cannot produce enough food for their people. However, a core problem is distribution rather than global production capabilities. Greed and violence are significant contributors to global hunger.

The Cities

Technology has also undergirded the astonishing growth of cities during the twentieth century. The modern city would be impossible without technological developments in food preservation, transportation, and communications.

At the beginning of the twentieth century, there were a quarter billion urban dwellers. Now, near the close of the century, the global urban population is approaching three billion people. Over 50 percent of humanity is becoming urban.

Multitudes of these city dwellers live in enormous metropolitan centers. Peking, China, was the first modern city to acquire a population of a million people. That was in 1770. The twentieth century commenced with twenty cities of a million or more people. Now demographers are identifying 433 such cities of a million or more.

A city of a million is hardly imaginable by the standards of previous centuries. But such cities are now considered rather small and tidy. In 1935 New York City became the first super-giant city with a metropolitan area of over ten million. By the year 2,000 there will be twenty-four super giants. Mexico City is now the biggest of all, having become a conglomerate of over twenty-five million.

Global Network

Cities are dependent on modern communication technologies. Modern transportation is one such technology.

When my father (born in 1911) was a lad growing up in Lancaster, Pennsylvania, he would run to the mud road going by his father's farm whenever a car went by. Any auto was an exciting thing to see in his early boyhood.

Nowadays even the most remote rural hamlets on earth are linked with urban centers through automotive or air transport. Although in many regions of the earth the donkey, ox, or water buffalo continue playing a role, it is rare to discover a hamlet anywhere which has no linkages with modern automotive transport.

The transportation revolution is phenomenal. Recently when my plane was on the runway in Montreal, awaiting takeoff for Luxembourg City, the pilot commented that two hundred planes would be departing North America that night for an Atlantic crossing to Europe. Half a millennium earlier, Columbus had taken nearly three months to sail the *Santa María,* the *Niña,* and the *Pinta* across this same Atlantic in his voyage to the New World.

On a recent flight from North America to Southeast Asia, I read the accounts of Adoniram Judson, the first missionary to Burma. It took him six months to travel the 12,000 miles from New England in North America to his destination in Southeast Asia. The turn-around time for mail was two years! That was only a century and a half ago. I was making the same journey in a day. My seat companion was a young Singaporean housewife, returning home after a half-week domestic shopping trip to Los Angeles.

Global Conversation

Telecommunications are equally astonishing. Having grown up in the hinterlands of East Africa, I saw my first telephone when I was ten. Today I can direct-dial the town near my boyhood African community.

In downtown Hong Kong, I can place my Visa card in a slot in a wall along Waterloo Road and in seven seconds receive cash from my bank in Mountville, Pennsylvania, including a full report on the status of my checking account. That seven-second transaction twelve thousand miles from home travels through satellites orbiting one hundred miles above the Pacific Ocean.

These instantaneous communications systems are creating an authentic global village network. The global communications network means that the tea shop conversation in Beijing, China, converges with coffee hour discussions in Toronto, Canada.

The whole world is involved in the global conversation, not just the peoples of urban centers. Whether I am in the small village of Migori, Kenya, or in Las Casas, Guatemala, or in Putusibau, West Kalimantan, the people listen to the world news on the radio in their native dialects. There is convergence in the dinner hour conversation in the homes of the earth's five to six billion people.

Not only radio has permeated remote hamlets. Television is there too. When the 1992 Summer Olympics opened, television announcers confidently proclaimed that three billion people were watching the opening games. In Egypt it is reported that 94 percent of the people have access to television. In China, with over a billion people, it is difficult to find a home anywhere without television. Much of the global village is meeting within a worldwide communication network.

Through global television networking, excellent education, information, and entertainment programing is now universally available. So is television trash. Satellite systems enable programs from Hollywood to cascade on homes everywhere around the world.

Television is creating a global village atmosphere. The most remote hamlets in China have access to MTV through satellite hookup. A friend reports seeing teenagers in a Guatemalan mountain hamlet glued to the television in the town hall. That night satellite accessibility was shocking this conservative peasant community with porn manufactured in the United States. Excellence and trash are equally available in our universal global village.

Global Culture

Modern communication systems are creating a global culture. English is the primary language medium of that culture. The opinion makers everywhere know English. That language is the door into modern culture.

That global culture is powerfully influenced by the ideals and worldview of the seventeenth- and eighteenth-century European enlightenment. There is astonishing convergence in the worldview of those who form and influence local and national cultural development, whether the decision makers are in Moscow, Lagos, Tokyo, or New York.

There is also a global pop-youth culture. MTV is now available throughout the world. Rock and roll made in England or North America is the primary glue which binds the global youth culture together. The youth wear oldish-looking blue jeans, often with whitish fold streaks in them. And English is the medium through which they communicate.

Pluralism

Modernity is also creating pluralism. People move from their home communities into cities. In the cities they meet people from other religious, racial, or cultural backgrounds.

Within my own community in eastern Pennsylvania, fifty years ago everyone was a professing Christian. Today that is no longer true. Locals are more free to profess atheism or agnosticism than in a previous era.

People have moved into our community who are Jehovah's Witnesses, Baha'is, Mormons, Sikhs, Taoists, Jainists, Muslims, Islamics, Buddhists, Hindus, Confucianists, Satanists, Communists, or even Zoroastrians. The global community of faith and ideology is within our neighborhood. We have become a pluralistic community. We cannot assume a Christian consensus.

That same phenomenon of pluralism is the global experience everywhere. Every urban center and many rural regions are experiencing pluralism. The era is vanishing when local communities could enjoy a consensus on values or beliefs. Healthy community relationships require that people must learn to live with diversity. The global community has become a pluralistic city.

Ethnic Pride

However, pluralism is always in tension with ethnic identity. That tension can be creative and dynamic; it can also become heinously destructive. Globally there is a resurgence of ethnic pride and identity. Uninhibited ethnicity which ignores the rights of others is terribly destructive of the web of relationships forming the core of modern global national and urban culture.

Mikhail Gorbachev introduced the winds of change known as

glasnost (openness) and *perestroika* (restructuring) into the U.S.S.R. These concepts opened the door for conversation, an exchange of plural ideas. Alas, a wolf came through that open door. That wolf was the powerful force of ethnic identities which communism had suppressed for more than seven decades. Gorbachev tried to contain and direct the explosive energy of ethnic pride. He failed; the Soviet Union unraveled.

Even after the Union had disintegrated, the former republics discovered ethnic forces had not abated. Most of the republics have struggled to maintain any semblance of statehood, for the various ethnic minorities within their borders demanded recognition and rights. Brushfire civil wars between ethnic communities have threatened the social fabric and well-being of communities throughout the region.

Ethnicity can become a demon. By 1991, the former communist societies of Yugoslavia and Somalia had become modern revelations of how terrifying that demon can become. In a pluralistic world, movements toward so-called ethnic cleansing become hellish; in Yugoslavia that hell has torn inter-ethnic families to shreds.

Communist ideology ignores ethnicity. Instead of ethnicity, communism views economic disparity as the key in human relationships. Thus communism represses ethnic differences; they just don't fit the ideology. It is not surprising that when the Communist Party lost control, the quest for ethnic identity among many groups threatened the well-being of the republics of the Commonwealth of Independent States.

The world was appalled at the ferocity of violence and destruction in the 1992 Los Angeles riots. Racism was the fuse which ignited that dynamite. White policemen who had beaten black Rodney King in a driving arrest were acquitted by a mostly white jury. A year later in a second trial, a more diverse jury found two of the defendants guilty and two innocent.

Ethnic strife mars many societies—Sri Lanka, Burma, Ireland, Lebanon, Guatemala, Ethiopia, and Los Angeles. The violence between Catholics and Protestants in Northern Ireland is a scar on the global witness of the church. However, God has created and commissioned the church to be a community of healing among the nations. It is a betrayal of the gospel when Christians are trapped in inter-community hatred and violence.

How tragic that the Orthodox Church of Serbia and the Uniate Catholic Church of Croatia did so little to bring healing to the Yugoslavian conflict after the collapse of communism. In fact, the

Orthodox-Catholic tensions contributed to the hostility and violence. If the church does not minister as a community of reconciliation, where is reconciliation to be found?

Modern societies must learn the art of living in a pluralistic world. Healthy nations must recognize that ethnicity is a foundation for wholesome human identity. It can function as a creative contributor within national or urban societies. Diversity of religions, cultures, and ethnicity is a foundational quality of healthy modern societies everywhere; they must nurture pluralism.

Wealth and Poverty

In any society, healthy pluralism undergoes critical strains when there is a significant gap in wealth between communities. That is also true within the global community.

For much of the twentieth century there was a critical polarization between the communist East and the capitalist West. A core ingredient in that tension was the disparity in wealth between these two economic systems. In the late 1980s and early 1990s, that polarization took on different expressions after the collapse of communism within Eastern Europe and the Soviet Union.

However, a deepening and tragic polarization is developing between the North and the South. Much of the Northern Hemisphere is developing huge free market spheres; the Southern Hemisphere is faltering seriously.

On a visit to Tanzania I experienced that gap in wealth between North and South. In a meeting with the elders of the congregation I had grown up in, they requested a bicycle for their pastor. The pastor was responsible for twenty-four congregations in a fifty-mile radius. He needed a bicycle. I thought the many members in his churches should purchase the bicycle for their pastor.

However, a quick calculation revealed that within that society the purchase price for a bicycle was equal to the cost of three new Ford Escort cars in the United States. In my town in the United States, a high school student can easily earn enough during Christmas break to purchase a bicycle; in Tanzania a bicycle cost a high school teacher's wages for a year.

This request revealed that something has gone tragically wrong with the Tanzania economy. Forty years ago when the pastor was a young evangelist, he owned a bicycle. Then he had a motor cycle. His enterprising spirit led him into some businesses, and he soon owned a pickup truck. Now he was walking and experiencing the humility of asking help to acquire a bicycle.

The statistics are appalling. Three examples illustrate the calamity. By 1990 the total annual gross national product (GNP) for the 530 million people in all of Africa south of the Sahara was U.S. $150 billion; that is equal to the annual GNP of Belgium, with ten million people. The people of Belgium enjoy a standard of living about fifty times higher than the Africans; the U.S. standard is 100 times higher.

In 1980 there were 500 million desperately poor people in the global village who lived on three dimes a day. By 1990 these poor had increased to 1.2 billion people. A critical crisis for the desperately poor is inadequate protein, which creates mental impairment.

In 1990 in Lima, Peru, the pay for a government civil servant was one-tenth of what was necessary to support a family of four at poverty levels.

Something has gone terribly wrong.

Many factors contribute to the economic catastrophe—corruption, excessive population growth, war and violence, policies which discourage investment, global debt.

The Rich Make the Rules

The debt issue deserves further comment. Ever since the 1960s, the debt burden of the poor nations has escalated, even though there has been minimal new lending for capital investment in factories or infrastructure such as highways. Yet the debt grows, because of the practice of adding unpaid interest to the debt principal.

Although the poor cannot pay the full interest on the loans, governments and banks work in concert to pressure the poor nations to pay as much as possible. They often squeeze the poor beyond measure. By the beginning of the 1990s, the squeeze was forcing the poor to transfer U.S. $150 million in interest payments to the rich every day.

To acquire funds for debt interest payments, the poorer nations are forced to raise the price of imports through taxes. As the local price for gasoline escalates through taxation, imports of gasoline decline. The same kind of taxation is applied to most imports, thereby discouraging importing foreign products. Thus the money earned from exports can be used to pay foreign interest payments rather than to pay for imports such as gasoline, medicines, paper, or machinery.

In these ways the rich countries are able to receive far more money from the poor countries than all aid and investments. For many years the overall net flow of wealth has been away from the poor South to the rich North.

The consequence for the poor nations is economic apocalypse. For example, it is normal in the poorest countries for gasoline to cost three, four, and even five dollars a gallon. In some of the poorest countries it now takes two months' wages of a high school teacher to fill the tank of a Honda car with gasoline.

A dollar a quart for gasoline discourages travel! Even bus fare to travel the eight miles across town for work is often impossible. Imagine a family of six in Nairobi trying to get to their church on Sunday. It might take two hours to walk, and Dad has bus fare for one person.

Another cause for the erosion of global prosperity is the bulging United States federal deficit. Throughout the 1980s, the United States government borrowed over $2.5 trillion. As the nation entered the 1990s, the borrowing had escalated to a billion dollars a day.

In September 1992, the International Monetary Fund issued a stern complaint concerning the policy of the United States government borrowing so much money. They cited two problems:

1. The escalating debt has kept global interest rates artificially high.
2. This horrendous debt has also sponged capital funds everywhere.

The whole global community had become starved for capital funds because of the flow of a billion dollars a day into U.S. Treasury bonds.

The situation had become especially disturbing because Eastern Europe and the Commonwealth of Independent States craved capital investment. The needed funds were not available. Global investment funds were tied up in U.S. government debt. The global famine of capital funds throughout the 1980s contributed significantly to a catastrophic decline in the economies of the poor countries.

We live in a global village. The U.S. debt harms not only the United States but the whole global economy.

A Discredited Communism?

The disintegration of the Soviet Union has resolved over half a century of brittle and dangerous tension between the Soviet empire and the Western powers. However, the dismantling of the Soviet-dominated military alliance known as the Warsaw Pact has not resulted in global peace. A year after the 1991 collapse of the Soviet Union, there were thirty wars raging in the global village. The number of refugees worldwide had escalated to over 30 million.

By 1993 the inter-ethnic wars in the former Yugoslavia had created four million refugees. In Somalia, post-communist interclan war, anarchy, and the accompanying famine threatened to kill half the people. Some anticipated a new world order when the communist flag was lowered from the Kremlin on Christmas Day, 1991. A year later the new world looked pretty grim.

The collapse of communism put all European societies under intense stress. The fabric of Western societies frayed as communities were overwhelmed by the huge inflow of refugees or immigrants. They were fleeing the economic apocalypse engulfing formerly communist societies—now encountering the shock of free enterprise systems. During 1992 Russia was a harbinger of what was happening throughout the region as inflation soared to 100 percent a month.

Six months after the communist flag was lowered from the Kremlin, I stood in a Moscow open market and wept. Hungry mothers and children were trying to sell items such as an old pair of shoes or an empty bottle for a bit of cash for food. Throughout the European continent, the euphoria of freedom from communism was tempered by hunger. The situation nurtured violence, for people had become desperate.

Death

In some regions of the global village, concerns about overpopulation have become non-issues. AIDS is killing thousands. At the epicenter of the AIDS epidemic on the western shores of Lake Victoria in East Africa, where AIDS first made its appearance, whole villages are now mostly depopulated. A few children and older people are all who remain.

Now AIDS has spread throughout the global village. In one country on the opposite side of the globe from the East African epicenter, over a quarter percent of the young men recruited for the army are HIV-positive (infected with the HIV virus associated with AIDS). In some societies half the people will die before they reach age forty.

No illness has ever been investigated as thoroughly as AIDS. Governments have thrown billions of dollars at the disease in research for a cure. Yet medical experts worry that a cure will never be found. That is the bad news. The good news, however, is that the virus is mostly transmitted through lifestyle patterns people can choose to change. In most cases transmission is preventable.

War, famine, and disease are not the only causes of death. Abortion also ends human lives in the wombs of mothers. In the United States there are a million abortions a year. In some industrial societies in Asia and Europe, abortions are contributing to population stabilization and even decline.

In societies where boys are especially valued and family sizes restricted by government policies, modern techniques for determining the sex of the fetus enable the mother to abort female embryos in favor of sons. This human-created pattern of selective death creates huge disparities in the ratio of boys to girls. Where will all those boys find wives someday? Abortion creates sadness within homes and societies everywhere.

The Good Earth Groans

The good earth groans under the curse of human exploitation. The litany of evils we inflict on our environment depresses—chopping down rain forests in West Kalimantan, flooding the Persian Gulf with oil during the 1991 Gulf War, pouring carbon monoxide into the air from inadequately controlled auto exhaust, dumping toxins into the rivers, poisoning sea and air and land and people with lethal radio activity from atomic plants and weapons, tossing plastics into the garbage. The whole global village is becoming aware that human survival on this planet requires that we care for the good earth.

The June 1992 Earth Summit in Rio de Janeiro revealed a global concern for ecology. Representatives came from 178 nations. One hundred heads of state participated; never before had so many national leaders met for a conference.

The participants were dismayed by reports of nations or communities who resisted the commitments of the summit. The United States was especially criticized for refusing to sign a bio-diversity treaty. The United States (then led by George Bush) conveyed that it considered economic growth more important than protecting endangered species or being unduly concerned for the environment. Yet those who resisted the mandates of the summit were a minority.

Is it right to exploit the earth for human economic progress? The Earth Summit called on all nations to care for and develop the good earth; our long-term well-being on earth depends on how people respond to that challenge. Governments cannot take all the responsibility. Each person needs to help care for the earth. That demands lifestyle disciplines and accepting personal responsibility for the environment in which we live.

Confronting Religions and Ideologies

The global village is experiencing astonishing transformations. The issues of modernity are placing enormous stress on all ideologies and religions.

That stress has discredited communism. Within the former Soviet Union and East Europe, people believed that communist ideology and government systems were incapable of responding adequately to the crisis of human rights abuses, economic decline, and ecological devastation. Communism was put to the test and found wanting. Global realities are putting all ideologies and religions to a similar test.

Modern challenges often press people into a rediscovery of their roots. People often believe the challenges of modernity are best resolved by rediscovering their religious cultural roots. Movements in that direction spawn renewed religious fervor.

A search for roots is a core reason for revival in religions such as Hinduism, Islam, Buddhism, Shintoism, African traditional religion, or Christianity. In China there is deepened interest in Confucianism. In Russia Orthodox Christianity is experiencing astonishing renewal. Religious renewal is a significant component of modernity.

However, modern societies are often uncomfortable with religious renewal movements. The test of modernity often reveals that religion is just as inadequate as an ideology such as communism.

For example, caste is the core of Hinduism. All Hindu philosophy is anchored within a worldview in which the caste hierarchy is the foundation. Brahmans are at the top and the Sudras at the bottom with some fifty thousand castes in between; those outside the system have no acceptable place within society.

However, modern mobility demands in-depth inter-caste relationships. The caste hierarchy just doesn't fit modernity; even an untouchable might do better in university than a Brahman. Modern pluralism also demands respectful relationships and equality with other religious communities such as the Muslims of India.

A healthy nation depends on healthy pluralism. For this reason a Hindu renewal movement such as the Bharatiya Janata is in collision with modern realities and the basis of nationhood. Such fundamentalist Hindu renewal movements are disconcerting to any communities in India that uphold healthy pluralism within a secular state.

North America is not exempt. In an editorial for *Christianity Today*, John N. Akers writes, "A recent poll reveals that one in three academics now view evangelicals as a 'serious threat to democracy' " (Sept. 2, 1988, 11). This perception is anchored in a concern that movements such as the Christian Coalition might succeed in imposing their ethic on pluralistic U.S. society through political power.

The moral crusades of some religious renewal groups in North America are narrow and highly selective. Public perception sees issues focused like this: Abortion is wrong, but the 1991 Desert Storm in which 100 thousand Iraqis died was justifiable. Free enterprise is right, but concern about the depletion of ozone in the atmosphere is ridiculous. Christians need to remember that single-issue moral campaigns are not the kingdom of God, nor can any political ideology introduce the rule of God on earth.

Modern people often embrace secular or humanist philosophies as a way to cope with modern challenges. Yet thoughtful people observe that secular ideologies have driven the world into disaster after disaster within the twentieth century. Nazism, Marxism, and capitalism have left a trail of tears. When in Russia I learned that with the KGB files now opened, it appears that Lenin and Stalin masterminded the slaughter of 60 million people in their determination to establish a communist utopia. Is secularism really the way?

Amid the clamor of modern times, there is a persistent witness to another way—the way of Jesus of Nazareth, who in his crucifixion cried out, "Father, forgive them, for they do not know what they are doing."

There is a community among the nations who believe that this crucified Jesus is Lord. Whenever this community lives in faithfulness to the one whom they confess as Lord, they become a people with healing for the nations. That anticipates the next chapter.

* * *

This chapter describes characteristics of our modern world. The well-being of all people is at risk. More than a billion people have already hit the sliding board into deep poverty. In many regions healthy patterns of pluralism are unraveling as interethnic and interreligious strife intensifies. We live in a tumultuous world where modern communications are enabling people everywhere to participate in the global communication network.

These are profiles of the modern world which form the context for mission. The next chapter, "The Global Church," explores the universal presence of the church within this modern context.

Reflection

1. Describe the economic, social, cultural and religious setting of your congregation. What difference does the presence of your church make?

2. Consider challenges that pluralism creates for your congregation and community? Can you think of ways in which the congregation should encourage healthy pluralism in your community? To what extent might pluralism erode the convictions of Christians in your congregation about Jesus Christ?

3. Compare the status of the modern global village with the descriptions of a world in trouble (recorded in Matthew 24 or Revelation 6—9).

4. Account for the discrediting of communism in Eastern Europe and the former Soviet Union.

5. Consider ways the modern global village confronts religions and ideologies with acute challenges.

6. What are the qualities of faith which could really help to bring healing to the nations in times like these?

7. What responsibility does your congregation or conference have for policies of government or business institutions as they affect the well-being of your country and/or the well-being of other nations?

* * *

Suggested background Scriptures—Matthew 24, Revelation 6—9, 22:1-2.

7

The Global Church

IMAGINE AN AMBASSADOR of Jesus Christ admonishing an assembly of the nations. Imagine the nations of the global village inviting counsel from the worldwide church. Astonishing?

Yet that is exactly what has happened. Pope Paul VI addressed the United Nations in New York City on October 4, 1965. Fourteen years later Pope John Paul II was also invited to address that global community of nations, on October 2, 1979.

A Different United Nations

Why would the nations of the world gathering at the United Nations invite an address by a representative of the global church? The peoples who comprise the United Nations are of varied religious and ideological commitments—Buddhist, Hindu, Shinto, Muslim, Marxist, secular, tribal religions, Christian. The United Nations is a revelation of global pluralism. Yet a core task of the United Nations is to tackle the issues which undermine the well-being of the global village.

The United Nations, the embodiment of global pluralism with a commission to guard the well-being of the community of nations, invited an address by a leader of global Christianity. Although half a billion Christians do not recognize the pope as their head, the Roman Catholic pope does nevertheless represent a billion Catholic Christians. The United Nations General Assembly invited this person to address them.

Why?

The reason is evident. The modern church is the most authentic global community. It is a remarkable "united nations." These believers in Jesus the Messiah live and work among the nations of the global village everywhere. They are members of all the nation-states on earth. Wherever these Christians live in faithfulness to their calling, they are a community of healing among the nations. They are light to the nations; they are a beacon showing the way through darkness.

We shall explore how this remarkable community has developed, and comment on the global mission of the modern church.

God's Strategy

What if Jesus had been born into a Mayan home in Central America? Or a Tamil home in South India? Or a Celtic family in Britain? Or the home of a Roman caesar and identified with imperial rule? Any such alternative would have trapped the gospel in a geographical, cultural, tribal, national, political, or sociological box.

God planned well for the growth of the church. The plan included geopolitical strategy. God didn't want Jesus locked into any box. He placed his Son in Palestine. That is the bridge between the continents of Asia, Africa, and Europe. Palestine is the crossroads of the world.

Israel located in Palestine was at the right place for maximum influence throughout the earth. God had called Israel to be a light to the nations; Palestine was an ideal location for that light to penetrate into Africa, Asia, and Europe. Jesus of Nazareth also lived within this same meeting place of the continents. God had planned wisely.

During the first decades of the church, unbelievers frequently scoffed at the notion that God's Son would be of the people of Israel and live within Palestine. Israel was a tiny nation; for most of the previous six hundred years these weak people had been colonized and often ruthlessly treated by great colonial powers. The Roman Empire ruled Palestine at the time of Jesus.

"Surely God would not condescend to place his Son in a poor family of Israel within occupied Palestine. That's just too ridiculous to imagine!" the scoffers taunted. "Palestine is such a tiny corner of the earth. God should have sent his Son to a great nation, not to an insignificant people."

"That's just the point," Christians such as Origen in Egypt insisted.

"God deliberately chose occupied Palestine for the homeland of his Son. The rule of Jesus is radically different from imperial rule."

Origen elaborates,

> Moreover, though the advent of Jesus was apparently in one corner, it was quite reasonable; since it was necessary that the one prophesied should visit those who had learnt that there was one God, and who were reading his prophets and learning of the Christ they preached, and that he should come at a time when the doctrine would be poured forth from one corner all over the world. (Young, 2)

By the time of Jesus, Israel had scattered from India to Spain. Wherever these people went, they carried their faith in one righteous Creator God who calls people to become his covenant nation among the nations.

As mentioned earlier, the Jews even translated their Scriptures into Greek. This is known as the Septuagint, which was completed in Alexandria, Egypt, at least a century before Jesus was born. Since Greek was read throughout the Mediterranean and Middle Eastern region, the Septuagint was helpful in Israel's efforts to be a witness and a light to the nations.

Israel considered all who were not of their peoplehood as Gentiles. Many Gentiles were inspired by the life and faith of Israel. Many believed; they were called God-fearers.

Sadly, by the time of Jesus, Israel had developed the notion that all Gentile God-fearers must submit to Jewish cultural practices to become full members of the covenant community. This included diet practices and dress codes. The men had to be circumcised, which was abhorrent to most Gentiles. So although many Gentiles from Africa, Europe, and Asia believed in God and sought to pattern their lives on the Ten Commandments, they could not become members of the covenant community of Israel.

Nevertheless, Israel was a preparation for the church. As the church expanded throughout the Middle East during those first centuries, the Gentile God-fearers eagerly sought membership in the church. Here at last they could find a spiritual home. They readily understood the gospel. Israel had prepared them to hear and receive the gospel.

The scattered witness of the people of Israel was not the only way God was preparing the world for the gospel. About the time Jesus was born, the Roman Empire had imposed peace throughout the entire Mediterranean and Middle Eastern region. The peace endured for two hundred years; historians call these two centuries the Pax Romana. Travel and trade flourished in the Empire and regions far beyond its borders.

The African theologian Origen observes,

> God was preparing the nations for his teaching, that they might be under one Roman emperor, so that the unfriendly attitude of the nations to one another caused by the existence of a large number of kingdoms, might not make it more difficult for Jesus' Apostles to do what was commanded them when He said, 'Go and teach all nations' (Matt. 28:19). It is quite clear that Jesus was born during the reign of Augustus, the one who reduced to uniformity, so to speak, the many kingdoms of the earth so that he had a single empire. It would have hindered Jesus' teaching from being spread through the whole world if there had been many kingdoms . . . (Young, 4).

God was preparing the world in other ways as well. The Greek language was spoken throughout the region. By writing the New Testament first in Greek, the early church was equipped to move from society to society with the message of the gospel.

Greek philosophy was critical of the polytheism of the traditional tribal and national religions. Yet there was no universal faith to replace those religions. The gospel provided that universal faith, just as it does in these modern times whenever people are seeking a faith and a community which can transcend tribal or national divisions.

When the Messiah was born about 2 millennia ago, the clusters of people within those regions of the world where Europe, Asia, and Africa met were seeking a universal faith and an authentic worldwide community. The gospel and the church fulfilled that quest.

We have noted that God planned well. He sent his Son into the world at the right place, among the right people, and at the right time. Yet it is not only in ancient times that we observe God planning well. Even today we discover that God arranges for his church to be present in the context of the right place, people, and time.

It is important for Christians to be aware of the opportunities God is providing for the advancement of his kingdom. Chapter nine explores the need for the church to be aware of the moments of opportunity God provides.

The First Christian Missionaries

The early church used the opportunities God had provided for mission. Yet the faithfulness of these first Christians was often costly. The church grew, but the missionaries often suffered for their faithfulness.

Church traditions describe John Mark, who wrote the Gospel of Mark, going to Egypt as a missionary. He preached fearlessly. People believed and the Coptic Church in Egypt was born. (Coptic means Egyptian.) Today, after nearly 1,300 years of Muslim rule in Egypt, Christians comprise about 10 percent of the population.

The Egyptian church honors John Mark as their martyr founder. According to traditions, the enemies of the gospel tied a rope around John Mark's neck and dragged him through the streets of Alexandria until his head severed from his body.

Other traditions describe Thomas, who was one of the twelve disciples of Jesus, sailing along the Red Sea preaching to the Ethiopians. He went on to India where he preached and planted churches. He was lanced to death by furious Brahmans on a hill eight miles southwest of Madras. That hill is still known as Saint Thomas Mount. The 2 million Christians of the Mar Thoma Church and the Orthodox Syrian Church of South India trace their beginning to missionary Thomas.

"Our church can never be destroyed," exclaimed Archbishop Silwa of Iraq, as he reflected on the ashes of war following the 1991 air raids against his country during Desert Storm. "Our church is founded on Jesus Christ. Our church was planted by an apostle of Jesus."

Some traditions describe Thomas planting churches in Iraq before going on to India. Other traditions claim that the disciple Matthew also planted churches in the Mesopotamia Valley. While missionaries John Mark, Thomas, and Matthew were sharing the gospel in Asia and Africa, Paul was heading into Europe, as described in the biblical book of Acts.

The apostles and disciples who were contemporaries of Jesus had a passion to share the gospel from nation to nation. Yet not just apostles shared the good news. Even slaves got into the act. The earliest evangelists among the Huns and Goths of Central Euro-Asia were slaves. All believers knew Jesus had commissioned them to share the good news.

Within two decades of the crucifixion and resurrection of Jesus, his disciples had laid the foundations for enduring churches within the three continents of Asia, Africa, and Europe. Within three centuries,

25 percent of the people in the Roman Empire were Christians. The church had spread from India to Spain.

Bardaisan of Edessa in Mesopotamia wrote in astonishment about "the new race of us Christians, whom Christ at his coming planted in every country and every region" (Young, 19).

By the sixth century, missionaries from Edessa (modern Iraq) had embarked on an astonishing missionary adventure. Although motorized sailing was still many centuries away, they commissioned missionaries to China, six thousand miles distant.

Persecution Didn't Stop Growth

The church grew amidst persecution. The Roman Empire, which brought peace throughout the Mediterranean and Middle Eastern region, had no sympathy for any movement which did not venerate the emperor as lord. The Christians could never accept that the emperor, government, or state had the ultimate authority. They insisted that there is only one Lord: Jesus Christ.

The gauntlet was cast. The faithful church was in collision with the Roman Empire on the issue of ultimate authority. Thousands died; they were thrown to the lions or bulls, beheaded, or burned alive.

Persecution continues in the modern church—more Christians have died for their faith in the twentieth century than in the previous 1900 years of church history. Some estimates are that 85 percent of my own Mennonite denominational family might have been killed in communist Russia. No one will ever know how many died; it is evident, however, that many suffered and died for their faith.

In every generation, the faithful church has experienced persecution in some region of the world. Yet the church continues growing.

Different Church Families

As the church has developed over the past twenty centuries, families of faith have formed. These are called denominations.

A core reason for denominations is that the church seeks to find a home within each cultural setting. Since cultures vary greatly, the church must also become diverse. The formation of denominations is usually caused by the church attempting to express the Christian faith in a particular culture or historical situation.

Israel and Gentiles

The decision that the church become diverse communities was deliberate. In less than two decades after the resurrection of Jesus, the apostolic church convened a conference in Jerusalem to decide whether Gentiles needed to follow Jewish practices. The Jewish people considered all other people Gentiles; they perceived that the world was inhabited by two kinds of people—Jewish and Gentile. The Jerusalem Conference decided that Jewish people should continue following Jewish customs, and Gentiles were free to continue their cultural practices.

The Jerusalem Conference also decided on a common ethical and faith center for all Christians. Thus within the first century the church decided to celebrate diversity. There would be different Jewish and Gentile expressions of the Christian faith. They also affirmed their center—Jesus Christ is Lord and Savior.

That decision guaranteed a core unity which also celebrated diversity. For the first few centuries, the church combined two very different communities of people. One had roots in Israel, the other was rooted in the Gentile nations of the world.

Sadly, as the church moved farther away from its roots in Israel, a deepening alienation developed between the Jewish and Gentile expressions of church. Eventually the Jewish church withered and died. Consequently, for many centuries the Gentile church has continued with little or no involvement by people whose roots are in Israel.

The alienation has been tragic. Within the European setting, a whole cultural system was poisoned by the alienation between Israel and Gentiles. One horrible consequence was the Holocaust, in which millions of Jewish people died in gas chambers during Hitler's regime.

The church misses a blessing when there is no relationship with believers whose heritage is Israel. Jewish believers in Jesus the Messiah are a presence of Israel within the church, thereby keeping Christians in touch with the Jewish origins of the church. They remind the church that the Old Testament has been the way God prepared the nations for the gospel.

In recent years a miracle is happening. Thousands of Jewish people have believed that Jesus is the Messiah. They have formed congregations of messianic Jews. These Jewish churches preserve Jewish customs but confess Jesus as Messiah and Lord. The messianic movement within the scattered people of Israel has revived the reality of a world church including Jews as well as Gentiles. That is good news.

The apostle Paul yearned for that day. He wrote that the inclusion of Israel within the church will be "life from the dead" (Rom. 11:15).

These modern Jewish believers affirm anew those ancient decisions of the Jerusalem Conference. They insist that they will remain Jewish; they do not seek to become Gentile-like Christians.

Denominations and Churches

The diversities within the Christian movement have created other differences in addition to those between Jews and Gentiles. There are basically three main church families—Orthodox, Catholic, and Protestant.

The oldest *Orthodox* churches trace their founding to the apostles of Jesus. These churches are present in all countries within the Middle East region where the disciples of Jesus preached. Missionaries from these churches planted Orthodox churches in far-off lands as well.

Many ancient Orthodox churches have experienced generations of pressure from Islam as well as religions such as Hinduism and Zoroastrianism. In much of the twentieth century, communist governments have persecuted Orthodox churches under their control. Suffering for Christ is the heritage of multitudes of Orthodox Christians.

Orthodox churches have often taken deep root within their national culture. We know these churches by the names of countries, such as Ethiopian Orthodox or Syrian Orthodox. Patience in suffering, fasting, prayer, and spirituality are qualities these churches often reveal. Two hundred million Christians are included in the Orthodox churches.

The Orthodox and Roman Catholic churches experienced a sad separation in the eleventh century. For many centuries before the separation, cultural and theological differences were developing between Eastern and Western Christians. Those differences culminated in division in 1054.

The *Roman Catholic church* is the largest and most universal Christian family with a global community of over a billion people. The vigorous missionary effort of the Catholic church has rooted this community within nearly every nation on earth.

The *Catholic church* believes that the apostle Peter, who was one of Jesus' disciples, founded the church in Rome. A core conviction of this church is that the pope is anointed with the spiritual authority of Peter. The authority of the pope provides this church with remarkable unity, even though it struggles with astonishing diversity.

The *Protestant* churches are a third Christian family. The Protestant movement began in Europe in the sixteenth century. The translation and printing of the Bible into several European languages helped to ignite a reformation. Martin Luther, Ulrich Zwingli, Conrad Grebel, and others called on the church to return to New Testament faith. The rupture which followed between these "protesters" and the Catholic church was sometimes violent.

The believers church movement gained momentum during the time of the Protestant Reformation. The Anabaptists were such a church. They taught that a person must be born again, and that new birth involves an adult commitment to Jesus Christ.

For this reason Anabaptists did not consider infant baptism helpful. Only those committed to following Jesus Christ in life should be baptized. The conviction that the church should be a fellowship of believers did not fit the church-state system, where everyone was counted as a Christian because all babies were baptized.

Nowadays the believers church movement is expressed in a variety of denominations, such as Mennonite, Baptist, or Christian Missionary Alliance.

The multiplication of denominations has been a characteristic of the Protestant movement. So have missions. Already in the sixteenth century, the Anabaptists within that movement planned and prayed for the evangelization of the whole world. Many Protestant groups have been missionary-sending communities during the past two centuries. Consequently Protestant churches have been planted around the world. Four hundred million people are affiliated with Protestant communions.

Many modern church communities have no bondings with any of the three main Christian families we have described. The translation of portions of the Bible into over two thousand languages has been one reason for the multiplication of denominational families. With their Bibles in hand, people simply begin churches with no particular global affiliations. There are 175 million such Christians.

The global Christian family is a rich and exuberant kaleidoscope of diversity. That diversity is a tremendous asset in world mission; you don't have to fit an alien cultural mold to be a Christian. The diversity of the church is astonishing. It is equally amazing that whenever the church is faithful to its calling, Christians experience unity because they all confess that Jesus Christ is Lord.

The Rise of the Muslim Nation

Nevertheless, the church often fails to express unity. Pride, selfishness, and divisiveness are not strangers within the church.

In the seventh century, divisions and hostility among Christians created a spiritual vacuum in the Middle East, and this provided an opportunity for the birth of the religion of Islam. The rise of Islam in Arabia is an unforgettable lesson for the church that divisiveness ruins Christian mission. Diversity enriches mission; divisiveness destroys mission.

Within one century of the birth of Islam, half the Christians throughout the world had come under the political and military power of Islam. That event curtailed the further missionary movement of the church into Africa and Asia for a thousand years. The pressure from Muslim governments led to a steady decline in church membership in all countries in which Muslims ruled. In those countries where people had no Bible in their mother tongue, the churches eventually died out completely. This occurred in Nubia (Sudan), Libya, and among the Berber peoples of the North African Maghreb.

Renewal of Mission

However, in the sixteenth-century renewal movements in European churches began to awaken an interest in world mission. The translation and printing of the Bible into European languages was one reason for this renewal. In 1380 the English received their first full translation of the Bible which John Wycliff brought to completion. Yet such translations were copied by hand; only a few ever saw a Bible.

The invention of printing changed that. The first book John Gutenberg produced on his newly invented press was an Italian translation of the Bible (1450). Soon low-cost printed Bibles were available in European languages everywhere. By 1520, there were eighteen German translations, two Dutch, four Bohemian, and eleven Italian. As people read their Bibles, the Holy Spirit brought renewal.

At the same time, navigators were improving the technology of sailing. European explorers were probing Asia, the African coasts, and the Americas. Columbus arrived in the Americas in 1492; Vasco da Gama circled the Cape of Good Hope in 1496. Soon the explorers could circle the Muslim empires of the Middle East by sailing around the tip of Africa and on to Asia.

Missionaries followed those explorations, although in some circumstances the missionaries were the first foreign explorers. The Catholic Jesuits led the way. In 1540 Francis Xavier sailed from Portugal for the Far East. He preached in India, regions of Malaysia, East Indonesia, and Japan—where multitudes were baptized prior to his death (while enroute to China). Xavier was the modern pioneer of a continuing global Catholic missionary movement which has created a worldwide Catholic Church of a billion people.

The Anabaptists were the pioneers of vigorous missionary renewal among non-Catholics. In 1527, only two years after their first baptisms in a Zurich prayer meeting, European Anabaptists met to plan for the evangelization of the world. Within two years of that conference, all but two or three of those who met there had been martyred. Their enemies sometimes cut out the tongues of these evangelists to keep them from preaching.

Amazingly, the Anabaptists did not despair. Within only five years of those Zurich baptisms, these congregations of believers had spread to five hundred locations. Thousands had confessed faith in Jesus Christ and received adult baptism.

Nevertheless, several decades of persecution did take a toll. In time the spirit of these evangelists was suffocated. The persecution was too severe; too many of the leaders were slain. Many were forced by their enemies to move into the hills away from people. They became the quiet in the land.

Two centuries later, eighteenth-century renewal movements among Protestant communities in Europe and England became the launch pad for the global missions movement which flourished during the nineteenth century. For example, during the eighteenth century, Halle University (in eastern Germany) produced at least seventy foreign missionaries! They were the pioneers who blazed trails for nineteenth-century missions.

However, it is the British William Carey who is considered the father of the modern Protestant missionary movement. He helped form The Particular Society for Propaganda of the Gospel Among the Heathen, then sailed to India in 1793. Today the name of his missionary organization seems frightful. But two centuries ago it attracted the imagination and commitment of some of Britain's finest young people.

Church renewal in the British Isles, such as the Evangelical Revival, provided the spiritual foundations which empowered British churches for a remarkable two centuries of missionary involvement. Evidence of that commitment is the size of the global Anglican communion—57 million members. This says nothing about communions such as the Methodists, Baptists, or Quakers who originated within Britain and whose missionary vigor has spread these churches into countries everywhere.

The Haystack and the Thunderstorm

Mission vision often begins in surprising ways. In the United States, a New England thunderstorm ignited a passion for world mission. Students from William College took refuge in a haystack during a summer thunderstorm. They prayed while the lightning cracked.

That is the famous Haystack Prayer meeting of 1806. As these young men prayed, God touched them, calling them to invest their lives in mission among people who had never heard the gospel. That is the beginning of the North American commitment to world missions.

The men in the Haystack Prayer meeting invested their lives in world mission. Later others joined in the commitment. They formed the American Board for Commissioners for Foreign Missions. These future missionaries enrolled in Andover Seminary to develop the biblical foundations and scholarship needed for fruitful missionary service.

Adoniram Judson was one of that group. He sailed for Burma; he is considered the father of the American world missions movement. It was a costly commitment. Many within those early-nineteenth-century missionary teams died. Judson himself witnessed the death of his children, and also the death of his first and then second wife.

There are many graves of adult missionaries and the little missionary children at the early mission centers in Burma. This is true of most early mission centers elsewhere in Asia and also in Africa. For many years missionaries going to Africa took their coffins with them; they rightly assumed that their obedience to God's call to mission would result in untimely death.

Missionaries and Culture

These missionaries combined piety with scholarship. Judson is an excellent example—he developed the first written Burmese grammar. He developed a massive lexicon. He translated the entire Bible directly from the Hebrew and Greek.

Throughout Asia and Africa, the nineteenth-century missionary scholars have been the pioneers in recording the grammars and vocabularies of the peoples among whom they served. Recording grammars, dictionaries, ethnographies, histories, or poetry was one way missionaries helped preserve the cultures of peoples against the threat from modern global culture. They knew that the oral traditions might be overwhelmed by the spread of modern global culture. In many settings, the churches the missionaries planted are primary pre-servers of the precious treasures of local culture.

If the language was not written, the missionaries reduced the language to writing and taught the people to read in their own tongue. The missionaries were the pacemakers for modern global literacy. The modern missionary movement has spawned amazing creativity in cultures.

Modern schools developed wherever the missionaries served. These schools permeated societies with the wonders of secular learning. Outstanding universities were founded by missionaries; some of these became renowned centers of scholarship—such as the American University in Beirut or the American University in Cairo. The church in mission in Europe and the Americas was also a primary pioneer in developing modern universities in those societies.

Modern medicine and grassroots economic development went hand in hand with the modern missionary movement. In Asia, Africa, and the Americas the missionaries and the churches were primarily responsible for introducing the wonders of modern medicines. In communities throughout these regions, the first modern hospitals and clinics were developed by the churches.

The same is true of commitments to authentic economic development. Missions introduced industries and whole new dimensions of agricultural possibilities. An example is the cocoa industry in West Africa.

Churches created as a result of modern missions became authentic transformers of society. For example, many centuries of Buddhism, Islam, and Confucianism in China did not abrogate foot-binding for Chinese women. This was the practice of binding each foot of a young girl with fabric so that her feet could not grow to normal size.

The reason for foot-binding was that Chinese society thought tiny dwarf feet for women were beautiful. Yet it was painful for the young girls. In adulthood women hobbled through life with tiny and sometimes gnarled feet.

Within decades of the widespread planting of churches in China, foot-binding ceased. It seems the Christian message that the whole person is created in God's own image influenced the society in ways that helped free women from foot-binding. Although church members comprised a tiny minority of the population, the gospel influenced Chinese culture as a whole in fascinating ways.

Another example of the gospel influencing society comes from India. In that society, widow suicide had been the norm for many centuries. The Hindu practice was for the widow to cast herself on the flaming funeral pyre of her husband. She joined her dead husband in death through burning. However, the newly planted churches in India influenced the culture to stop this practice. With the support of the British colonial administration, widow suicide ceased.

These are examples of the positive contributions of the modern missionary movement. There has also been violation of people and cultures. There is no need to elaborate; ample books have been written about that deep wrong. Some of the critique is exaggerated; some is true.

A Gikuyu graduate student friend in Kenya did his thesis on the Presbyterian missionary effort among his people. A summary of his findings is an example of both the good and wrong of the missionary movement.

He said, "We rightfully critique the inclinations of the missionaries to believe that their Western culture was superior to that of the Gikuyu people. They did sometimes act in wrong ways toward my people.

"For example, they pushed for an instant abrogation of female circumcision. That is the excision of the clitoris at the time of puberty. The missionaries did not understand the cultural reasons behind that practice, and the way they worked at this issue created a disaster.

"Nevertheless, all those old people I have interviewed who remember the first missionaries spoke with great appreciation for them. There is no exception to the appreciation, by both Christian and non-Christian Gikuyu."

Multiplication of Mission Centers

The modern missionary movement has become global with multitudes of missionary centers.

A Hong Kong pastor hopes that his congregation can enable a missionary to serve in Mongolia.

A Kenya church is commissioning a missionary-student family for university ministry in China.

A Singapore pastor describes plans his congregation has to commission one hundred missionaries within one decade.

K'ekchi' churches in the mountains of Guatemala are planning to send a missionary to Belize.

A congregation in Tegulcigapa is equipping a young man to become their missionary among the Turks of Germany.

A Romanian pastor is developing a missionary training center to equip men and women for mission within the southern republics of the former Soviet Union.

There are already more than 40,000 cross-cultural missionaries commissioned by the younger churches.

Panorama of the World Church

During the twentieth century, the worldwide church has experienced the most phenomenal growth in history. At the beginning of the century, there were about half a billion professing Christians. At this writing there are one and three-quarter billion professing Christians. During the decade of the 1990s, the number of professing Christians has been increasing by 30 million people each year.

We use the term "professing Christian" which is in contrast to actual church membership.

Ask a person, "What is your faith?"

"I am a Christian," responds the professing Christian.

That response says nothing about the degree of commitment. Perhaps she was baptized as a baby but has never been confirmed and never attends church. We need to recognize that millions of professing Christians are not seriously committed to Jesus Christ. Nevertheless, when a person confesses she is a Christian, it does say something important about the direction she is facing.

In some societies the number of Christians is declining. This is true in Europe. In most Western societies where communist governments have ruled, there has been a significant decrease in the percentage of people professing Christian faith.

Halle, in eastern Germany, is an example. As mentioned above, that university town was a vigorous missionary-sending community during the eighteenth century. A statue of George Frederick Handel stands in the town square; this man, the author of the choral masterpiece, the *Messiah,* was born in the city. However, today fewer than one out of two hundred people are related to any church.

"Materialistic philosophy has destroyed any awareness of the person as a unique being; people have no more worth than the stones in the street," lamented an Indian Lutheran who was visiting Halle.

"My people became Christians because of the witness of missionaries from this city," exclaimed the Indian believer. "Alas, today it is difficult to find any faith in Halle!"

In other societies, the ingathering into the church is almost unbelievable. This includes some formerly communist countries in eastern

Europe and the Commonwealth of Independent States. Albania is an example of a society where the church had ceased to function under the ruthless repression of communism. Since the fall of communism, the thirst for the gospel has been astonishing.

Educated estimates are that by 1993 there were over 72 million Christians in China. When the communist government took power in 1949 there were only 5 million Christians. The ruthless communist policies toward Christians in China contributed to serious decline in the churches—by 1970 there were only 2 million Christians remaining in China. With greater freedoms, within two decades the number of Christians in China had increased thirtyfold.

At the beginning of the twentieth century, there were about one million Christians in Africa. By the close of the century there are over 300 million African Christians.

The twentieth century has experienced the most remarkable in-gathering of peoples into the church since the first century. During the twentieth century, the worldwide Christian community has increased by 1,300 million people. As the century ends, about a third of the in-habitants of earth are professing Christians.

Not only have the churches grown, but the Christian message is reaching a larger percentage of people than ever. In 1900 about half the people on earth had never heard of Jesus Christ. These people could not become Christians. By the end of the century, church growth research estimates are that about 17 percent will have no awareness of the gospel. There has been good progress during the twentieth century in reaching unreached peoples with the gospel (Barrett, 54).

However, the church has not yet fulfilled God's plan for every people group to have the opportunity to believe in Jesus Christ. By the year 2000 there will still be well over a billion people who cannot believe in Jesus Christ. These people comprise about three thousand groups wherein there are no thriving churches. Cross-cultural evangelism focused on these unreached people must be a priority for the church as we enter the twenty-first century.

God Loves Each Person

However, concern for unreached people groups in regions beyond must not eclipse the need for every Christian congregation to reach its own neighborhood with the gospel. Furthermore, we recognize that all such statistics as described above are about persons. God loves each one.

Jesus compared God to a shepherd looking in the mountains for one lost sheep, even though ninety-nine sheep were safe in the sheepfold. He described the shepherd's huge joy when he found that lost sheep. That is a description of our missionary God. He seeks the person who is lost. In the account of the father and his two alienated sons, Jesus describes our Father God throwing a great party when his lost child comes home (Luke 15).

Fifteen-year-old Chuck had no difficulty believing God had a party when he came home to his Father's house.

Chuck telephoned me at work. He wanted to talk. So that evening we met for a milkshake at Friendly's Restaurant.

"I want to believe in Jesus Christ," Chuck began. "I am making a mess of my life."

We prayed together.

"Thank you, Jesus, for dying for my sin," Chuck said to our Savior. "I need you, because I am going in the wrong direction. I want you to be my captain. I want to come home, to be a child in God's family. Amen!"

After the prayer, we tried to keep on drinking our milkshakes. Chuck was laughing and crying.

"I can't finish this strawberry shake," he grinned in amazement. "I'm too happy. Doesn't the Bible say somewhere that God has a party with the angels singing when a sinner comes to Jesus? That's not hard to believe."

Christians join in the party of joy with God and the angels whenever a person says "yes" to Jesus Christ. Healthy churches grow because, person by person, people are coming home to God their heavenly Father. Each person converted and baptized deserves a party!

Sadly some churches never have an occasion for that kind of party. They never experience the joy of the shepherd who found his lost sheep. They never seek and never find lost people.

Do Alive Churches Always Grow?

However, rapid membership growth is not necessarily the proof of faithfulness or that the church is filled with the Holy Spirit. Sometimes churches grow because they have become popular clubs, not because they are faithful to Christ.

Some churches grow because they have become completely absorbed into the larger culture; there is no difference between the church members and the larger community. There is no cost to being a member. That kind of church is not a sign of the presence of the kingdom of God; it is neither salt nor light in its community.

The church is called into faithful ministry and witness even when there is slow growth in membership. In some societies a faithful church or missionary might be present for years with no one joining the church. In those settings, it isn't harvest time yet. The missionary is preparing people for the harvest that will come someday.

That is what happened on the coasts of Kenya during the mid-nineteenth century. Missionaries served for three decades; after all that time the church numbered seven people. More missionaries died than there were converts. Then, slowly a change began. People began to comprehend the gospel. Today 80 percent of Kenya is Christian.

In some societies the church has served in mission for several centuries and has never experienced large growth in members. This is especially true in some Buddhist and Muslim societies. Some secular societies are also persistently resistant to church growth. For many centuries cultural, sociological, and theological systems might block the planting of thriving churches in some societies. In those circumstances, God calls his church to extraordinary patience and faithfulness.

Faithfulness

Fifty years after my parents had first gone to Tanzania, my father, stepmother, and I visited Bumangi where my parents had first served as missionaries.

The church was filled with seven hundred people. They killed a cow so all could have beef to eat for a wonderful feast. We were filled with joy as we heard of the gospel expanding throughout the whole region.

A few months later I visited Mogadishu, Somalia. That is a Muslim country. My family and I had served among these people just about as long as my parents had served among the Zanaki. Yet there was no feast. We met quietly with disciples of the Messiah in a home. There were only about a dozen people present. We did not sing, for that would call attention to our meeting.

Was the mission in Somalia less important than the mission among the Zanaki?

* * *

This chapter describes the missionary movement following the Pentecost birthday of the church. God had planned well for the timing and place for the church to begin. From their first base in Jerusalem, the first missionaries moved outward, becoming a model for all later missionary outreach. Missions is a commitment the church has sometimes neglected but also recovers whenever the Holy Spirit revives the church.

As the church grows, it experiences significant diversity. In the Jerusalem Conference (Acts 15), the early church decided to affirm cultural diversity with unity in her commitment to Christ. The diversities in the church have contributed to the formation of a variety of Christian families, sometimes called denominations.

During the twentieth century, the church has experienced amazing global growth. The church is now a truly universal community. The worldwide presence of the church give Christians special responsibilities, for the church is the most authentic global community.

Diversity tests the faith of the worldwide church. The next chapter, "The Rock," describes the foundation of the church in a world of diversity.

Reflection

1. Consider reasons for the United Nations inviting a representative of the worldwide church to share comments.

2. Account for the fact that the emergence of Islam in the seventh century put back the missionary outreach of the church in Asia and Africa for one thousand years.

3. Account for the amazing growth of the church worldwide during the twentieth century.

4. In what ways might your church's faithfulness hinder church growth in your community?

5. To what extent should the potential for growth influence decisions concerning missionary assignments?

6. What responsibility does your congregation have for those peoples where there is no Christian presence?

7. Describe your congregation's participation in the joyful party of welcoming people into the family of our Father God.

* * *

Suggested background Scriptures—Isaiah 11:1-10; Zechariah 9:9-10; Matthew 24:14; 28:18-20; Acts 1:7-8; Revelation 5:9-10.

8

The Rock

"CHRISTIAN MISSIONARIES are a trifle arrogant and quite narrow-minded indeed, wouldn't you say?" expounded my seat companion on a flight from Caracas to Miami.

My companion was British. He spoke flawless Queen's English. I was a bit self-conscious with my heavy-tongued U.S. version of his native language.

I had just mentioned to this worldwide business traveler that I had been visiting missionaries in Caracas.

Are Religions Basically the Same?

He patiently explained, "All religions are basically the same. Each is a path to God. Muhammad, Buddha, Jesus, Krishna, Confucius, Zoroaster, Moses, and all the other religious prophets teach us to love each other. When we do that, it will all come out right in the end."

"How interesting!" I exclaimed.

If my companion is right, then Christian missionaries are misguided fools. Is he right?

I gave him a bit of a jolt. "I have a Ph.D. in religious studies and have taught comparative religions for many years in universities in North America and East Africa."

"How delightful to know you. It's not every day I meet a specialist in world religions!" my perplexed companion interjected. He was bewildered, for he could not comprehend how an academic could be a missionary.

Then I administered a second shock, "I was never aware that the destiny to which the religions invite us is the same. Neither have I noticed that world religions teach basically the same truths.

"The Christian faith is distinctive in many ways. Yet at the very core of that distinctiveness is Jesus Christ crucified. All other religions and philosophies of humankind have never imagined that any Creator God would love people enough to suffer for them.

"Such love is beyond human imagination. Yet that is precisely the astonishment of the gospel. God sent his one and only Son to earth and we crucified him.

"Instead of revenge or condemnation, Jesus cried out as he died, 'Father, forgive them, for they do not know what they are doing!' "

About that time my companion realized that he had urgent reading to complete before landing in Miami. This distinguished gentleman is not alone in his perceptions that all religions are basically the same. Our world is awash with that falsehood.

Hinduism offers personal oblivion as the human destiny, after thousands of tragic reincarnations. Buddhism offers emptiness as the ultimate goal, also after going through a marathon of rebirths. Christ offers eternal personal bodily life after death. Muslims anticipate a final judgment when the righteous will be rewarded in paradise and the evil punished in hell.

Both Buddha and Confucius doubted there is any God or gods. They believed that even if there is a god, he has no relevancy to the human situation now or after death. We are on our own. In Hinduism nature is divine; there is no possibility of a personal God who is other than nature. Jesus had a profound personal relationship with God the Creator. Muhammad urged people to submit to God.

Krishna seduced milkmaids and led his clansmen into battle. Muhammad fled from suffering in Mecca to become a general and a statesman in Medina from whence he could subdue his enemies in battle. Zoroaster perceived the world as two camps in hostile confrontation. This conflict was an extension of the battle between peaceful agriculturalists and warlike nomads. Buddha abandoned his young family and social responsibilities to escape the world, so he could find personal enlightenment.

Jesus actively engaged the world and confronted evil in the social and religious systems. The consequence was crucifixion. He chose the path of nonviolent, active, confrontational love.

Indeed world religions are different! Religions don't even invite people to the same destiny.

We will explore the relationship of the gospel and world religions more adequately in chapter 12. In this chapter we discern the foundation of the church and how the church should express her mission in a pluralistic world.

Christendom Fought Pluralism

Our world is filled with many religions and ideologies. Christians are only one faith community among many other religious communities.

However, for many centuries Christians in the West had significant political and cultural influence in their societies. The term Christendom described the union between European societies and the church. Five hundred years ago there was no distinction between church and society in Europe.

The church-state system in Christendom could not condone pluralism. Catholic doctrine taught that anyone who was not included in the church was doomed to hell. Therefore, it was a kindness to use force and even violence to prevent people from leaving the church. Christians who differed with church doctrine were dangerous, for they were leading people to hell. In some circumstances the authorities used the sword to compel those outside the church to be baptized.

Persons or communities who differed with church doctrine were tortured and killed, often by burning at the stake. William Tyndale is just one of multitudes of martyrs who died for their witness against the church-state system. His primary sin was translating and printing an English version of the Bible. He was burned at the stake in 1536.

Jews were also harassed. In 1492 all Jews were expelled from Spain. Only five centuries ago, Christendom could not tolerate pluralism.

A Response to Pluralism

Today all of that has changed in Western societies. The transformation began with the European Enlightenment of the seventeenth and eighteenth centuries. European intellectuals were dismayed by many aspects of Christendom. They detested a Christian church which abused its privileged position. They called for respect for the freedom of the person.

The United States was founded on the principles of the Enlightenment. The Constitution insists on the separation of church and state. Many other modern nations have followed the U.S. example. In various ways, they recognize a difference between religious communities and the state. It is rare to find any government requiring its people to belong to a particular religious community. Most modern governments affirm pluralism.

During the past three centuries, the political power of the church has declined significantly in all Western countries. In many Western societies, the church has become almost irrelevant to the direction their cultures are going. In pluralistic Western societies, the church is only one voice among many. That is a dramatic change from the era when the church controlled people's minds and actions.

Modern mobility also creates pluralism. Half a century ago no one in my community in eastern Pennsylvania in the United States had ever met a Muslim. Today there are several mosques in our area. Our immediate neighborhood includes Jewish, Muslim, Hindu, Buddhist, and secular people. Only a third of our neighborhood are relating to any church. We have become a pluralistic community.

The enlightenment and modern mobility have pushed Western societies to accept pluralism. A critical question for Christians is this: how do we interpret pluralism?

In a pluralistic society, it is tempting for Christians to become relativists. That is what has happened within Western culture as a whole. The truth is only relative to your own culture. So there are many truths. Relativism says Jesus is Savior for Christians and Buddha is savior for Buddhists, and both are equally true.

Is Truth Relative?

North American philosopher Allan Bloom published a best-seller entitled the *Closing of the American Mind* (1987). His first chapter opens with this comment:

> There is one thing a professor can be absolutely certain of: almost every student entering the university believes, or says he believes, that truth is relative. If this belief is put to the test, one can count on the student's reaction: they will be uncomprehending. That anyone should regard the proposition as not self-evident astonishes them, as though he were calling into question $2 + 2 = 4$. . . .
>
> The relativity of truth is not a theoretical insight but a moral postulate, the condition of a free society, or so they see it. . . . That it is a moral issue

for students is revealed by the character of their response when challenged—a combination of disbelief and indignation. (Bloom, 25)

Relativism is invading the church. It is not just out there in the larger society. In recent years Christian theologians have written a number of books encouraging Christians to become relativists. The Protestant John Hicks in England, and the Catholic Paul Knitter in the United States are two of these theologians.

Their argument is amazing. They observe that in the era of Christendom we could believe that Jesus Christ is the only Lord and Savior of humankind. That conviction made sense because our societies were Christian. Now society has become pluralistic. Our neighbors are not all Christians.

These theologians of relativism observe that in a pluralistic world Christians are discovering that we are only one among many. Therefore we need to develop a theology which also affirms that Jesus is only one Savior among many. It is especially astonishing that these scholars insist that Jesus never intended his disciples to develop the misguided notion that he is the one and only Son of God. Any notions that Jesus is Lord are a huge misunderstanding.

There are tragic errors in these theologies of relativism. One error is Eurocentricity. Just because Christians in the West are now discovering that they are a minority community in post-Christian pluralistic Europe or North America does not mean that this is the first time Christians have been a minority in a pluralistic world.

Most Christians in other regions of the world have always been a minority in a pluralistic world. In many settings the church is not only a minority community; it has been a persecuted minority community for centuries.

Devoted to the Truth

"My church in Damascus worships on Sundays in Aramaic, the same language which Jesus Christ our Lord spoke," explained the black-robed and turbaned archbishop of Syria. A large dark cross was on his necklace, a constant reminder of the suffering of Jesus.

He continued, "My church has endured two thousand years of persecution. We have always been a minority in a hostile world. But my church will never die, for it is founded on Jesus Christ, the eternal and true foundation."

The archbishop of Damascus represents hundreds of millions of

Christians who have always been a minority community living among peoples of other religions. The worldview of Western Christians who have only recently discovered pluralism is provincial and narrow when they urge a theology of relativism, because now in these modern times Christians are discovering pluralism. Modern Western Christians might be meeting pluralism for the first time, but this is not true for the world church.

Actually Jesus never anticipated that the church would have positions of power within society. He warned that Christians would live like sheep among wolves. They would be *in* the world but never *of* the world. People would hate and persecute and kill Christians. Christendom was an aberration for the church. Christendom never was the church as Jesus anticipated.

The Church Present Within Pluralism

The New Testament vision of the church is a community among communities. It is a new people *from* all the nations; it is a community living *among* the nations. In the last book of the Bible God revealed to John a vision of the church, a people serving God "from every tribe and language and people and nation" (Rev. 5:9).

Churches lose their power wherever Christians begin to suspect that Jesus is only one Savior among other saviors. Why suffer or witness for Jesus, if he is only an ideal man? Many others have also lived excellently. Christians who have not in their "hearts set apart Christ as Lord" develop a limp witness; such churches wither (1 Pet. 3:15). They will not endure in times of testing.

God calls the church to introduce Jesus Christ to people within our pluralistic world. The church should invite people to believe in and follow Jesus Christ. But the church must respect the freedom of the person to make his own choice.

Governments and Pluralism

The church also functions as a conscience in society. Christians should encourage government leaders to rule justly and honestly. The church witnesses to government, inviting the authorities to work for the well-being of everyone, including those who have no political power. In a pluralistic world, the church should not hesitate to be a witness to the truth of the gospel and a conscience for righteousness to all social institutions including government authorities.

"Never thank the government of Kenya for religious freedom," admonished Mwai Kibaki, minister of finance in the Kenya government, to a university assembly in 1977.

Kibaki continued, "When you thank government for freedom of conscience, then government begins to think it has the right to take that freedom from you. It does not have that right, for God himself has given you the right to choose. Never surrender that right; freedom is God's gift to you."

God created the person with a free will. Governments should therefore respect the person's freedom. That must be a foundational Christian commitment. We therefore urge governments to affirm pluralism. Because all modern nations have multiple religious communities within their borders, it is wise for Christians to favor secular governments which affirm the freedom of all communities to practice their different faiths.

The Church in Restrictive Settings

However, even in situations where a government is restrictive and circumscribes the witness of the church, Christians need to continue commending Christ before those who have not believed in him. In restrictive circumstances that witness must be unobtrusive. Yet there is always a way. The Holy Spirit nudges Christians in the way of gentle, patient, prayerful persistence.

The district commissioner of a Muslim town I was teaching in called me to his office. He hit me with a broadside: "Muslims in the school in which you are teaching are becoming Christians. The law of this country forbids propagating the Christian faith. I am launching an investigation, and I promise you that what you are doing will stop!"

I prayed silently, "Lord Jesus, you promised that when we are on trial before government officials you will tell us what to say. I'm listening!"

I began, "Sir, it is a privilege to be a guest in your country. As a guest I respect the laws of your government. However, I have a problem, and I need your counsel."

"What is your problem?" the commissioner inquired, leaning forward.

"As you know, I am a Christian. A special gift God places within the soul of any disciple of Jesus, the Messiah, is joy and love. I cannot abandon that gift.

"Occasionally students come to me and they say, 'We observe a special quality within you. You are a joyful person, and you have much love. We believe that quality comes from your faith. We also want to believe.' "

I paused, and then asked, "What shall I do? Can I deny them the gift of faith in the Messiah if they choose to believe in him? Can the government prevent such a person from believing? If you choose to become a Christian, can I or the government prevent you?"

"Of course not!" the commissioner almost shouted. "I am a free man. No government can tell me what to believe."

"I think you understand my problem. What shall I do?"

By this time his anger had turned to joviality. "You are doing well. The investigation is called off. Go in peace!"

The church is a miracle. Even in restrictive societies, God calls forth a church. In 1991 a pastor in a setting of war, famine, and severe restriction shared the words of a song he had written. This is an English version.

> I will never deny my Savior.
>   If they put me on a mountain
> And it snows on me,
> I will never deny my Savior.
>   Or if they take my wife from me
> And all my friends forsake me,
> I will never deny my Savior.
>   Or if I am hungry and naked
> And they throw me into the sea,
> I will never deny my Savior.

God Declared: This Is My Son

The Christian confession that Jesus is the Son of the living God is not some concoction theologians have invented. The notion that the Creator of the universe would send his Son to earth where he experienced crucifixion is too amazing for theologians or philosophers to imagine. This is God's action, and it is a surprise only he can reveal.

During the three-year public ministry of Jesus, God himself declared from heaven that this Jesus is his Son. Imagine the astonishment of those who heard that announcement. Listen to the first proclamation from the heavens.

"You are my Son, whom I love; with you I am well pleased," a voice proclaimed from heaven at the time Jesus was baptized (Luke

3:22). At that time the Holy Spirit descended on Jesus like a dove from the heavens which opened above him. This was at the inauguration of his public ministry.

Now, listen to the second proclamation.

"This is my Son, whom I love; with him I am well pleased. Listen to him," a voice from the cloud proclaimed when Jesus and three of his disciples were together on the Mount of Transfiguration (Matt. 17:5).

Peter, James, and John were with Jesus on that mountain. Thirty years later Peter was still astonished by what they heard and saw that day. He wrote a letter to the churches describing that event. This is what he recorded.

> We did not follow cleverly invented stories when we told you about the power and coming of our Lord Jesus Christ, but we were eyewitnesses of his majesty. For he received honor and glory from God the Father when the voice came to him from the Majestic Glory, saying, "This is my Son, whom I love; with him I am well pleased." We ourselves heard this voice that came from heaven when we were with him on the sacred mountain. (2 Pet. 1:16-18)

These accounts testify that God himself has proclaimed that Jesus of Nazareth is his beloved Son. It wasn't just Peter, James, and John who were with Jesus on the Mount of Transfiguration when they heard the voice from the cloud. The two central prophets of the Old Testament, Moses and Elijah, also appeared with Jesus and the three disciples on that mountain. Their appearance was a resurrection miracle, for Moses and Elijah had lived many centuries earlier.

These two honored prophets encouraged Jesus concerning the crucifixion he would soon face. Moses was the prophet who led Israel from slavery in Egypt and gave them the Ten Commandments at Mount Sinai. He formed Israel into God's covenant community. Elijah was the miracle-working prophet who called Israel back to God at a time they were worshiping false divinities, including sacrificing their babies. Moses and Elijah—they were the greatest.

Then a cloud descended over the mountain, Moses and Elijah vanished, and God himself proclaimed: "This Jesus is my beloved Son. Obey him."

God made a special point there on that mountain. He wanted the disciples to get the core of the gospel clear. Jesus is not one among others. Jesus is the one and only Savior and Lord. Even Moses and Elijah are not equal to Jesus.

The event on the Mount of Transfiguration was God's way of confirming a conviction which had already seized the disciples. As they lived with Jesus, the Spirit of God was opening their minds to understand who this man was.

The Disciples: You Are the Christ

Eight days before Jesus climbed that mountain with Peter, James, and John, he asked his disciples a probing question.

"Who do people say I am?" asked Jesus.

"A wonderful prophet, perhaps a resurrected prophet from long ago," the disciples responded.

Then Jesus put it straight to the disciples, "Who do you believe I am?"

Simon Peter answered, "You are the Christ, the Son of the living God!"

Jesus was overjoyed, and exclaimed, "Blessed are you, Simon son of Jonah, for this was not revealed to you by man, but by my Father in heaven. And I tell you that you are Peter, and on this rock I will build my church, and the gates of Hades will not overcome it" (Matt. 16:13-18 paraphrased).

What a day that was. Jesus was overjoyed that his disciples recognized who he really was. Yet he quickly cautioned them that he would be arrested and crucified. That was incomprehensible for the disciples. They could not conceive of the crucifixion of the Christ, the Son of the living God.

Jesus Made a Confession

A few months later Jesus was arrested in Jerusalem, just as he had predicted. He stood trial before the highest governing authority in Israel, the seventy-one-member Sanhedrin. Caiaphas, the high priest, arose to question Jesus. The high priest would be similar to the chief justice in modern nations.

"Are you the Christ, the Son of the Blessed One?" asked Caiaphas.

"I am," said Jesus. "And you will see the Son of man sitting at the right hand of the Mighty One and coming on the clouds of heaven."

The high priest tore his clothes in rage; some spit on Jesus, blindfolded him, and hit him with their fists.

That two-word confession by Jesus, "I am," was the clincher in that court. That jury of seventy-one was determined Jesus must die. Later, after further proceedings involving the Roman government, Jesus was crucified on a cross between two criminals.

A Costly Confession

Confessing Jesus as Lord is costly.

It was costly for Jesus himself to confess in that Sanhedrin that he was Son of the living God.

It was a costly confession for the disciples of Jesus. Shortly after the crucifixion and resurrection of Jesus and the formation of the church, James (who had been with Jesus on that mountain) was beheaded due to confessing Jesus as Lord.

Confessing Jesus is also costly today. In the twentieth century alone, millions have been imprisoned, tortured, and killed because of that confession.

Yet all who confess Jesus as Lord experience him to be the only one in all history worthy of being Lord.

Jesus Christ the Foundation of the Church

On the Pentecost birthday of the church, when Peter preached the first Christian sermon in history, he proclaimed, "Therefore let all Israel be assured of this: God has made this Jesus, whom you crucified, both Lord and Christ" (Acts 2:36).

That day three thousand people repented and made the confession of faith in Jesus crucified, who is both Lord and the Anointed One of God (Christ).

Jesus Christ is the rock on which the church was founded on that Pentecost day, just as Jesus had announced several months earlier when Peter confessed, "You are the Christ, the Son of the living God!"

Shortly after Pentecost, the temple authorities were becoming vexed because so many people were believing in this Jesus whom they had crucified. In great agitation the police arrested and imprisoned Peter and John. The next day they were brought before the Sanhedrin, just where Jesus had been brought a few months earlier. There sat the high priest Caiaphas in his judgment chair, just where he had been the night he asked Jesus if he was the Son of God.

The trial began. Peter and John knew they might be condemned to death just as Jesus had been. Nevertheless, Peter stood and spoke his astonishing defense.

Full of the Holy Spirit and with great boldness, Peter proclaimed concerning Jesus, "He is the stone you builders rejected, which has become the Capstone. Salvation is found in no one else, for there is no other name under heaven given to men by which we must be saved" (Acts 4:11-12)!

It is a miracle that the Sanhedrin didn't condemn them to death on the spot. Instead they sternly warned these two uneducated fishermen from Galilee to stop talking about Jesus.

Peter and John responded, "Judge for yourselves whether it is right in God's sight to obey you rather than God. For we cannot help speaking about what we have seen and heard" (Acts 4:19-20).

It wasn't just the disciples who had been with Jesus on the mount who possessed the bold conviction that he was the Son of the living God. That confession was the foundation for the entire church.

Twenty-five years later Paul, who himself had been a member of the Sanhedrin, wrote a letter to the church in Corinth. Paul was now a Christian missionary; the risen Christ had confronted him on his way to Damascus to arrest Christians. Some years after his conversion, the church in Antioch called him and commissioned him to become a missionary.

Corinth was a European church a thousand miles from Jerusalem. This church existed in a society which celebrated pluralism with a vengeance. The Corinthians were even more dogmatic than Allan Bloom's students in their conviction that truth was relative. Their religions venerating many gods reinforced that conviction.

Paul wrote an astonishing proclamation to this church living amidst incredible moral and religious pluralism: "For no one can lay any foundation other than the one already laid, which is Jesus Christ!" Paul exclaims (1 Cor. 3:11).

What did Paul mean? People do build on other foundations.

Other Foundations

However, all other foundations crack. That is what Bishop Kariuki told skeptical university students in Kenya.

When I was teaching world religions in the Kenyatta College of the University of Nairobi, I took my class to meet Bishop Obadiah Kariuki. This man had been tortured and persecuted by the Mau Mau because of his confession that Jesus is Lord. The students listened to his story.

Then came question time. "We are now educated. And we have learned that there are many foundations on which to build one's life. You have chosen Jesus as your foundation. We young and educated people shall choose other foundations," explained a self-styled intellectual.

The bishop took his Bible and held it high. "Go ahead and build on whatever foundation you wish. You are free to choose. I guarantee, however, that every other foundation will crack. In time your house will fall. Jesus Christ of the Scriptures will never crack."

Sometimes that crack in a foundation is revealed in ghastly ways. The collapse of communist systems in the closing decade of the twentieth century is a revelation of an irreparable crack in an ideology that offered salvation to the whole earth.

A Muslim professor has been my dear friend. We often discuss the question of foundations together, sometimes in university classrooms.

On one occasion my colleague explained, "Islam is the practical religion. If you hit a Muslim on one cheek, he will hit back so hard you'll never hit him again. The Christians are naive, however. If you hit a Christian on one cheek, he will turn the other cheek, because that is what Jesus taught. That is foolishness. You cannot build a healthy society on that foundation."

I responded, "However, if you hit back, then your opponent will try to hit you even harder. The consequence of hitting back is that the cycle of violence never stops. Jesus stops the cycle, for he died rather than take vengeance. The cross reveals the way to stop the cycle of violence; it is the way of love for the enemy."

Is Christ an impractical foundation as my colleague insisted? Christians confess that Christ is the only true foundation. Does that foundation withstand the test?

Bishop Obadiah Kariuki looked us in the eye and said, "I have tested Christ, and say with certainty, he is the one foundation which will never ever crack."

The Three-Legged Stool

Jesus is like a three-legged stool. If one leg is missing, then the stool is not very helpful. The three legs of our christological stool are incarnation, crucifixion, and resurrection.

The *incarnation* is God with us in Jesus of Nazareth. That means much more than the virgin birth and Christmas story, important as they are. We must take the whole life and teachings of Jesus seriously. The ethics of the Sermon on the Mount is also good news in any society!

In the *crucifixion* of Jesus, we experience forgiveness. As sinners we deserve punishment. Jesus took our place. We are forgiven. The cross is also a revelation of the way Christians should confront evil. The kingdom of God breaks through as we confront evil in the spirit of suffering love.

The **resurrection** is the guarantee that Jesus is Lord. He has revealed the impotence of the powers of death, whether they are demons or human authorities. The resurrection is also the promise that we shall sometime rise from the dead. The resurrection is the assurance that Jesus and his church are triumphant over evil and death.

When Christians confess that Jesus Christ is the only foundation, they should mean what they say. Too often Christians invent a Christ who has no relationship to the Jesus of the Scriptures. The real historical Jesus of Nazareth is the fulfillment of the Old Testament; his life and ministry is recorded and expounded in the New Testament. He is the one on whom we must build.

Multitudes of Christians claim they would die defending the inerrancy of the Bible—but then ignore Jesus of the very Scriptures they defend. Some Christians are distracted by the traditions of their church or theology or creeds. Others assume that Jesus is too complex for ordinary people to understand, so they leave it to the clergy to define their faith.

Jesus declared, "But I, when I am lifted up from the earth, will draw all men to myself" (John 12:32).

I regularly read one of the gospels in my devotional reflections. I want consistent exposure to all the angles of this one whom God has appointed. We must seek to be formed into his image rather than attempt to chisel Christ into our image.

The Fish

The fish was the logo of the early Christians. In times of persecution the fish was especially helpful. When a Christian was conversing with a person she did not know, it might be dangerous to ask outright, "Are you a Christian?" If the person was not a believer, he might report the Christian to the authorities for arrest. So Christians used the fish logo as a secret way of asking the question, "Are you a Christian?"

While conversing, the Christian inconspicuously drew an outline of a fish on the ground with her toes. If her conversant responded by also drawing a fish, then they both knew that they were believers in Jesus Christ. The fish was the secret sign of recognition used by the Christians.

Why did they use the fish sign?

The Greek word for fish is *i-ch-th-u-s*. Those five Greek characters are also an acronym for five Greek words, which when translated into English mean, "Jesus Christ God's Son Savior."

The fish reminded Christians that Jesus Christ God's Son Savior is the only enduring foundation.

* * *

This chapter describes the foundation of the church—Jesus Christ. Christians confess that Jesus is the only true foundation.

Yet the church exists in societies where people build on many other foundations. It is therefore tempting for Christians to accept the relativistic philosophies of modern times. The church must find ways to give authentic witness that Jesus is Lord within a pluralistic world.

The next chapter describes the four pillars which comprise fruitful witness in our pluralistic world.

Reflection

1. In what ways does your community reflect pluralism?

2. In a pluralistic society, what responsibility do Christians have to keep undesirable businesses or clubs out of your community or the city block where you live?

3. To what extent should global mission agencies concern themselves with human rights in the countries where their missionaries serve? Think of missionaries you know who are serving in situations where human rights abuses exist. Find out how they are responding to these situations.

4. How should a Christian respond to those who insist that Jesus is only one among many?

5. How does a person discover that Jesus Christ is the one and only beloved Son of the living God?

6. Reflect on Jesus as the only true foundation.

7. As a witness to the uniqueness of Jesus Christ, how can one keep from seeming arrogant? Or is it all right to be arrogant about faith?

* * *

Suggested background Scriptures—John 1:1-18; Matthew 24:14; 26:63-64; Acts 4:12-20; Romans 1:16; 1 Corinthians 3:11.

9

The Four Pillars

"PHOEBE, I am calling you to go to Africa as a missionary," the Lord spoke quietly into the heart of a twelve-year old Mennonite Kansas farm girl.

Phoebe was astonished! She was filled with joy. For the next two decades, she set her face in the direction of fulfilling that mission. Three times suitors sought her for courtship.

"Will you go to Africa?" she queried each one.

"No," they each respectfully declined. She never married.

Phoebe planned for mission. Her denomination had no mission commitment in Africa, so she sent regular tithes to the Mennonite Board of Missions designated for mission in Africa. She went to college training as a nurse and to seminary for biblical studies.

Phoebe's tithes put the mission administrators on the spot. The U.S. economy had moved into a deep depression. It did not seem wise to begin a new mission in unknown regions when finances were so scarce. Yet Phoebe's tithes kept coming. At every annual meeting the mission board directors struggled with the problem of Phoebe's tithes.

And Phoebe kept praying. Over a decade after she said "yes" to becoming a missionary, her denomination finally decided to begin a mission in Africa. However, others were chosen as the pioneers. She was heartbroken.

Later she was offered a new position in the nursing profession in

Colorado. "What shall I do?" she asked the Lord.

"Wait for ten days before responding," the Holy Spirit gently instructed.

Just before the ten days were completed, she received a letter from the mission board. Reverently she opened the envelope.

She read, "We are looking for a nurse, mature in spirit and Christian commitment. Would you consent to go to Africa?"

We can guess that tears of joy and praise stained the letter of response and acceptance.

For nearly forty years, Phoebe served as a pathbreaking missionary helping to lay the foundations of a thriving church in Tanzania, East Africa. Other missionaries joined the Tanzania team. Africans shared the vision for mission, and the church spread to many regions of the nation.

Soon Mennonite missionaries were serving in other East African nations as well, including Ethiopia, Kenya, and Somalia. Sixty years after the first missionaries arrived in Tanzania, the total membership of the Mennonite churches in the region was ninety thousand.

Jesus compared faith to a mustard seed. In faith a twelve-year-old Kansas farm girl had said "yes" to God's call to mission in Africa. In time that mustard seed became a surprisingly spacious tree.

Phoebe's story is a revelation of the four pillars which comprise fruitful mission. They are pray, plan, praise, and partner.

Pray

It was in prayer that the Holy Spirit called Phoebe for a specific mission. The Holy Spirit does not always call in the way he called Phoebe. Yet fruitful and joyful mission requires the confidence that we serve in harmony with God's appointment.

It was nearly two thousand years ago in a prayer meeting in Antioch, Syria, that the Holy Spirit said, "Set apart for me Barnabas and Saul [Paul] for the work to which I have called them" (Acts 13:2).

That particular prayer meeting and call was the beginning of an unfolding mission which expanded into regions of Asia and southern Europe.

Mongolia

Prayer and mission always flow together. When we pray, God often surprises us. That is what happened to Jane.

"Tell me about Mongolia," requested Jane, an eighteen-year-old high school graduate.

I was perplexed. "May I ask why you wish to know about Mongolia?" I inquired.

"After my conversion, when I was about twelve, I wanted to invest my whole life in a thank-you to Jesus. During that time I picked up a *National Geographic* magazine that featured Mongolia. As I read it, I felt compassion for these people. I sensed the Holy Spirit inviting me to invest my life in sharing the gospel with the Mongolians."

"Did you know that only two years ago there was no church in Mongolia?" I asked her. "However, the communist government in Mongolia has changed recently. The new government is welcoming Christian missions to serve in Mongolia so that the people can be spiritually and morally recreated. Our mission board is exploring possibilities."

Jane listened with wonder at the plan of God unfolding.

"I know of no place on earth more difficult for a Western missionary than Mongolia," I continued. "It is bitterly cold. Houses are poorly heated. It is remote and vast, far into the heartland of central Asia. The language is complex."

With tears of joy and commitment, Jane responded simply, "Tell me how to plan and prepare."

Empowerment

In prayer we receive those nudges from the Holy Spirit that become a calling for mission.

In prayer we also receive empowerment for mission. In prayer the Holy Spirit fills us with his presence so our efforts are empowered and fruitful.

In prayer the Holy Spirit can reveal sin to us so that we can confess our wrong, repent, and become free for fruitful mission.

In prayer the Holy Spirit reveals the way we should serve. He enables us to plan wisely; otherwise our efforts in mission can become just fuss and activity.

Blasio Kigozi

In 1935 Blasio Kigozi learned in fresh ways the meaning of prayer. This Buganda teacher in Ruanda, Central Africa, was discouraged. The students had gone on strike. Blasio was tired of trying to live the Christian life. He locked himself in a hut for a week to pray and fast.

Blasio left his hut a transformed man. He called a school assembly, and proclaimed a word from the Lord: "Repent!"

The Holy Spirit fell on the school assembly convicting people of sin. They wept in repentance. When the Anglican Church council heard of what had happened, they called Blasio to rebuke him for this fanaticism.

Blasio shared with the council that the Lord had given him a message for the church leaders, "Repent and be born again."

The conviction of the Holy Spirit fell on the church leaders. They wept before the Lord in repentance. This was the beginning of a mighty movement of the Holy Spirit in Central and East Africa.

After Blasio's week of fasting, he first went to his wife and family and put matters right with them. With his sins confessed and forgiven, Blasio became a person available for the Holy Spirit.

His ministry lasted only a few weeks, for soon he took ill and died. Yet the convicting fire of the Holy Spirit has spread throughout the churches of Central and East Africa.

Katuru Hill

A decade after Blasio's week of prayer, the fire of the Holy Spirit fell on the churches of Musoma District in Tanzania on the eastern shores of Lake Victoria. Although I was only a child, I remember those days well. My parents arose at 4:00 in the morning and joined others in the grass-thatched church for prayer. They were participants in a network of believers throughout the region joining in regular early morning prayer.

On a Sunday morning, the Holy Spirit touched the Shirati congregation on Katuru Hill. People wept before the Lord in deep repentance. A woman at the back ran from the church crying that they were throwing stones at her.

For many days people from the surrounding region who were resisting the Holy Spirit avoided coming near the church building. In awe they confided with one another that the fire of God had fallen on Katuru Hill.

This outpouring of the Holy Spirit happened during a time when mission programs were mostly at a standstill. World War II raged, and it was difficult to acquire supplies such as gasoline or paper. Since the missionaries couldn't do anything else, they had time to join with African colleagues in prayer. Those were the days when the foundation of the church in East Africa was formed, for Jesus Christ revealed himself in unforgettable power.

Plan

Phoebe's prayer would have come to nothing without planning. She prayed and planned. She sent her tithes designated for mission in Africa. In that way she helped move an apathetic denomination into a new mission frontier. Her planning involved personal preparation for the mission God had appointed for her. Her prayers inspired her to focus and plan her life in accordance with God's leading.

Revival

Blasio Kigozi's week of prayer led to a great revival. Yet the revived Christians soon discovered that they were returning to their old ways of indifference to Christ and lukewarm compassion for others. As they prayed about their spiritual coldness, the Holy Spirit enabled them to develop a plan for continuous renewal. The plan is still working throughout Central and East Africa today.

This is the plan. Believers meet regularly for confession of sin, reflecting on the Word of God, praying together, renewing their commitment to Christ, planning for mission, and praising the Lord. God has honored that plan by continually renewing the church. Renewal is continuous when we walk in fellowship with Christ and one another. The plan encourages that walk.

Meserete Kristos

Christians in Ethiopia have also learned how important planning is for fruitful mission.

For about two decades the Mennonite mission in Ethiopia had been involved in medical, educational, development, and evangelistic ministry. Slowly a church developed. The Ethiopian believers named the church Meserete Kristos (Christ is the foundation).

Christ the foundation (1 Corinthians 3:11) was the favorite sermon topic for the sixteenth-century Dutch Anabaptist leader, Menno Simons, whose name was affixed to the Mennonite church. The Ethiopians recaptured that theme in their church name.

One church youth group meeting in the town of Nazareth took the name Heavenly Sunshine. The group rented a small building made of corrugated metal sheeting for youth meetings. That was in 1964. While they were in prayer, the Holy Spirit came on them, giving them a passion to share Christ with those who did not know salvation. They planned for the evangelization of Ethiopia, and they permeated the entire Meserete Kristos church with new life.

After a communist government took over Ethiopia, these believers had to go underground. When they saw signs of impending persecution, they organized themselves into cell groups in accordance with the political zones of the cities. Each group had three leaders, so if one was arrested, there would still be leaders in the group.

Groups met secretly. They alternated places and times of meeting so the authorities would have difficulty detecting them. Group leaders met one-on-one with the central church leaders, but for many years the cell group leaders never had opportunity to meet together.

After a decade the government changed, and the Meserete Kristos church was legalized. At their first public leadership meeting, they were amazed to discover that their church had grown from five thousand to fifty thousand believers during the ten years underground.

Meserete Kristos is a praying church which also plans well. Thoughtful planning by the central leaders enabled it to continue as a growing church even when cell group leaders could never meet together.

It is important for the church to plan for mission. The plan includes being alert to the opportunities for mission which God is providing for the local and global church.

Mountville Mennonite

Our congregation in Mountville, Pennsylvania, learned something about the importance of planning for mission. Mountville is a growing community; people are moving into it from other areas of the world. Most are young families. These new arrivals in our town are in transition and often open to the gospel. This is a moment of opportunity for mission.

We found that investing in the moment of opportunity demands planning. Rarely does anyone consider believing in Christ just because there is a church in the community. The church must plan for mission within the local community as well as beyond the local church. Without a plan, little or nothing happens.

Our congregation made plans. We acquired the record of housing purchases from the recorder of deeds. Every month we visited every new home in a three-mile radius of the church. We planned events like an evening at the bowling lanes. Every church member was encouraged to invite a neighbor who was unchurched. The young mothers in our congregation began a weekly event for mothers and their children. Occasionally as many as fifty community mothers have been present.

The congregation has frequent congregational potluck dinners right after Sunday worship. On those Sundays people are encouraged to make a special effort to invite guests. We find it is thoughtful for everyone to wear name tags on those Sundays so no one is embarrassed by not knowing the name of the person one is eating with. These modest plans have helped our congregation double in membership over the past decade.

The plan gets the church moving. However, it must never become a straitjacket that prevents creativity and adaptability. As we move forward, we discover surprises and even obstacles which invite a change of direction. We must be prepared to plan fresh directions at any time.

Negligence

The history of mission includes sad accounts of churches neglecting significant opportunities because they had no vision or plan for mission. One such missed opportunity occurred in Asia seven centuries ago.

In the thirteenth century, Marco Polo of Venice traveled to China with his father and uncle. For more than two decades, Marco served in the court of Kublai Khan. After twenty-four years, Marco returned home with a letter from Kublai Khan addressed to the pope of the Catholic Church.

"Send us one hundred missionaries," the letter requested.

But the missionaries never went. The regions of China and Mongolia ruled by Kublai Khan subsequently became mostly Buddhist and Muslim.

Just as God planned for the salvation of the world and acted on that plan by sending his Son, so the church must plan for mission. Prayer meetings alone do not lead to the conversion of people or the feeding of the poor. As we combine prayer and planning, mission develops fruitfully.

Focus

Our plans need to be inspired by and made with the counsel of the Holy Spirit. The need in the world is overwhelming. No church can do all that should be accomplished. Each church and person needs discernment informed by the Holy Spirit to determine priorities and focus.

What is God's appointment for our particular church? Should we focus on evangelism, compassion for the poor, or justice and peace commitments? Should we put most of our resources into mission in the home community or in regions beyond? Should we share mission resources with churches already established or seek to bring the gospel into communities where people have never heard of Christ? Such questions inform our planning for mission.

Two considerations help define the plan for any congregation—gifts and need. When Grace and I were invited to help pastor the small, declining congregation at Mountville, we promptly convened a congregational meeting. We asked two questions. First, what gifts for mission has God bestowed on this congregation? Second, what needs in this community and within regions beyond could those gifts most fruitfully serve?

We discerned two particular gifts among us—hospitality and finances. The finances we invested mostly in outward mission providing support for missionaries. The hospitality we invested in making friends with unchurched neighbors. As our congregation grew, we discovered increasing diversity of gifts within our group which provided resources for a broadening scope of mission.

Mission Agencies

One congregation alone cannot plan adequately for the world harvest. There are people groups who will never hear the gospel and impoverished communities who will never be touched with the compassion of the church unless congregations work together. That is the role of mission agencies.

Congregations and denominations support mission agencies so a cluster of congregations can do together what no one congregation could do alone.

Some mission agencies are accountable to denominations or a cluster of congregations. Others are parachurch agencies. These agencies organize around a particular vision and have their own board of directors. Being free of denominational restraints, such agencies can often function with considerable flexibility and focus. An example is the Summer Institute of Linguistics, which reduces languages to writing as a preparation for translating the Bible.

Parachurch agencies are active in modern global missions. Such agencies need to consciously seek connections and accountabilities with local churches. Otherwise mission can become separated from congregational life.

Mission agencies should also enable wealthy congregations to share resources for the poor of our world. Mission agencies remind congregations to look beyond their local community as they pray and plan for mission among those who are poor, suffer injustice, are in conflict situations, or have not yet believed in Jesus Christ.

Mission agencies are entrusted with the responsibility to plan for mission within the global harvest. Such agencies need to give special attention to peoples who have never heard of Jesus Christ and communities where there is no thriving indigenous church. Reaching these unreached peoples might require extraordinary flexibility and creative imagination.

Nonresident Missionaries

The Southern Baptists have given leadership to the idea of nonresident missionaries. These missionaries focus prayer and planning toward a specific people among whom it is difficult to place traditional residential missionaries.

For example, Eastern Mennonite Missions has appointed a nonresident missionary for Vietnam. That person's responsibility is to keep informed on developments in Vietnam and help facilitate the modest mission commitments which have been possible in that communist regime. His task is to pray and plan concerning Vietnam.

Every Congregation

Every congregation should have the privilege of participating in local and global mission. No church is too impoverished to experience the blessing of mission within regions beyond the local experience.

Mission agencies have a special responsibility for planning mission in ways that enable a wide variety of local congregations to experience the blessing of mission beyond the local community. Such agencies need to plan mission in a way that includes all of God's people, not just those with significant financial resources.

Denominational as well as parachurch mission agencies need to respect the fact that the local congregation is the basic mission community. Authentic mission planning must involve conversation between congregations and agencies. Mission agency structures should encourage that conversation.

It is not wise for congregations to surrender to a mission board their congregational responsibility for planning for mission. Neither is it wise for a congregation to determine its mission commitments independent of conversation with mission agencies in touch with world mission developments.

Planning Growth

In recent years mission experts known as missiologists have developed excellent plans for church growth. The School of World Mission at Fuller Theological Seminary (Pasadena, California), has been an imaginative leader in the church growth movement. Church growth missiologists counsel missionaries on priorities. The inclination is to concentrate missionary outreach toward people who are especially responsive to the Christian faith.

The counsel of church growth mission experts can be helpful. However, there are two dangers people should consider when planning for church growth and mission.

First, an overconcern for growth might nudge a church into a popularity contest. We must recognize that disciples of Jesus are not always popular. Jesus is not a Santa Claus who gives whatever we want.

Second, an emphasis on growth can discourage churches or missionaries who are working in a society where few people are responding to the gospel. Many mission agencies actually avoid sending missionaries into societies where they expect slow church growth.

Resistant Groups

A sad consequence of such a policy is that many people groups considered "resistant" to the gospel never have opportunity to hear of Christ. Missionaries avoid these peoples. Consequently the overwhelming majority of the global missionary team is ministering within Christianizing societies.

Mission among Muslims is an example of avoiding a mission commitment which requires patience. There are about 900 million Muslims. Fewer than nine hundred missionaries serve with a focus on mission among Muslims. That equals one missionary for one million people. Frequently churches present in Muslim societies avoid explaining the gospel.

Muslims have tragic misconceptions about the Christian faith! How will those misunderstandings ever be corrected when the global church is doing so little about sharing the gospel faithfully among Muslims?

No wonder the Muslim community seems resistant; most have never had an opportunity to hear the astonishing biblical account of Jesus Christ. Too often world mission agencies simply avoid considering Muslims when developing their plans for mission.

Churches in mission too often avoid secular humanists. People with a secular humanist worldview often experience greater difficulty considering the gospel than groups such as Muslims or Buddhists. This worldview is the basic orientation of Western universities. The philosophy pervades Western culture, yet the church largely avoids conversation with secular humanist people .

Secular humanists have drunk deeply from the philosophies of the seventeenth- and eighteenth-century European Enlightenment. This worldview is suspicious of all faiths. Human reason is the only reliable basis for truth. People are mostly good. Wise social organization and education will create a secular salvation. That is all people really need or desire—a good life now.

The gospel is exceptionally good news for secular humanists. Yet a credible Christian witness is seldom heard within the centers where the secular humanist worldview is communicated and assumed—the universities of the Western world.

Mission plans should not ignore those who seem disinterested in the gospel. Planning must include mission among especially responsive people. Nevertheless, those whose culture has created barriers preventing their acceptance of the gospel also deserve to hear a patient, sensitive witness concerning the gift of new life in Jesus Christ.

Praise

Pray and plan—these are the first two supporting pillars for fruitful mission. Praise and partner—these pillars are also essential. We now explore the pillar of praise, for mission is joyful.

Have You Heard of Joy?

Thai believers who have come out of Buddhism have discovered how central joy is for fruitful mission. That is the conviction shared by a former Buddhist monk.

Wan Phetsongram was once a Buddhist monk in Bangkok, Thailand. After his conversion to Christ, he left the Buddhist monastery and prepared for pastoral ministry. The Holy Spirit has anointed his ministry; every month he is baptizing two hundred Buddhist converts to Christ.

Since Thai Buddhists have resisted the gospel for many generations, we asked him why this is changing.

With a monkish grin, pastor Phetsongram needled a bit, "The Western mind is not capable of explaining the gospel in a convincing manner to the Thai Buddhist mind. Our perception is that Western thinking is superficial. Thai thinking is deep. However, Thai Christians need the encouragement and biblical foundations of the Western church."

"In what ways is the gospel attractive to Buddhists?" I persisted.

"Have you heard of the Holy Spirit? One fruit of the Spirit is joy. There is no joy in Buddhism. However, believers in Jesus Christ are baptized with joy. Our worship is a crescendo of overflowing praise and joy. The joy and praise in the life of Christians is powerfully attractive!"

Pastor Phetsongram is right. Joy that produces praise is vital to fruitful mission, not only among the Buddhists, but in every culture.

As the church moves forward in prayer and planning, the Holy Spirit anoints believers with praise. Muslims often comment that Christian congregations in worship sound like people having a party. Indeed they are enjoying a party. A universal characteristic of faithful churches everywhere, in every culture and circumstance, is joy and praise.

Amor Viviente

Joy permeates the Amor Viviente (Living Love) Church in Honduras. These Christians even experience joy in fasting! They have an annual week for prayer and fasting. Some members take their week of vacation at that time so they can invest all their energies in prayer. They meet for prayer in their hundreds of growth groups throughout the city of Tegucigalpa.

Midway through the week the congregation is invited to a united prayer meeting. Fifteen hundred were present for that prayer event in February 1992. These prayer warriors convened on a mountainside above the city of Tegucigalpa to conclude the fast. Two thousand were present.

The Holy Spirit spoke, "Don't take yourselves so seriously. Enjoy the Lord. Praise him. Have a party! The Lord will fulfill the kingdom of God. Your responsibility is to follow the Lord and enjoy him. So rejoice!"

Joy in Suffering

Even in circumstances of suffering, God has a way of giving his people a party. Have you noticed the holy joviality and gentle laughter, mingling with tears, usually present in the worship and conversation at the funeral of a person who has loved the Lord? The sadness is touched with joy. That is a mystery of the Christian faith.

As God's people celebrate the grace of our Lord Jesus Christ, people are baptized with praise. When we praise the Lord, the Holy Spirit is freed to anoint the mission of the church with fruitfulness.

Partner

Churches in mission exercise prayer, plan, and praise. Missionaries should also partner with other Christians. Missionary Paul whose service is described in the biblical book of Acts demonstrated this spirit of partnership.

A Cross-Cultural Team

"Come over to Macedonia and help us," a man implored Paul in a night vision when he was in Troas, at the end of his missionary journey through the Anatolia Peninsula (Acts 16:9).

With expectation Paul boarded ship for Macedonia in Europe. However, he did not sail alone; he was traveling in a team of four—Paul, Silas, Luke, and Timothy.

This was an excellent cross-cultural missionary team. Luke was a European Greek who understood his native environment and culture well. Paul came with a deep biblical heritage. Timothy had a Greek father and Jewish mother. He was an authentic cross-cultural person who moved comfortably from one culture to another. Silas had solid Jewish roots. This remarkable team quickly found their way when they arrived in the large Macedonian city of Philippi.

Later, when the Asians Paul and Silas were imprisoned, Timothy and Luke with European connections were free. I imagine that during the night of that imprisonment, Luke and Timothy were working their contacts in Philippi, encouraging release for their Asian companions. By morning the magistrates had decided to let Paul and Silas go free.

Team partnerships are much stronger than individual efforts in mission, especially when some members of the team are in prison!

E1 to E4

Whenever possible, cross-cultural evangelism should involve cross cultural teams. The E1-to-E4 principle helps us understand why this is important. E refers to evangelism. E1 are the people culturally closest to you. E2 are people culturally more distant. E3 would be more distant, and E4 very distant. It is most possible to evangelize E1 people. It is most difficult to evangelize E4 people (Engel and Norton).

Paul in Macedonia was meeting an E3 situation, but for Luke, Macedonia was E1. He was completely comfortable. Although Paul was the preacher, Luke counseled him on the proprieties of Macedonian life.

My father and mother had not studied the E1-to-E4 principle before they went to Tanganyika as missionaries in 1936. But their biblical intuition informed them of this principle. When they moved into the Zanaki society, Jonah Itini accompanied them. Jonah was probably the only Zanaki Christian on earth.

Jonah was a cross-cultural Zanaki, for he had moved into another society and married a Jita woman. He heard and believed the gospel while living among the Jita. He and his Jita wife, Leah, teamed up with my parents for the first cross-cultural evangelical witness among the Zanaki. When my parents needed counsel on cultural or religious matters, Jonah was a wise partner. The Zanaki people were E4 to my parents, but E1 for Jonah. They formed a powerful team.

One reason it is important for local congregations to keep on growing is that the believers within a church soon become E1 to one another but have few meaningful connections with people who are not Christians. The outsiders are all E2 or even E3. The Christian community feels uncomfortable relating to those who are not Christians. Perhaps in the workplace the Christians will even sit together over lunch, for they feel uncomfortable with the conversation of their fellow workers.

However, a new believer experiences his nonbelieving friends as E1. As time goes on, the new Christian will become more involved with her church community. In time a distance often develops between the new Christian and her non-Christian friends. They have become E2.

It is for this reason that new Christians are among the best evangelists within any congregation. They still have close relationships with non-Christians. Experienced Christians need to partner with and encourage new Christians to reach out invitationally to their non-Christian friends. They are a special gift to any church.

Global Network

The greatest resource the modern global church possesses is the reality that it is now a global church. One century ago this was not true. When Adoniram Judson went to Southeast Asia, the entire team were Western Caucasians. There just were no Southeast Asian Christians. No wonder they struggled so heroically for many years with so few conversions.

In contrast, the mission agency with which I work is preparing for mission outreach in an unevangelized region of Thailand. Churches in the region are partnering with us. The team will also include Thai evangelists. North Americans will be included in the partner team.

The twentieth-century development of a genuinely global church is a marvelous resource for world mission. It is no wonder that the world church is now experiencing an amazing ingathering of people. As churches partner in mission, they discover that the quantity and diversity of laborers for the world harvest in our time is unprecedented.

However, marshaling the rich diversity of laborers for the harvest requires a deepening commitment to partnering with varieties of Christian communities. Suppose a Korean Presbyterian mission agency is planning mission among Muslims in the Republic of Kirghizia in the southern regions of the Commonwealth of Independent States. It would be helpful to link people resources with churches already present. That would likely require forming partnerships with churches within adjacent communities or republics. A mission in Kirghizia involving partnership between the Korean mission agency and local churches will likely be far more fruitful than it would be if the Korean missionaries worked independently of nearby churches.

International partnerships might form within denominational communities. The Anabaptist Mennonite and Brethren in Christ denominations have formed regional, continental, and global consultations which bring together leadership of all Anabaptist synods or denominations. These international consultations are an excellent arena to develop partnerships and networking for mission.

Thus when the Muria Synod in Indonesia was contemplating their first international mission, the Asia regional consultation helped develop the partnership patterns necessary for a Muria Synod initiative in Singapore. They also invited a North American agency to share in that partnership.

Fifteen Anabaptist denominations within the North American context involved in world mission and service have an annual missions and service conference for consultation. This meeting is the Council of International Ministries (CIM). That meeting provides opportunity for consultation and networking for expanded mission.

Variety Enriches

Partnership in mission is enriched when efforts include a variety of denominations and agencies. The Lausanne movement for world evangelism is becoming an increasingly significant consultation for partnership in world mission. Both the World Evangelical Fellowship and the World Council of Churches bring together different expressions of the worldwide church for consultation and partnership.

In many regions of the world, Christians form councils in which the varied expressions of the body of Christ can encourage one another and weave networks for mission.

* * *

This chapter describes four pillars, or four P's, of fruitful mission—prayer, plan, praise, and partner. In *prayer* we cultivate a joyful and right relationship with God. The Holy Spirit is able to guide in mission. We experience empowerment for the task.

In prayer we discern the *plan* for moving forward in mission. Without planning, not much happens in mission. God honors planning.

Mission is like a party. It is permeated with joy. *Praise* and joviality give mission buoyancy, even in the most difficult circumstances.

Every congregation and every missionary must remember that no one is called by God to be a lonely laborer. *Partnering* with others is vital. No one can do the job alone.

All of this calls for leaders with vision who empower congregations for mission. That is the theme of the next chapter.

Reflection

1. Reflect on ways your congregation uses the gifts of prayer and planning in developing its mission.

2. Account for the importance of praise in fruitful mission. How does your congregation experience joviality in mission?

3. Explain the E1-to-E4 principle. Discover the unevangelized groups of people within your region of the world. Applying the E1-to-E4 principle, develop a plan whereby your congregation could participate in reaching one such group with the gospel.

4. Consider an E4 community in a distant country which is not evangelized. In what ways could your congregation partner with others in cross-cultural mission among these people? In what ways could a mission agency be helpful in that commitment?

5. Using the four pillars of fruitful mission, develop a mission proposal for your congregation.

* * *

Suggested background Scriptures—Matthew 9:38; Mark 11:24; John 17:4; Acts 16.

10

Leaders Who Empower

I MAGINE A CHURCH COMMUNITY of six thousand people where half the pastors do not have a second grade education and where you could count on one hand the leaders who have completed sixth grade! That is what we experienced when meeting K'ekchi' Mennonite Church leaders in San Pedro Carcha in the Alta Verapaz highlands of Guatemala in 1993.

Leaders with Beautiful Feet

Six North American leaders sat in a circle with twenty K'ekchi' pastors. We from the north were trained people with M.A. and Ph.D. degrees. Yet in four days of conversation, we discovered we needed to become the students. These pastors were wise and capable leaders.

While trained pastors of North American churches were struggling to lead their congregations into 10 percent growth over a decade, K'ekchi' pastors with a year or two of school were forming new church districts and experiencing a doubling in membership every five years.

The K'ekchi' pastors had dressed in their best for the meeting, yet the shoes they wore were old and shabby. These were the shoes of pastors who had walked thousands of miles carrying the gospel from hamlet to hamlet within the mountains and valleys of Alta Verapaz.

"Your worn shoes reveal that you have beautiful feet," we exclaimed at the climax of our three days of conversation.

Many years ago the prophet Isaiah exclaimed, "How beautiful on the mountains are the feet of those who bring good news, who proclaim peace, who bring good tidings, who proclaim salvation" (Isa. 52:7).

The K'ekchi' pastors laughed jovially as they kicked their feet into the air to inspect the evidence of shoes which contained beautiful feet.

A quality of K'ekchi' leadership is the conviction that all who are gifted and anointed for pastoral ministry or other ministries within the church should have opportunity to express and develop those ministries. Characteristically a pastor will step aside from his visible leadership position after several years to give others the chance to develop their pastoral gifts.

Pastors with experience might move into communities without churches and begin new congregations. Or they might just rest awhile until ready to accept new leadership responsibilities. The theme which guides these wise K'ekchi' pastors is this: enable all who are anointed for leadership to develop their gifts.

One advantage of the K'ekchi' leadership pattern is that people become sympathetic toward their leaders. When many within a congregation have personally experienced the responsibilities of leadership, they understand the challenges a leader faces.

Another advantage of the K'ekchi' leadership style is that every congregation becomes a center for leadership formation. The pattern enables each of the 120 K'ekchi' congregations to call forth many leaders and provide in-service training within each congregation for pastors, evangelists, teachers, missionaries, or development workers. The K'ekchi' churches are multiplying leaders!

Leadership Patterns

The New Testament reveals flexibility in the leadership patterns of the early church. When widows needed assistance, the church chose seven assistants to administer the feeding program so that the apostles could continue giving their full attention to "prayer and the ministry of the word" (Acts 6:4). Soon persons emerged who provided spiritual oversight for clusters of churches. Leadership developed in response to the needs of the church in mission.

New Testament Guidance

These leadership patterns developed into three overall functions:

1. Bishops for the oversight of clusters of churches.

2. Pastors for the ministry of the Word of God within congregations.

3. Deacons for the administration of compassion ministries.

All leaders served as evangelists and missionaries.

Throughout the centuries church communities have mostly based their leadership patterns on variations of the roles developed within the early church. Yet there is great diversity in the ways oversight of churches, pastoral ministry, and care for the poor are carried out.

Cultural Patterns

However, the manner in which these leadership functions are developed should converge with normal patterns of the culture. The traditional K'ekchi' leadership system is egalitarian. Within the traditional system, leaders are continually stepping aside to give others opportunity for developing leadership skills. Thus it is appropriate and not surprising that the church has developed similar patterns.

In Confucian Asian and Bantu African societies, leadership patterns are hierarchical and stable. In Korea, Paul Y. Choo pastors the world's largest congregation, with well over half a million members. He operates a tight ship. At every level of leadership, people know to whom they are accountable. Choo's system converges with traditional Korean family leadership patterns.

Most of the language groups south of the western hump of Africa are within the Bantu family of languages. Everywhere in Bantu Africa, churches have developed hierarchical leadership patterns. If the missionaries came from communities such as the Quakers, which had egalitarian systems of leadership, they discovered that it was impossible to transplant their system into Bantu society. As far as I know, wherever the missionary influence declined, the leadership patterns across Bantu Africa developed hierarchical patterns. The Anglican and Catholic models of leadership fit Bantu African patterns well.

Why has that happened? Because leadership patterns in Bantu society were anchored in the chief. Churches throughout the continent have also developed a chief style of leadership.

That is the way it should be. A church should develop leadership patterns consistent with the culture in which the church is developing.

Coming Down the Ladder

However, the New Testament reveals that in Christ a revolution must take place in the spirit of leadership, no matter what the authentic pattern might be. The new spirit which Christ introduces is that of a servant. And that is a revolution.

The Disciples Seek Status

For three years Jesus taught and modeled servant leadership among his disciples. He struggled to communicate this core quality of leadership within the kingdom of God: the leader must be a servant. The disciples could not comprehend. It is amazing how resistant these mostly peasant disciples were to any notions of becoming servants. They could not imagine that leaders in the kingdom of God would ever need to serve others or suffer.

"If Jesus is the Messiah, he cannot be a suffering servant." They all agreed about that.

They also knew that if Jesus was the Messiah, then they were in for a giddy climb with him to the top of global leadership and power. As soon as they understood that Jesus was indeed the Messiah, the Son of the living God, they began a nasty jockeying for position. Thus, while Jesus was beginning his journey south from fame in the northern regions of Galilee to certain crucifixion in Jerusalem, the disciples argued along the way about who was the greatest among them.

The disciples' quest for status and power saddened Jesus.

Two Dramas by Jesus

Twice Jesus used drama to get the attention of the disciples about being servants. He used these dramas when the disciples' bickering about greatness had become especially obnoxious.

Drama one occurred in Galilee. Jesus took a young child and stood her among the disciples. Then Jesus said, "I tell you the truth, unless you change and become like little children, you will never enter the kingdom of heaven. Therefore, whoever humbles himself like this child is the greatest in the kingdom of heaven. And whoever welcomes a little child like this in my name welcomes me" (Matt. 18:3-5).

Drama two unfolded in Jerusalem. During the Last Supper with his disciples—in the evening just before his betrayal would result in his trial, crucifixion, and death—the disciples were at it again. Whispered talk eddied from corners of the large dining room table.

"I am the greatest."

"Don't be so sure of yourself. I know I will be the chief administrator in Jesus' cabinet."

In profound sadness, Jesus took a basin of water and a towel. He removed his outer garment as a servant does when preparing for menial work. He moved around the table from person to person, washing the feet of each and drying each foot with the towel. He also washed the feet of Judas, who planned to betray him that night. Some ancient Christian traditions say that Judas was the first person whose feet Jesus washed and John the last. Then he returned to his place.

Jesus explained, "You call me 'Teacher' and 'Lord' and rightly so, for that is what I am. Now that I, your Lord and Teacher, have washed your feet, you also should wash one another's feet. I have set you an example that you should do as I have done for you" (John 13:13-15).

Servant Leaders Are Surprising

Servant ministry is the touchstone of authentic Christian leadership. The inclination of the human spirit is to try to climb the ladder of authority and control. The mind of Christ invites a movement in the opposite direction. Servant leaders climb down the ladder (Phil. 2:1-11).

Writing from a Roman prison, the apostle Paul counsels the church in Philippi, "Do nothing out of selfish ambition or vain conceit, but in humility consider others better than yourselves. Each of you should look not only to your own interests, but also to the interests of others. Your attitude should be the same as that of Christ Jesus" (Phil. 2:3-5).

A servant leader spirit is a good news revolution in any culture. Although the K'ekchi' people are egalitarian in their leadership pattern, the servant leader mind of Christ is creating an amazing revolution in the core of their culture.

"Why are many K'ekchi' believing in Jesus Christ?" I asked half a dozen K'ekchi' elders during a dinner of meat broth and tortillas.

We were enjoying lunch after a three-hour Sunday morning worship which included prayer for the sick, singing, a wedding, baby dedication, preaching, gifts and affirmation for the good work of the pastor, and testimonies.

Immediately an elder answered, "Most Christian husbands don't beat their wives. Christ brings a new attitude into the souls of the men who are believers. They respect and love their wives. They are concerned for the well-being of their families. They avoid drinking. There is peace in the homes of Christians. Many families want that kind of peace and become Christians."

The same servant leadership spirit of K'ekchi' men which is bringing peace into their homes is also beginning to free women for community and church leadership. In some congregations women are invited to lead in aspects of the worship service. That is an astonishing revolution not imagined even five years ago.

Servant Leaders Reveal Reconciliation

We enjoy climbing the ladder of status and power. We resent coming down, especially when we meet the cross of suffering at the foot of our status ladder. Yet the way of the cross is the only way for fruitful leadership in the mission of the church.

When leaders climb the status ladder, there is alienation. When they come down the ladder, there is reconciliation. The whole church is led toward reconciliation when leaders are experiencing it.

A pastor in Kenya and his bishop in Tanzania had experienced a break in relationships. Consequently, the entire church was suffering a deep malaise. Twice the bishop had sent a message to the pastor inviting him to come and make peace. Once he had even sent his wife in a vehicle to personally bring the pastor to the bishop's home for reconciliation and a goat feast.

The pastor could not bring himself to accept these invitations. Within African hierarchical leadership patterns, the pastor's nonresponse to these invitations was a grievous affront to the bishop.

After some two years, intermediaries persuaded the pastor to meet the bishop on neutral ground halfway between their homes; each would travel a hundred miles. However, everything within the African chief system would say that this arrangement was wrong. The pastor himself should come to see the bishop.

The bishop met with pastors within his home community for counsel.

They advised, "According to our tradition, the pastor must come to you. However, for Jesus' sake, you must go to him wherever he consents to meet you."

On the set day the two men met at Kisii in western Kenya. The meeting continued for three hours.

The bishop took charge, just as any responsible chief should do. Yet he functioned as a servant chief.

"My brother, I have come today to ask a question. For Jesus' sake, will you forgive me for whatever I have done to offend you?" asked the bishop.

The pastor responded by expounding about his grievances. He was climbing his ladder higher and higher.

For a couple hours that afternoon the bishop climbed further and further down his bishop's ladder.

"But, my brother, can you forgive me?" the bishop persisted. The bishop was washing, as it were, the feet of his brother pastor.

Finally in the late afternoon, the aged bishop arose from his seat and walked over to where the younger pastor sat.

Looking into the pastor's eyes, he asked yet once more, "For the sake of Jesus, will you forgive me, my brother?"

The pastor began sobbing. He stood, and the two men embraced. We heard words of remorse, repentance, and forgiveness. We wept with joy.

That evening the oral grapevine carried word of the reconciliation to scattered clusters of believers. They sang hallelujahs of great joy.

A few days later the two men met alone to work through the issues which had separated them. Within several months the bishop had arranged for the ordination of bishop partners, one of whom was the pastor from Kenya.

That kind of servant leadership equips the church for authentic mission. It is a revelation of the way of the cross, which results in profound reconciliation. When we climb ladders, we move further and further apart. Ladder climbers cannot experience reconciliation. Yet when we follow the example of Christ and come down our ladders of pride and status and power, we experience reconciliation with our sisters and brothers.

Servant Missionaries Gain Trust

A servant spirit often paves the way for fruitful ministry even among people who might seem hostile to the gospel.

Seek Counsel

A team was developing a Bible correspondence course for Muslims. After the first drafts were completed, the author took the course to a Muslim fundamentalist, who was quite opposed to Christian witness in his community.

"As you know, we are those whom the Koran describes as the people of the Book," the author said. "We have developed a correspondence course based on the Scriptures in our possession. We hope this course will help our Muslim friends understand our faith and convictions which are based upon the Book God has entrusted to us.

"While we insist that the course must be true to the Scriptures known as the Bible, we are also concerned that we express these truths in ways which do not offend our Muslim friends.

"Would you consent to evaluate this course? If there are portions which are offensive, help us express our faith in a way which can be understood."

"I will gladly assess the course for you," the Muslim sheik responded.

The next week the author returned to the sheik's home.

"This course is good!" he exclaimed. "However, there is one section which chagrined me—the one in which you describe the Fall of humankind."

The Muslim sheik then helped the author formulate that chapter in a manner true to biblical faith and less offensive to Muslims. It is Christian theologians who talk of the Fall, not the Bible. The sheik and the author agreed to use the phrase "turn away from God."

The concept of turning away from God is not Muslim doctrine. It is biblical. Yet if "the Fall" was expressed in those terms, Muslims could hear it.

A decade later, some five thousand Muslims in East Africa had enrolled in that course, with little or no objection from the Muslim community. By first listening as servant learners before publishing and circulating the course, the writing team had gained credibility with Muslim leaders.

Be Like Lambs

Servant leadership gives credibility and power to the mission of the church within the world.

On one occasion Jesus commissioned seventy-two missionaries. He told them, "Go! I am sending you out like lambs among wolves" (Luke 10:3).

Lambs are harmless and gentle, yet bold and persistent.

Later the missionaries returned to Jesus with joy, exclaiming, "Lord, even the demons submit to us in your name" (Luke 10:17).

Who Should Be Leader?

The servant leader discerns who is best suited for the roles and responsibilities of the church and mission. The servant leader rejoices when a person emerges who is anointed for leadership or ministry. She is not threatened by the abilities of others. She enables and empowers people for service.

The Holy Spirit has taught the Amor Viviente Church in Honduras a revolutionary insight on leadership.

After a week of fasting, the Holy Spirit counseled them, "The church does not need leaders, only servants."

The chairman of the church had been a key person in laying the foundations for this growth movement fifteen years earlier. However, in light of the counsel from the Lord concerning servants, he climbed right down his leadership ladder.

The chairman asked, "Is there someone else whom the Lord has anointed for leadership of this movement? Is there a servant who could minister as chairman of the church more fruitfully than I can?"

The answer was, "Yes!"

So with joy the chairman resigned. A new chairman was appointed.

When I was in Tegucigalpa I experienced peace and joy and power in that church.

"Leadership is not something we grasp," they explained. "We must become servants to one another and the church. We all work together to discern who the Lord has anointed for various servant ministries. The Holy Spirit releases gifts for mission and ministry when we minister as servants rather than as bosses."

Nurturing God's Call for Mission

It is important that every congregation nurture a climate which enables people to hear the Holy Spirit and respond to his call for mission. The Holy Spirit is moving around the world. He pauses and calls here and invites there. He invites people to participate with him in mission. He calls and anoints leaders.

It is a colossal tragedy that few people are tuned in to the Spirit. The call of the Spirit is futile when no one listens. The world sinks deeper into the hell of human sinfulness. The progress of the kingdom of God is hindered because people are deaf to the Spirit's counsel.

"Who is the Lord calling as missionaries within your congregation?" missionary Adrian asked a pastor in a church where he was preaching for a week.

"I can't think of anyone," the pastor responded.

"Are you praying that the Lord of harvest will call laborers from your congregation?" Adrian asked.

"No, not really."

Adrian chided gently, "Hasn't the Lord commanded us to pray for laborers?"

Later the pastor confided that as he prayed about laborers, he thought of two couples. Within a year that congregation had commissioned these couples as missionaries.

"What will you do after graduation?" professor I. B. Horst asked David when he was a college senior.

"I plan to go for my doctorate."

The professor paused, then commented slowly, "That might be all right. Don't forget, though, that the Lord has called you to be an evangelist."

David knew he was right.

Missionaries Ed and Gloria King prayed and fasted for the salvation of youth in Tegucigalpa, Honduras, who were self-destructing through wrong lifestyle choices. They invited these exuberant and undisciplined youth to a weekend retreat. The Holy Spirit spoke; many were converted.

Then came the shock.

"God is calling you to be pastors!" Ed exclaimed. "I will train you."

They have never forgotten the surprise of that announcement. Yet that is exactly what Ed and Gloria did with the team working with them. They equipped these undisciplined youth to become evangelists and pastors. These same youth are the founders and pioneers of the Amor Viviente Church, which has experienced phenomenal growth.

Every congregation, pastor, and Christian should pray that the Lord will call laborers from within the congregation for mission; they should encourage people to hear and respond to God's call for mission.

Servant Leaders Equip Every Member

Servant leaders attempt to equip every member for service and mission. Children experience the joy of involvement in the ministries of the church. Both men and women are empowered to invest all their gifts and anointing in the ministries of the church and within the community. The elderly are encouraged to invest their talents in mission. The youth develop their gifts for the good of the body. All people are freed and empowered.

Equipping Youth

In my home congregation, a twelve-year-old girl once preached during a worship event led by the youth. No one will ever forget that sermon. Using her dolls in the pulpit as props, she preached on Christian love from 1 Corinthians 13.

In Nairobi, Kenya, a congregation in the slums of Eastleigh was in decline. An experienced ordained American missionary joined the congregation. "At last we have a preacher," the leaders exulted. They were youthful with little leadership experience.

"I shall not preach," missionary Don Yoder announced.

"Why not? We desperately need a preacher," the leadership team protested.

"I shall not preach because you are not yet very good preachers. If I preach, you will never learn. Instead let us work together evaluating each sermon you preach so you can improve. When I consent to preach, you will know you have become good preachers."

Two years later, Don Yoder preached his first sermon. These youthful leaders were delighted. All had become good preachers. That missionary was a fruitful servant leader!

In modern times there are increasing opportunities for young people to gain experience in cross-cultural mission, evangelism, and service. Youth With a Mission provides discipleship training and cross-cultural mission experiences for thousands of young people. There are many such mission-training opportunities for young people.

The agency I serve, Eastern Mennonite Missions, has developed summer cross-cultural mission-training experiences for high school students—the Summer Training Action Teams. There is also the Youth Evangelism Service (YES) training for young adults, which extends for six months or longer and provides in-depth mission training and exposure. School of Witness further equips young people for pastoral and missionary service.

Pastors and congregations need to help young people called to mission discern the focus for their ministry. The discernment might include an internship where the person's gifting and stamina under test is developed and assessed. It might be necessary for the person to develop particular tools for the task, such as medical, agricultural, business, or teaching skills—tools which require formal academic training.

Developing the Gifts

Living and witnessing for Christ is at the core of all mission commitment regardless of the task. Persons who are not living invitations to Christ in their home community won't become missionaries by crossing an ocean. Pastors and congregations should nurture persons experiencing a call for mission, helping to equip them with confidence for evangelistic service regardless of specialization.

The happiest experiences we have had in commissioning missionaries occur when their congregations have worked intentionally in equipping young persons for mission. This includes a congregational assessment of the strengths and weaknesses of missionary candidates, as well as in-service training and oversight in the congregation itself.

Character and Spiritual Formation

Character is critical. A key dimension of equipping a person for mission is character formation. Integrity, chastity, patience, love, kindness, simplicity of lifestyle, control of temper, a positive spirit, and consideration of others are fundamental.

African friends tell of missionary Jim. He was so hot-tempered the people he had come to evangelize detoured around his house, lest they be victims of his tantrums!

"One day Jim came to the end of himself," they reminisce. "He wept in repentance. The Holy Spirit began to transform his character. Then we enjoyed visiting in his home, for we had no more fear of his temper."

Paul the missionary commanded those among whom he ministered, "Whatever you have learned or received or heard from me, or seen in me—put it into practice. And the God of peace will be with you" (Phil. 4:9).

The Ministry of Women

The role of women in leadership is a disturbing debate in many churches in societies everywhere. How should churches find the way through the debate?

We are convinced that Jesus Christ liberates women. To the amazement and chagrin of his Jewish contemporaries, Jesus related to women in a manner which freed and empowered them. In male-dominated Jewish culture, people were astonished that Jesus appeared first to women after the resurrection. It was women who first proclaimed his resurrection.

Where were the male disciples when the women went to the tomb to put spices on the body of Jesus early on the first day of the week? The women knew they would need men to roll away the stone that covered the opening of the rock-hewn tomb. Yet not one male disciple accompanied them. Probably the men were hiding, fearing for their lives. No wonder the resurrected Jesus met the women first.

"There is neither . . . male nor female, for you are all one in Christ Jesus," summarizes Paul in his letter to the Galatians (3:28).

However, within the New Testament, local proprieties and sensitivities helped to define the role of women in the church. In some circumstances women were commanded to be silent and not even speak in public worship assemblies (1 Cor. 14:35). In other circumstances women served as prophets. Phoebe was a deaconess of the church in Cenchrea (Rom. 16:1-2). Priscilla and her husband, Aquilla, are both recognized as effective teachers of the Word (Acts 18:24-26). Apparently the early church as a whole was flexible concerning the role of women in the church.

In modern as in biblical times, women serve faithfully in mission within all frontiers of evangelism, church planting, and service. They serve in the most difficult situations, often braving dangers and depravation for the sake of Christ. In their faithful ministries, they demonstrate that in Christ there is neither male nor female.

The authentic church takes root in particular cultures. Cultural diversity therefore creates varieties of churches, including different perspectives on appropriate roles of women and men. For this reason any church is wise to be flexible in defining the specific roles of women. A fruitful church will relate constructively to its own culture.

Yet in every circumstance the faithful church must give witness that in Christ there is neither female nor male. The Holy Spirit empowers both women and men for fruitful ministry, regardless of their specific roles. The church should seek ways to recognize and bless the faithful ministry of women.

Acquiring Tools for Mission

How does formal leadership training fit into these themes of servanthood and spiritual formation?

The projection of formal educational systems into K'ekchi' society might interrupt their authentic and highly effective patterns of leadership formation. There is almost no relationship between pastoral formation and formal education in K'ekchi' culture. At present a high school education has little relationship to the leadership qualities needed for pastors within their culture.

In time, however, that will change as congregational members gain greater educational sophistication. The K'ekchi' told us they need effective elementary schools within their communities to teach literacy to their people. They need nurses, agriculturalists, and teachers. They want teachers of the Word of God to equip them for more effective pastoral ministry. These dimensions of ministry do require the tools which formal education provides.

However, formal education does not provide spiritual or character formation. Even a seminary education does not assure that a pastor will be equipped for fruitful mission. Nevertheless, in many societies formal training does provide useful tools for leadership and mission. Colleges, seminaries, and graduate schools help provide those tools.

Here are examples of helpful tools. Insights into anthropology are critical for fruitful mission in many cross-cultural situations. Skills in counseling are necessary. An appreciation for the arts such as song, design, folklore, and paintings are helpful. There are technical skills like tropical agriculture, intermediate technology, and medicine which formal education provides.

Insights into modern urban sociology can help the city pastor lead a congregation more fruitfully. Our interpretation of the Bible should be informed by an understanding of history, culture, and theology. It is important to understand the history of the people with whom one works. Formal education can provide a wealth of helpful tools for the person in mission. In some settings the host government will not issue a visa unless the missionary has the tools and credentials provided by formal education.

How Many Workers Are Needed?

How many laborers for the world harvest should a congregation equip? This is the answer: every member.

Paul writes, "It was he who gave some to be apostles, some to be prophets, some to be evangelists, and some to be pastors and teachers, to prepare God's people for works of service, so that the body of Christ may be built up" (Eph. 4:11-12).

"I am a full-time missionary," John Bender told me.

John is an electrician who has worked with a rough-and-tumble building construction team for thirty years.

"The opportunities for being a missionary on my job are unimaginable," he exclaimed. "Every day I live on the frontiers of mission."

Lily Rohrer would have been a frustrated cross-cultural missionary. Divergence from the eighty-year tradition of our congregation saddened her. Yet when I visited her at her home, I discovered the dining room table strewn with odd shapes of cloth. She was sewing.

"What are you doing?" I inquired.

With animation she described her project. "I am sewing dresses for orphan girls in Bangladesh."

This was Lily's mission. She was sewing with all her might for orphans on the opposite side of the world.

The world harvest is enormous. Every member must be marshaled as a laborer. And every congregation should nurture the call among members for those who will move beyond the boundaries of the local community for mission within the world harvest in regions beyond.

A minimum and easily attainable goal for every congregation is to equip one person out of every fifty members for mission or pastoral ministry. A congregation of a hundred people would equip two people for the world harvest. When these persons were commissioned, the congregation would commence equipping two more people.

While equipping persons for specific pastoral or missionary ministry, the congregation must also train every member for involvement in the mission of the church. Some, like Lily, will sew for the poor.

The congregation must never forget that the Holy Spirit invites every congregation on earth to be a pastoral and missionary training center.

The Holy Spirit Empowers for Mission

I was drinking tea in Semarang, Central Java, with Yesaya Abdi, the church administrator of the Muria Synod.

Yesaya confided, "Although my father is a preacher, he never studied in seminary. During the years of raising his family, in the late evenings after we children were in bed, he would sit by the lantern and read the Bible. He asked the Holy Spirit to teach him the meaning of the Scriptures.

"As the Holy Spirit instructed my father, he would weep. The pages of his Bible became stained with those tears. Then on Sunday he would rise early and go by bicycle from church to church throughout central Java preaching the Word which the Holy Spirit had burned into his soul. The people were fed, congregations nurtured, and many converted."

Yesaya paused, "That is the way my father always preached, with fire in his soul. But you and I have gone to graduate school. When we prepare sermons, we read commentaries. We preach excellent sermons. But do we weep with joy and wonder as we consider the truths we are preparing to proclaim?

"Too few tears stain the pages of my Bible. We modern pastors don't have to ask the Holy Spirit to teach and empower us, for the commentaries do that for us. Alas. May the Holy Spirit anoint us also!"

January 15, 1993, was the twenty-sixth anniversary of the ordination of Zedekia M. Kisare as bishop of the Tanzania Mennonite Church. As he was then in his early eighties, the Mennonite churches of East Africa planned a commemoration in his home community of Shirati, a village sprawling over Katuru Hill on the eastern shore of Lake Victoria.

Fifty-nine years earlier the first Mennonite missionaries to East Africa placed their tents under a gnarled tree on Katuru Hill. A very youthful Kisare stood nearby and offered help. The missionaries discovered that he had met Christ in neighboring Kenya, and his family had recently moved to Shirati in Tanzania. Kisare rejoiced that fellow Christians had come to his community. He joined the missionary team as an assistant and an evangelist.

Now nearly six decades later, I sat with Kisare as church leaders shared their appreciation for these years of fruitful ministry—seventeen years as an evangelist, sixteen years as pastor, twenty-six years as bishop.

Bishop Kisare leaned toward me and spoke in a low voice, "In 1942 the Spirit of God came upon the congregation gathering right here on Katuru Hill. We wept all day before the Lord in repentance; the Sunday morning worship extended all day and late into the night. That day the Holy Spirit burned within my soul and began to form me for these years of ministry.

"Many times since that day the Holy Spirit has burned within me as he has called me to renewed repentance, empowered me, and formed me for the ministry of the gospel of Jesus Christ whom I love."

* * *

This chapter describes the nature of servant leaders who empower the church for mission. All congregations should be praying forth laborers for mission and equipping those laborers so they will be fruitful.

While preparation for mission often requires the acquisition of the tools provided by formal education, spiritual and character formation are foundational to fruitful mission.

Congregations should equip every member for involvement in some dimensions of mission. Every congregation should also call, equip, and commission laborers for the harvest in regions beyond the bounds of the congregation.

Mission requires laborers; fruitful mission also requires a rich variety of other resources. The next chapter explores the grace of generosity as it relates to mission.

Reflection

1. In what ways are the leadership patterns within your congregation different from those of the K'ekchi'? In what ways might there be similarities?

2. What is your opinion on the observation that leadership patterns within the church should develop in ways that are in harmony with the local culture? What leadership structures would be in harmony with your culture?

3. Describe ways Jesus taught servant leadership to his disciples. Why was a servant spirit so difficult for them to accept?

4. In what ways is your congregation equipping every member for involvement in mission? Consider how your church could do better.

5. Consider the likelihood that the Holy Spirit is calling people within your church for pastoral or missionary service. In what ways should you and the congregation encourage and equip people for these kinds of ministry?

* * *

Suggested background Scriptures—Matthew 9:37, 38; 18:3-5; Luke 10:2; Acts 13:1-4; John 4:25-26; 13:1-17; 20:17-18; 1 Corinthians 12:12-31; Ephesians 4:11-12; Philippians 2:1-11; 4:9.

11

Grace and Generosity

"SOMALIS ARE SUFFERING because of war and famine. One brother lost his leg when a mortar shell hit him," I told the Grace Church on Hong Kong's Waterloo Road.

At once, pastor Daniel Ngai arose and stood at the podium.

"Let us pray for these people right now," he suggested.

After the prayer, he added, "I believe we should contribute our offering today for these suffering sisters and brothers."

That Sunday in October 1992, the forty who were present shared in an offering for sisters and brothers whom they had never seen. The gift came to $787.

I delivered that gift to the fellowship in Somalia in January 1993. It included a letter of greeting and encouragement written in Chinese and translated into English. The gift and letter were a sign that churches in other areas of the world prayed for them in their suffering. After the letter was read, there was silence.

Then the pastor spoke. "I remember in 1965 we here in Mogadishu heard of the suffering of sisters and brothers in Vietnam. At that time they were also suffering because of war, just as we are now.

"We did the same thing that the fellowship in Hong Kong has done for us. We also gave an offering for our Vietnamese brothers and sisters, and we wrote a letter.

"Now when we are experiencing extremity, God has heard our cry through the generosity of our brothers and sisters in Hong Kong whom we have never met. Sometime we will meet them in heaven. Then we can give a proper thank-you."

The Somali congregation was small, and the believers were in deep poverty when they gave that gift for Vietnam. It was about $5.00.

Forwarding the money to Vietnam was complex. Some wondered whether it was worth the effort. But it was a precious gift.

Jesus said, "The widow's mite was a greater offering than all the great gifts given by the wealthy" (Luke 21:3, paraphrased).

What Is Giving for Mission?

Only a tiny portion of North American congregational resources are invested in mission. Other causes might be good but are not mission. A fundraiser for the church's youth to have a weekend in the mountains, purchasing new carpets for the Sunday school, or paying the heating bills is not mission.

Even supporting the pastor is, in some circumstances, not mission, unless the pastor is involved in outreach beyond the congregation or equipping the congregation for mission. Resources of time, personnel, talent, or finances invested for such ministries are for the well-being of the local congregation where we worship. Those resources nurture us and our Christian friends. That is a valid investment—but it is not mission.

Mission is the commitment to reach people outside the cozy circle of congregational life. Mission is engagement with the poor and the disadvantaged. Mission is a commitment to the widows and orphans, the homeless and the imprisoned, the drug addicts and the AIDS victims, the teenage gangs and unwed mothers, the lonely and depressed, the hungry and ill, the self-sufficient and wealthy who are not within the circle of congregational life.

Mission is especially concerned with reaching people who have not confessed Jesus Christ as their Lord and Savior and have no relationship with the church. Mission is extending God's love beyond ourselves and our congregation.

Who Shares Resources for Mission?

Whenever the Holy Spirit creates a congregation, God's plan is for that congregation to become a center of local and world mission.

For this reason the congregation is the primary resource-sharing center for mission. Giving for mission in the context of worship provides Christians with an opportunity, right within the worship experience, to respond generously to the gift of God's grace.

Sharing for mission should become a core conviction of every new church planting. For this reason it is wise for new church plantings to have special prayer, during the first public Sunday worship, for those laboring for the world harvest. Some new congregations give their first offering for world mission. That prayer and offering for mission beyond the new congregation is a statement of vision for mission in communities near and far.

Why Give for Mission?

The gift of God's grace is the reason we desire to give for mission. Just as Christ became poor so we might become rich, so we also are now invited to become poor so others might become rich (2 Cor. 8:9). Giving generously for mission is our response to the gift of God's generous grace to us.

It is important that pastors and denominational leaders recognize and emphasize that fact: we want to give for mission as a response to God's generous gift to us.

When a person meets Jesus Christ, she longs that as many others as possible also gain the privilege of believing in him. A person who has been touched by the boundless generosity of God's grace in Jesus Christ wants to share generously with any who are hungry and poor and oppressed.

Investment in mission is not rooted in excitement. Mission is blood, sweat, sacrifice, tears, disappointment, and risk—with joy. Mission is solid commitment. It is the decision to lay down one's life, if need be, in gratitude to Jesus Christ.

For that reason, if people have the opportunity of designating gifts for mission, they will often give far more than the tithe. They will give sacrificially. For mission and compassion, many Christians will give until it hurts.

Planning for Resources for Mission

Sometimes congregational and denominational leaders feel nervous about the exuberant way their people want to give for missions and service. They might describe generosity for mission as excessive emotionalism. They fear that generosity for mission will divert resources away from programs for the congregation or denomination.

The Within Budget Plan

Unified budgets are one way to guide and control people's giving patterns. At the beginning of each budget year, decisions are made about how the budget pie shall be divided. Mission gets one portion of that pie. Each ministry of the church gets a portion of the pie. People give to meet the budget.

On the surface, the plan seems excellent. However, in most circumstances giving for mission declines in the unified budget system. Why? There are several reasons.

1. Ministries serving Christians in the congregation get priority in the budget.

2. Most people give less exuberantly to a budget plan than for designated giving.

3. The budget is complex and impersonal. It erodes the sense that this dollar will help that particular ministry happen.

4. There are some ministries a person will give for sacrificially, and others that the same person will support only with a modest gift. The unified budget takes such choice away from the giver.

5. People believe that once the budget has been met, they have fulfilled their responsibilities. There is no call for stretching beyond the modest and achievable goals outlined in the budget.

6. People surrender responsibility for the investment of their resources to other decision makers. There is, therefore, little sense of personal responsibility for supporting community or global mission needs. It is easy for persons to assume that when they have contributed their tithe or firstfruits to the budget, they have no further responsibility.

The most obvious strength of the unified budget plan is reliable prediction of the amount of resources for all ministries of the church, including mission. That is good for responsible planning.

A modification of the unified budget is to develop a budget for the life of the congregation but plan special offerings throughout the year for mission and service beyond the congregation. Those offerings would be open and represent above-budget generosity for mission. Gifts designated for the world harvest are invested in the congregation's commitment to local and world mission.

The Bust-the-Budget Plan

Leaders and congregations should encourage sacrificial and generous commitment to mission. Congregational giving plans should provide opportunities for sacrificial giving for mission and service. Congregations should encourage bust-the-budget generosity for mission and personal commitment to mission.

Twice a year Southern Baptist congregations have just that kind of giving event for missions. These are above-budget offerings for the world harvest. Baptist mission leaders have informed me that half their annual missions contributions come from those two special offerings. On those Sundays, members across the denomination are encouraged to give sacrificially, generously, and joyfully for the world harvest.

Most congregations supporting Eastern Mennonite Missions have an open offering for missions the first Sunday of every month. People on monthly salary have the most money at the beginning of the month. That is when the mission offering is planned—as a sign in the soul of the congregation that the firstfruits offering, the best we can give, should go for mission beyond the congregation. Often congregations will plan yet another missions-related offering later in the month, for hunger or short-term mission for youth.

These offerings are not within the congregational budget. As the Holy Spirit prods, people give. We are amazed by their generosity. Even the children get involved.

Two Surprising Plans

Children often share with surprising generosity.

Sunday morning four-year-old Jacob heard of the need for money for missionaries to serve in the world harvest. He went home and emptied his piggy bank of most of the money he had saved. He placed his precious gift in an envelope. The next Sunday was the missions offering. He was ready.

Jacob put his gift in the offering plate for missions.

"I think Jesus is happy. I am happy, too," whispered Jacob in his mother's ear.

Not only children often share generously; sometimes the wealthy in the church also give with sacrificial generosity.

"I have chosen not to buy a new car or a top model," explained the millionaire founder and owner of a major industrial enterprise in Lancaster, Pennsylvania.

He explained, "By choosing to live modestly, I have more resources to share for world mission and the poor in our world."

Some People Have No Vote

The tragedy of most congregational and denominational budget planning is that the poorest of the poor and those who have never heard of Jesus are never present when budgets are decided. One-fifth of the people on earth have never seen or heard of a Christian church. They have no vote when congregations divide the money pie. The unreached have no voice.

Neither do the poor have a voice. One hundred million teenagers are homeless. Not one of them are ever present to help affluent congregations plan their financial priorities. The one billion hungry people in our global village are not present when the board of directors of affluent churches carve up the budget pie. The poor might get crumbs as leftovers after all the other needs are met, but that is all.

The clamor of needs felt within the affluent church most often overwhelms any serious commitment to mission beyond the fellowship of the congregation.

A Coffin Versus Life

The statement "Of course, we all know everything we do is mission" is a nail in the coffin of a dead commitment to mission. When everything is mission, nothing is mission. Mission then dies.

God sent his Son, the Christ. As God sent Christ, so he also sends us into mission. Mission is sending and being sent into the world. A plush auditorium, polished sermons, and practiced choirs don't count as mission projects.

"The harvest is plentiful, but the workers are few. Ask the Lord of the harvest, therefore, to send out workers into his harvest field. Go! I am sending you out like lambs among wolves," commanded Jesus (Luke 10:2-4). Going and enabling people to go in mission is an eternal investment!

Frequently congregations have mission commitments that have little direct relationship to denominational mission and service agencies. They are reaching out to their community in vigorous mission, and often discovering ways to do mission in regions beyond the congregation as well.

Within the Mennonite Church, regional conferences sometimes also invest in mission. Eastern Mennonite Missions is one such conference-based mission agency. It is good that conferences and congregations become involved in hands-on mission within their local community as well as in distant places.

Nevertheless, there is continuing validity for energetic denominational commitment to global mission and service. Denominational mission agencies are well situated for developing networks for mission with churches in other lands, especially churches with which the denomination has a historic link.

A Tiny Burger and Small Coke Each Week

However, the per-member contributions to global missions in my denomination is declining. The funds, talent, and personnel resources invested in congregational life are escalating. By 1990 the giving for missions through our denominational mission board was about $1.00 a week per member. Giving for service and development through Mennonite Central Committee was about $.70 a week per member. I am told by mission and service leaders in other denominations that $1.70 a week per member for global mission and service is generous.

Really?

I went to McDonalds the other day. Small fries took all but a penny of the $1.00 weekly budget for missions. The $.70 for relief and development could purchase the smallest Coca-Cola available. Yet the average North American per-person income, including children, has to be at least $300 per week.

Is three nickels a day for global missions and a dime a day for global hunger a good way for North Americans to lay up treasures in heaven?

Would I be comfortable inviting Jesus of Nazareth into my home? What would he say about the car I drive? How would he feel about my wardrobe? What about the perfumes and ointments in the bathroom?

A rule we do well to follow is this: if my poor brother in the world church family were with me when I was shopping, would I be comfortable with how I spent my money?

The poor do have their times of celebration. Jesus also enjoyed celebration. He was not an ascetic. Yet he lived in a manner that the poor could identify with.

As disciples of Jesus, we are called to live generously. The economic law of missions is this: the less I invest on myself, the more I have to share that others might live.

What Is in Your Home to Share?

Honduras is one of the poorest countries in the Western Hemisphere. Yet the Amor Viviente church in Honduras expects all members to tithe. Then they have special offerings for the mission of the church in addition to the tithes. Above that there is the annual exuberant giving-for-missions event.

In response to God's wonderful grace, members are invited to offer a sacrifice of praise for investment in world missions. Most members go from the church service to their homes and select a gift of great value. Voluntarily they sell the gift and give the proceeds as a sacrifice for mission. It is unusual to see a television set in those homes. Yet peace abounds.

Their generosity has blessed them with the need to live simply. They sacrifice unnecessary material trappings as an offering of praise, so others might hear the gospel.

A Message for North American Churches

"We have a message for the churches of North America," counseled Yahya Chrismanto, the mission director for PIPKA of the Muria Synod in Indonesia.

We were considering the multitudes of Southeast Asia who had never heard of Jesus Christ or seen a Christian congregation. We were looking at a map of the region. Yahya had been explaining the various areas in which PIPKA missionaries served, mostly among unreached peoples within Indonesia.

Yahya continued, "There are hundreds and thousands of villages and towns throughout this region of the world where there is no church. When I visit North America, I discover that every town and village has at least one church.

"You are debtors to Asia. These people also need to hear of Jesus Christ. Otherwise they can never believe in him. We and other Christians throughout this region are doing the best we can. But we cannot accomplish the task alone.

"We need your partnership. God has blessed you with people resources and finances. You also have a rich and deep Christian tradition. Now is not the time for North American churches to retreat in their commitment to mission."

Investing in Mission

There are five key resources every congregation should invest in mission.

First, information. Keep mission information flowing. If the women are having a ministry to young mothers and children in the community, have the women give occasional reports. Perhaps the young people are inviting their unchurched school friends for a night of bowling; inform the congregation.

Provide ways for the congregation to keep informed about missionaries or volunteers serving in nearby cities or abroad. If your congregation's global mission commitments are expressed primarily through a particular mission agency, keep up-to-date news of your mission agency's ministries in front of the church. Hold forth a consistent and informed vision of mission.

Second, prayer. Whenever the congregation meets for worship, there should be prayer for the world harvest and for laborers for the harvest. Any missionaries supported by the congregation or commissioned by the church should be remembered by name in prayer every week. No church should ever support or commission a missionary if there is no commitment to regular intercessory prayer for her.

The prayer should also focus on areas of the world harvest where the congregation is already involved through offerings and personnel it has invested in mission, probably through the mission agencies with which the congregation partners. However, it is also important to pray regularly for people groups who have never heard the gospel.

Two helpful resources for prayer for unreached peoples are:

Operation World: Handbook for World Intercession, Operation Mobilization, 121 Ray Avenue, Hawthorne, NJ 07506.

Global Prayer Digest, U.S. Center for World Mission, 1605 Elizabeth Street, Pasadena, CA 91104 (1-818 797-1111).

Current news also helps develop the mission and service prayer focus for the congregation.

I experienced such informed prayer one dark night in the Philippines. I climbed a steep ladder into a loft in the slums of Old Santa Mesa, Manila. It was prayer meeting night. About thirty were present, mostly young people.

"Lord save the people of San Francisco from destruction from the earthquake," they were praying, some nearly in tears. That was the night of the San Francisco quake.

Third, talent. Mobilize the gifts in the congregation for mission. If an impoverished person in the community needs a new roof, mobilize the carpenters in the congregation to place a roof on that house some Saturday. Should there be a call from the Salvation Army, World Vision, Lutheran Relief, Mennonite Central Committee, or some other relief agency for dresses for Somali orphan girls, mobilize the seamstresses in the church for a sewing party.

Fourth, people. Encourage every young person in the congregation to invest a minimum of a summer in church-related voluntary service away from the congregation. Build mission interest into the young people through information sharing, exposure, and personal involvement in mission-service work. Provide mission-related discipleship training experiences for the young people.

Keep alert to whom the Lord is calling within the church for long-term missionary service. Nurture, test, and evaluate such callings. Equip called persons for mission.

Fifth, finance. Encourage generous and sacrificial giving for mission. Keep informed about the ways in which the generous offerings of the congregation are being invested. Report on what is happening in the mission and service ministries the congregation supports with these gifts.

Encourage a minimum of a tithe for the support of the congregation and mission. Especially in affluent Western societies, a tithe is a pittance. Congregations in affluent North American, European, or Asian societies should stretch toward giving for mission which far exceeds tithing.

In most societies there are wealthy people, or people with estates and retirement resources. It is important to help these people get good counsel on how to invest their resources in a manner which provides for their needs as well as for investment in mission. Good counsel can save money while providing for one's own needs as well as for mission.

"I have just sold a plot of land and want to invest all the proceeds for mission," the joyous farmer announced as he entered the office of the mission treasurer.

"However, I need to keep one third of the proceeds for taxes."

"Have you deposited the funds from the sale of your land into your bank account?" asked the treasurer.

"Yes, but here is the check for two-thirds of the sale price."

The treasurer received the funds with appreciation. He did not have the heart to comment that if the cash from the land sale had not been mixed in with the donor's personal bank account, there would have been no taxation. All the money could have been given for mission if it had been deposited directly with the mission board.

Most mission agencies have expert financial advisers who can provide counsel which would save a potential donor from such a mistake. There are also excellent deferred-giving plans advisers can help a donor develop. Congregations serious about mission resources should help their people discover these financial counselors.

Many people will never have much of an estate. Yet they might have modest savings accounts. Money placed on deposit in a bank is all right. How much better, however, to invest savings in mission.

Many mission agencies in North America do have plans whereby people place their savings with the agency. The funds are then loaned at reasonable interest in mission-related real estate, such as the purchasing of church buildings. The congregation should encourage the members to consider that kind of savings investment.

God is calling every congregation to be a center of world mission. That means that the congregation generously shares resources for mission as a response to the gift of grace and salvation we have freely received through Jesus Christ.

Hinkletown

Hinkletown Mennonite Church (which has about 300 members) joins with many other congregations in a Christmas season act of generosity for world mission. I was invited to share in one of those early December events.

Excitement permeated the church. For months people had been preparing for this act of exceptional generosity. Pastor Warren Good reminded the congregation of the multitudes who had not yet heard of Christ and of the poor of our world who needed the touch of Christian compassion which our mission and service workers share.

"In heaven someday we shall meet brothers and sisters from many countries who have learned of Christ and been touched with Christian compassion through these gifts for mission," explained the pastor.

Just before the sermon, people were invited to come forward with their gifts. These were deposited in two huge boxes on either side of the pulpit. Everyone came. Old people with canes and walkers hobbled forward. Tiny children, who had to be hoisted high by parents to reach the collection boxes, also went forward. We sang mission songs during this gift processional. Then ushers took the boxes for counting the money while I began to preach.

After the sermon the pastor entered the pulpit. There was hushed silence. The pastor was overcome with emotion. Then he said, "Our missions offering today is $158,000."

I wept. I looked around. Almost everyone was weeping with joy and amazement. We sang a song. Then we prayed.

I know the angels in heaven also wept and sang with joy that day. All had done their best and shared with boundless generosity. God's call to mission is not a burden; it gives great joy.

The closing sentences of the Bible say, "The Spirit and the bride [church] say, 'Come!' And let him who hears say, 'Come!' Whoever is thirsty, let him come; and whoever wishes, let him take the free gift of the water of life" (Rev. 22:17).

Mission is congregations and the Holy Spirit cooperating, serving among the peoples of our world and inviting them to come to Christ through whom we receive the gift of everlasting life.

* * *

This chapter describes God's generous gift of grace in Jesus Christ as the foundation for generous giving for mission.

There are practical ways a congregation can encourage generosity for mission—information sharing, informed intercessory prayer, investing of the congregation in mission, calling and commissioning people for mission, and sharing finances. Giving plans should not restrict but rather free people for generous investment in mission.

As congregations commission people for mission and service, new expressions of the church are created. These new churches must become rooted in the local culture. That is explored in the next chapter, "Cultures and Religions."

Reflection

1. Reflect on the gift of grace within your own life. In what ways are you responding in thankfulness for that gift?

2. Develop a proposal for your congregation to implement the five-step plan for investment in mission—information, prayer, talent, people, finance.

3. What do you think about Yahya Chrismanto's message to North American churches?

* * *

Suggested background Scriptures—1 Corinthians 16:1-4; 2 Corinthians 8—9; Philippians 2:19-30; 4:10-20.

12

Cultures and Religions

BLACK FRIDAY brings good news to retail stores across the United States. On this Friday after each Thanksgiving Day, Christmas shoppers buy so many gifts that retailers' books are back in the black.

That is astonishing! The biggest shopping day of the year, which helps save many stores from bankruptcy, occurs because people throng to buy gifts for others.

Why does American society go on this exuberant gift-buying spree? The origin is obvious. Christians desire to share gifts with others as a response to God's present to all humankind—the gift of Jesus Christ, born in a cattle stall in Bethlehem. Gift giving at Christmas is a way of expressing thanksgiving for God's unspeakable gift.

While we deplore the commercialization of Christmas, there could be worse uses of money than purchasing gifts for others. Suppose Black Friday happened because people went shopping for new clothes and gadgets for themselves. How sad that would be. However, our most enthusiastic spending occurs as an act of generosity. The birth of Jesus inspires this gift giving.

Signs of Truth

All cultures possess signs which point toward a greater truth. Christian anthropologists and theologians refer to these signs as truth paradigms. Christian missionaries should give attention to these signs. They point toward the gospel. Gift giving at Christmas is a sign that "God so loved the world that he gave his one and only Son."

It is not surprising that the gospel will have significant influence on cultures or religions exposed to biblical faith. In such cultures one will discern signs of the gospel everywhere, even in the literature of the society. But even where people have never been in contact with the church or biblical faith, truth paradigms are present.

"The word is near you; it is in your mouth and in your heart," records Paul the missionary (Rom. 10:8). Paul is referring to people who have not yet heard the gospel. He observes that the truth is near them. The Holy Spirit is working in all cultures, attempting to prepare people to hear and receive the gospel.

Paul observes, "For since the creation of the world God's invisible qualities—his eternal power and divine nature—have been clearly seen, being understood from what has been made, so that men are without excuse" (Rom. 1:20).

If there were no truth paradigms in a culture, then the gospel would be complete nonsense. At the same time, if the gospel is shared in a way which bypasses these truth paradigms, it is then understood as bad news. For the gospel to be received, it must connect with and become a fulfillment of the signs of truth present in the culture.

For example, during the Christmas gift-buying spree at Park City near my home, Christians sing Christmas carols in the center of the mall. When my congregation participated one evening, some members scattered throughout the mall to pray unobtrusively, while others were available to converse with shoppers who stopped to hear the carols. In this way we connected with a sign of truth in our culture.

Rejecting Truth

Even though we share the gospel in a manner which connects with the culture, people may not be ready to believe in Christ. This is because all societies contain human sinfulness and rebellion against God.

In our rebellion, we frequently distort truth paradigms. They then actually point away from the truth. That has happened with Christmas gift giving. Fables about Santa Claus distort the truth of Christmas. Furthermore, the notion that Santa will only give children gifts if they are good denies of the grace of God, which is at the core of the original Christmas story. God's gift does not depend on our goodness.

The Scriptures proclaim, "God demonstrates his own love for us in this: While we were still sinners, Christ died for us" (Rom. 5:8).

People create cultures which reject the truth at many different levels. Sometimes a lie inspires an entire cultural system. For example, Nazism created the Holocaust with death for millions of Jews. The Marxist analysis of evil justified the slaughter of tens of millions of people. The Shinto myth drove the Japanese nation into World War 2 and horrible atrocities. The U.S. notion of manifest destiny has inspired obnoxious U.S. arrogance and several wars. The Hindu caste system is based on a wrong understanding of human nature; so is racism or South Africa's experiment with apartheid.

Missionary Paul wrote in his letter to the Romans, "For although they knew God, they neither glorified him as God nor gave thanks to him, but their thinking became futile and their foolish hearts were darkened. Although they claimed to be wise, they became fools" (Rom. 1:21-22).

We do well to examine our cultures. Are they informed by truth? Or by deception?

The Cultural Onion

In addition to truth paradigms, missionaries must try to understand the worldview of people—how they see the universe and their place in it.

Paradigms help unlock the mystery of the worldview of a people. The worldview is at the core of every culture. Other aspects of culture form layers around the cultural core, like the layers of an onion. Values, practices, and artifacts (the things a culture makes) are additional layers moving outward from the worldview cultural core. These four layers of culture all hang together; they form the integrated cultural system of a society. The worldview powerfully influences the outer layers of a culture.

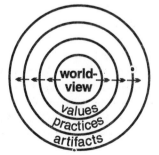

The most obvious expressions of a culture are the artifacts. These things which people produce and use change the most readily. A person might readily switch transportation artifacts from a donkey to a bicycle.

However, a worldview, such as the belief that the dead ancestors will bless you for pouring beer on the ground for them every evening, is much more persistent. Although the worldview culture core is the most resistant to change, it is within that core that Jesus Christ seeks to make his home. Authentic change in a culture must happen at the worldview center. Change at any other layer of the culture is less significant.

We shall now explore two examples of communicating the gospel in cultures and religions where there has been little or no Christian influence.

The first account is of the Zanaki of Tanzania. These people functioned within the ontocratic worldview we explored in the first chapter (*ontocratic* is a worldview in which nature and divinity or the divinities are united). They had never heard of Abraham; they did not have an awareness of God as the transcendent covenant-making Creator.

The second account is of the Muslim Somalis of the Somali Republic. These people live within the transcendent worldview we also explored in the first chapter. They consider themselves the heirs of the faith of Abraham; all Somalis trace their genealogy to Muhammad and from there to Abraham.

These two examples represent the diverse worldviews described in the first chapter: (1) ontocractic and (2) transcendent.

The Zanaki: a Tribal Religion

The Zanaki are a tribal Bantu society of about 20,000 people living in the hills east of Lake Victoria. Theirs is a tribal religion. They would not imagine sending a missionary anywhere. You cannot convert into the Zanaki tribal religion. They perceive that each tribe has its own religion, and the Zanaki have theirs as well.

Tribal and National Religions

The Zanaki are representatives of tribal religions everywhere. However, some religions are national systems. These encompass a variety of tribes within one national religious embrace. Japanese Shintoism, Chinese Confucianism, and Indian Hinduism are three significant examples of national religions.

Both national and tribal religions never seek recruits from outside their societies. A person not born as a Japanese can never become a Shintoist. There are no Confucian missionaries traveling the world trying to convert people to Confucianism. That is impossible because Chinese nationality is the essence of Confucianism. To be Hindu, one must be born into a Hindu caste. A person cannot convert into a caste. Neither tribal nor national religions commission missionaries; they never seek converts.

Some might object to this sweeping observation that tribal and national religions are not missionary. The exception seems to be some modern neo-Hindu missionary movements. There are also Hindu philosophers who invite people into the insights of Hindu Vedanta philosophy.

Yet these Hindu philosophers do not invite people to convert to Hinduism. Rather they invite participation in some of the spiritual or psychological disciplines that Hindu yogas practice in their quest for enlightenment. The New Age movement, for example, has been greatly influenced by Hindu Vedanta philosophy. Yet New Age is not Hinduism.

One becomes a participant in these tribal or national religions only through birth into the system. The Zanaki have never tried to recruit anyone into their faith system; such notions are just unthinkable in tribal or national religions. Yet the Zanaki belief system is sophisticated and comprehensive.

Zanaki Beliefs

The Zanaki believe in a Creator God. However, something went wrong in the relationship between God and the Zanaki in the ancient past. Consequently, evils such as witchcraft plague their society. It is impossible for the previous relationship with God ever to be restored. They therefore have no hope of harmony with God or of genuine peace in their society.

For this reason they need the help of ancestral spirits, nature spirits, and other divinities. God is of little help; other divinities and especially the ancestors have become important. In their quest for well-being, people offer animal sacrifices and oblations (offerings) to the spirits and divinities.

Magic has become significant as a way to manipulate the divine forces in nature. Witchcraft uses magic for evil; it has become rampant and frightening.

Since their former harmony with God is broken, they know God won't pay attention to the well-being of the person at the time of death. It is doubtful that the ancestor or nature spirits can help either. Therefore the only way to provide for existence in the next life is through one's children.

Children remember the departed parent. Through the memory and offerings of food and beer they offer their departed parents, children assure continued existence of the parent's spirit after death. Any adult who has no children is to be pitied, for if he dies he will go into oblivion.

The primary goal of life is to produce as many children as possible. This is the drive behind polygyny (having many wives). A man will practice polygyny to have many children. Through his children he will acquire a good existence in the next life. God won't pay attention to his plight after death; only his children will be concerned for him.

The Cultural Onion

Applying the four layers of our cultural onion to these aspects of traditional Zanaki culture and religion, we find the following.

The outer layer—*artifact*. Each family homestead has several round houses.

The second layer—*practice*. A wife and her children occupy each round house.

The third layer—*values*. Each wife and the man of the family desire that the homestead be filled with as many children as possible.

The inner core—*worldview*. Many children are necessary to assure a good life for the parents after death.

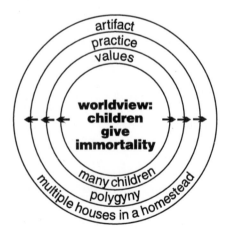

Signs of Truth

In this cultural system we discern truth paradigms, signs pointing toward the gospel. We mention a few of these signs of grace and truth.

1. The myths of their ancestors all agree that something has gone wrong between God and the Zanaki.

2. They offer animal sacrifices, but these efforts will never bring about a full healing of their distorted relationship with God.

3. Some expression of personal spirit-life may exist after death. There is much concern about the quality of that next-life existence and ways to prepare for the inevitability of death.

4. The quality of existence in the next life depends on being re-membered. Someone must remember you; otherwise you will go into oblivion.

In what ways is Jesus Christ good news within the Zanaki worldview? Usually the missionary is not sure what a people are perceiving when Jesus of Nazareth crosses the path of their worldview for the first time.

As the missionary listens to the response of a people to the biblical accounts of Jesus, she learns how the gospel is addressing their worldview as good news. She also learns how Jesus the Christ is transforming the worldview. Jesus always disturbs a culture.

What Difference Does Jesus Make?

This is what the missionaries heard as they lived among the Zanaki:

"Our ancient myths told us that God was too busy for us, and that the break between God and the Zanaki would never be healed. In a most unexpected way, Jesus has changed all of that. We now know God as our friend, who has appeared among us in Jesus the Christ and walks with us, understanding our suffering and joy.

"We always knew that our animal sacrifices did not bring true healing between us and God; now we understand that these sacrifices were signs in our culture preparing us to understand that Jesus is the perfect sacrifice for our sins. Through Christ crucified for our sins, we experience forgiveness and a right and joyful relationship with God.

"Jesus has broken the power of the spirits and divinities. The Holy Spirit, who is the Spirit of Jesus, lives in every believer. He never does us harm and always works for our good. The Holy Spirit is far more powerful than any of the divinities or spirits we have venerated. We should burn all the charms we have used to protect us from witchcraft or to manipulate the spirits. [After church, bonfires for such paraphernalia were an occasional event. Such fires were punctuated with songs of praise and testimonies concerning the triumph of Christ over the powers.]

"Jesus has risen from the dead and has promised that we also will rise sometime from the dead. The next life will be far better than simply having our spirits wandering around. It will be a personal bodily resurrection.

"Jesus will never forget us. We therefore don't need children to give us an existence after death. If the Son of God introduces us by name to God when we die, then death holds no fear. All will be well.

"Because children are not necessary for the next life, a man does not need to marry more than one wife. Even a person who has never married can enter heaven. Let a man marry one wife only. Let a husband and his one wife raise only as many children as they can care for."

A New Kind of Tribe

"We are Zanaki, and that is good. However, the church is a worldwide community, and so we are now not only Zanaki. We are part of a new kind of tribe called the church (Eph. 2:16). God is bringing people from every tribe and language into this new community of people redeemed by the Lord Jesus Christ."

This is what missionaries heard Zanaki people say about the difference Jesus made within their society and worldview. Jesus, the Christ, was creating a good news revolution among them.

The Somalis: a Muslim Society

The Hamitic Somalis are mostly camel-following nomads who inhabit the northeastern Horn of Africa. The Islamization of the people of this region of Africa began over fourteen hundred years ago, when Muhammad was still in Mecca. During the twelve years of persecution in Mecca (610-622 A.D.), Muhammad sent several hundred of his followers to settle in Zeilla on the northernmost coast of Somalia.

From that small colony of Zeilla and subsequent Muslim settlements, Islam spread through the Horn of Africa. The Somalis were one of the few Muslim societies who never needed to deal with pluralism; until recent decades all Somalis were Muslim.

A Christian Presence

After World War 2, portions of Somali-inhabited regions came under United Nations Trusteeship. The United Nations Charter assures religious freedom. It was within that context that Catholic and Protestant missions could operate. The Christian missions developed quality medical, educational, and development programs. My own family became a small part of the Christian mission presence.

Soon after Somalia's independence in 1960, it became illegal to propagate any religion except Islam. Yet the humanitarian ministries of Christian agencies such as Sudan Interior Mission, the Catholic Mission, or Somalia Mennonite Mission provided an image for the Christian faith which in time did provide room in the society for the emergence of unobtrusive Christian fellowships.

The Massihiin

The Christian Somalis are known as the Massihiin (disciples of the Messiah). Quality Christian presence and ministry, undergirded with much prayer, was foundational to the emergence of these fellowships. They were miracles of God's grace and the power of the Holy Spirit.

During the first years of the 1990s, the tiny fellowship in Mogadishu became a mustard seed of the kingdom of God in a society desperately needing a reconciling spirit. Jesus referred to the church as salt and light. These brothers and sisters from different clans were salt and light revealing the way for healing in a nation deeply wounded by interclan civil war. The believers demonstrated that being reconcilers was a fruitful witness.

Islam

Islam is very different from the faith of the Zanaki. Islam is not a tribal faith like that of the Zanaki, nor is it a national faith. Islam is one of the world's three universal missionary religions. The other two missionary faiths are Buddhism and Christianity.

Thus when Muslims and Christians converse about religion, they are meeting as persons representing missionary faiths. Although Muslims and Christians might try having dialogue only for the purpose of better understanding, both realize that if they are true to the foundations of their respective faiths, they must desire to invite others.

Muslims frequently ask about the meaning of Christian mission presence. Such occasions provide opportunities to express the faith within us, with the gentleness and respect missionary Peter had counseled in biblical times (1 Peter 3:15-16).

Late one evening Yusuf Ali came to our home. "Give me a book that explains the Christian faith clearly," he asked with blunt integrity.

I looked through the several hundred volumes on my bookshelf. There were books on Islam, culture, anthropology, Somalia, missiology, sociology, history, religion, and education. There were many theological books. Some were written by Muslims. None communicated the gospel gently and clearly in terms of a Muslim worldview.

"I have nothing to give you," I replied.

Dismay and disbelief etched his face as he gazed at my many shelves of books.

In a flash I made a commitment. "But we shall write that book for you. School will close in two weeks. We will write during the school vacation. Give us three months."

Three months later when Yusuf returned for the new school year, I gave him a mimeographed copy of the first draft of a biblical study series for Muslims. After further development and revisions (and the help of a team of students), that series developed into the *People of God* correspondence course, which has been translated into at least a dozen languages and is communicating the gospel among Muslims in several dozen countries around the world.

Faith and Culture

While preparing the *People of God* curriculum, we asked ourselves, "What is the core of the Muslim worldview and the nature of Islamic culture?"

There is a prominent *artifact* in every Muslim community. It is the mosque. Every mosque has a *qibla*, which is a niche in the direction of the *Ka'abah* in Mecca. The artifact of mosque with *qibla* is a key to understanding Islam. We shall now probe the other layers of the Muslim cultural onion—practice, value, and worldview.

The Muslim *practice* is to gather within the mosque for prayers five times daily. The men have their own meeting. If women gather for prayer, they must be separate from the men, perhaps within their own mosque. Of course, not every Muslim can leave work for the five prayers at the mosque. In that case the faithful will pray right where they are, or say extra catch-up prayers later in the day when they have time.

The participants in the mosque prayer stand in straight rows, all facing the *qibla*. They bow in unison and kneel prostrate with their foreheads on the floor. Devout Muslims often have a carbuncle on their foreheads. The five daily prayers include cycles of prostration (*rakas*) within each prayer time. There is some variation among Muslim schools of law on the total number of daily prostrations required; fourteen is a minimal expectation.

Repeating the *Fatiha* (opening) in Arabic is required in these prayer experiences. That is the first chapter of Koran. The repetition of the Arabic *Fatiha* while prostrated before God is the central component of Islamic worship. This is an interpretation in English.

> In the name of Allah, the Beneficent and the Merciful.
> Praise be to Allah, Lord of the Worlds:
> The Beneficent, the Merciful:
> Owner of the Day of judgment.
> Thee [alone] we worship; Thee [alone] we ask for help.
> Show us the straight path:
> The path of those whom Thou hast favored;
> Not [the path] of those who earn Thine anger nor of those who
>   go astray. (Koran: *Fatiha*, by Pickthall)

Submission to the will of God is the *value* revealed in these prayer practices. Islam is the desire to submit to the will of God. That is the central value in all Islamic culture. Muslim societies seek to bring every area of culture under the will of God.

The *worldview* is that God who is merciful reveals his will to humankind. Facing the Ka'abah in prayer is in response to that worldview. According to Muslim teaching, the Ka'abah area was Adam's first home. The Ka'abah is a large black stone in Mecca; before Muhammad this stone was the center of Arabian polytheism.

Muslims believe it is at the Ka'abah that God revealed his will to Adam. Islam is the guidance God sent down to Adam. By facing the Ka'abah in worship, Muslims submit to the same guidance God revealed to the father of all humankind, Adam.

However, people easily forget God's guidance. Therefore, God has chosen to reveal his guidance in the form of books of revelation. They are:

The Torah of the prophet Moses.
The Psalms of the prophet David.
The Gospel of Jesus the Messiah.
The Koran of the prophet Muhammad.

This is a summary of four layers of the Islamic cultural onion, beginning with the outer and most obvious aspect of the culture:

The *artifact* of the mosque with its *qibla*.

The *practice* of prayer five times daily facing in the position shown by the *qibla*, which indicates the direction of the Ka'abah in Mecca.

The *value* of submitting to the will of God which is Islam; that is the reason for bowing prostrate in prayer.

The *worldview* of God revealing his guidance first to Adam at the Ka'abah, then in books of revelation.

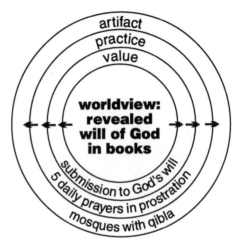

Obstacles and Stepping Stones

The Koran is the summary of all other Scriptures. Therefore, most Muslims never read the previous Scriptures, which Christians have in their Bible. However, the Koran reminds Muslims that there are a people who do possess the previous Scriptures.

The Koran refers to those who possess the first books of revelation as the People of the Book. The Koran counsels Muslims to seek counsel from the People of the Book if they experience difficulties in understanding the Koran!

We invite Muslims to consider that counsel. For example, the Koran refers to Jesus as the Messiah. Yet the Koran never develops the meaning of that mystery name. We remind Muslims that we have the previous books of revelation in our possession. We invite our friends to explore with us the meaning of Messiah.

That is the stance we developed in the *People of God* correspondence course. Being aware of the Muslim worldview, we built the course on those books of biblical revelation the Koran recognizes—Torah, Psalms, and Gospel. The unifying theme throughout the courses is the mystery of the meaning of the Messiah. The course attracts much interest because it builds on biblical accounts mentioned in the Koran but never developed in these Muslim Scriptures.

For example, the Koran admonishes that the flood in the time of Noah is a warning of God's judgment on sinners. Yet the account of Noah is not developed in the Koran. The event is a mystery. Therefore, the *People of God* introduces the fascinating account of Noah and the flood as recorded in the Torah of the prophet Moses. Muslims are delighted.

The course begins with the account of Creation in the first chapter of the Torah (Gen. 1). It concludes with the invitation to faith in the concluding biblical verses (Rev. 22). Thus lesson by lesson the participant walks through the biblical drama of God's salvation acts. Yet the primary sources for the study are the biblical books a Muslim already recognizes as Scripture.

Good News; Not Bad News

The Zanaki and Somali accounts are two small windows on communicating the gospel within cultures. There is much more to these two accounts than we have described. Yet the approach to culture we have presented is always valid.

We must learn to listen to the heartbeat of people and enter into their worldview. Otherwise we might be communicating bad news rather than good news. The Holy Spirit wants to empower the communication of the gospel in such a way that in every culture Jesus Christ crucified and risen shall become the revolutionary surprise of salvation.

An "Acts 15" Event Among the Maasai

As a people invite Christ to make his home within their cultural core, how does he speak into their worldview? How does his presence begin transforming the values of their culture? The practices? The artifacts?

The Maasai warriors of Ogwedhi Sigawa in southwestern Kenya are becoming Christian. I was invited to participate with them in an "Acts 15" meeting. They wanted to sort out some gospel and culture issues, just as the early church had done in the Jerusalem Conference in A.D. 48.

Be Free

We read the biblical Acts 15 account of the Jerusalem Conference, and decided to follow the same agenda as that conference.

1. What is the Holy Spirit doing?

2. What expressions of our culture are affirmed by Christ and the Scriptures?

3. What expressions of our culture need transformation or rejection?

4. What decisions about these matters are good to the Holy Spirit and to us?

First, all participants described their conversion and salvation in Christ. We learned of drunkards being transformed and warriors laying aside their weapons. We rejoiced.

(I was sorry that no Maasai women were present. In traditional culture women never participated in discussions with men, and in this meeting the traditional practice continued.)

Second, we listened to the Maasai describe expressions of their culture which the gospel was affirming or even strengthening.

"The ornamental beads our women wear are beautiful and so good!" exclaimed a young man.

The Maasai women bedeck themselves with thousands of beads strung in huge plaited necklaces.

"Yes," another fellow affirmed. "They are daughters of the King of the universe. In our traditions the daughters of chiefs are especially gorgeous with their necklaces. Christian women should dress like the daughter of a chief!"

The conferees became animated as they spoke of other wonders of their culture—hospitality, respect for elders, the belief in the Creator God, and their cattle. They spoke with delight of their foods, such as milk mixed with blood.

I wondered, *Is that diet biblical?* We were listeners, although invited to walk with these new Christians in their discernment.

Third, we moved to themes Christ critiqued.

An elder spoke immediately, "We must stop the practice of a young man killing another man before he is worthy to marry. That must cease!"

We agreed!

A young man quickly added, "And we must stop swapping wives. It is right to be hospitable, but not to the extent of offering your friend your wife for his overnight stay in your home. That must end."

These were sober discussions. They talked through the issues carefully and with wisdom. They named other practices they had to abandon as disciples of Jesus Christ—witchcraft, alcohol, going to the spirit festivals conducted by the shaman, and sacrifices to the ancestors. All these decisions related not only to obvious practices, but to their worldview cultural core.

"And polygyny must stop!" exclaimed an elder.

"Why?" we asked.

"Because polygyny is contrary to the way of Christ," the elder continued. "My wives are jealous of one another, and it is that way in all polygynous homes. There is no peace."

The conference invested the rest of the day discussing how the church should respond to those who were polygynous when they became Christians. It was not easy.

Be Gentle

"Remember, Christ treats a culture gently," counseled a new Maasai believer. "Keep the goal clear. But move gently. Otherwise we will tear our culture to pieces and destroy ourselves as a Maasai people."

These new Christians possessed wisdom. Not all the issues were resolved that day. They will need more "Acts 15" meetings. Yet by the end of the day, their bishop summarized the discussion. Using the phrase from the Jerusalem Conference he noted that it had seemed "good to the Holy Spirit and to us"

1. to bless wonderful qualities in Maasai culture.

2. to reject other dimensions of Maasai culture.

3. to put several difficult issues to prayer for further discernment in the future.

Often that day we opened our Bibles to receive the counsel of the Scriptures. Occasionally the Maasai asked counsel from those of us from elsewhere. It was important to them that representatives from the global church be present as a sounding board. They sought to avoid moving into some far-out orbit the global church could not bless. They treasured their credible participation within the global church family.

Yet they addressed the issues with confidence, for they knew that ultimately they themselves must make the decisions in obedience to the Holy Spirit and the counsel of Scripture. The decisions about gospel and culture made that day were their choices. It was a good day, a turning point in the life of the Maasai churches in Ogwedhi Sigawa.

204 God's Call to Mission

* * *

This chapter describes the cultural onion with its four major layers—the worldview core, the values, the practices, and finally the artifacts. Cultures are organized; the religion most often is an expression
of the culture in all its levels.

There is truth and falsehood in every culture. The missionary
seeks for signs of truth. The evangelists and missionaries should build
on those truth signs as they communicate the gospel.

As case studies, we explored the two quite different cultural and
religious systems of African traditional religion and Islam. Yet in both
the gospel is good news.

As a church is formed in any society, the believers must sort out
what aspects of culture should be included in the church and what excluded. The Maasai of Kenya discovered that the Jerusalem Conference described in Acts 15 is an excellent blueprint for how to do it.

The final chapter describes mission among the Quechua and how
they in turn became a church in mission.

Reflection

1. Reflect on signs of truth within your culture.

2. Reflect on ways in which deception has influenced aspects of
your culture.

3. Describe the four layers in the cultural onion. Reflect on ways
your society's worldview forms your culture.

4. Explain why the manner of interpreting the gospel among the
Zanaki and Somali has been quite different.

5. Consider ways in which an "Acts 15" approach to the issues of
the gospel and culture could help your congregation.

* * *

Suggested background Scriptures—Matthew 5:10-12; 25:31-46;
28:18-20; John 17:14-18; Acts 14:17; 15:1-35; 17:24-28; Romans 1:16-
32; Ephesians 1:10; 2:11-22; 4:1-5; 6:11-18.

13

The Quechua

THE MOST AMAZING and revolutionary event in history forms the center of Christian mission.

> For God so loved the world that he gave his one and only Son, that whoever believes in him shall not perish but have eternal life. (John 3:16)

The church engages in mission because of an astonishing promise and commission which the Son of God has given to his disciples.

> "Peace be with you! As the Father has sent me, I am sending you." (John 20:21)

Thus far our exploration has described various dimensions of "God's call to mission." This chapter describes a modern church in mission among one particular people—the Quechua. It is the account of the Quechua also becoming a people in mission.

The New Testament book of Acts shows the early church's commitment to mission. We will discover that Acts never stops. Acts continues wherever the church lives in obedience to God's call to mission.

The Call

In the mid-1980s, a church planters' retreat in the village of Liberty (in central Pennsylvania) drew three dozen men and women from the cities and towns of northeastern United States. Pioneer church planters, they gathered as battle-weary troops needing refreshment and encouragement.

Their emerging churches never had enough money. Some of the church planters had no reliable salaries. A few supported themselves like Paul, the tent-maker missionary described in the book of Acts. Because they were inviting their neighbors to faith in Christ and forming new churches, most were teaching people who knew nothing about the Bible and had never known Christian role models. They had more than sufficient responsibilities.

Yet as these church planters prayed together, the Holy Spirit laid a burden on them for people who were unreached by the gospel. Although the United States has one congregation for every 1,100 people, at least 3,000 major people groups on earth have no indigenous churches among them. Thousands of villages, towns, and cities in the world have never had a church.

One fifth of the people on earth cannot believe in Jesus Christ, for they have never conversed with a Christian or seen a Bible. These are the one and a quarter billion unreached people who have been denied any awareness of the good news described in John 3:16.

When we gathered at Liberty House of the Lord for prayer, the Holy Spirit seemed to be saying something important. We listened, opening our souls to the mind of the Holy Spirit.

Then in a quiet voice one of the pastors said, "Sisters and brothers, I discern that the Holy Spirit is saying we need to act. I feel the Lord is calling us to send missionaries to an unreached people in Peru."

I was astonished.

There was a spirit of quiet solemnity as I explained my amazement. "Just this week I read a term paper written by one of my students in a church growth class at Messiah College. He described the work of Wycliffe Bible translators among the Quechua Indians in the high Andes of Peru. He lamented that church planting missionaries were not using these newly translated Scriptures to share the gospel, evangelize, and plant churches among the Quechua."

"Praise the Lord for that confirmation that we should consider Peru," the group responded in spontaneous unison.

As we continued praying, the Holy Spirit revealed that several from the group should go to Peru to investigate. That was the beginning of an incredible adventure in mission among unreached villages in the Cusco region of Peru. Most of that investigative team still serves on a commission known as Servants of Love to Peru.

Three dozen young churches or church plantings partially support this mission with prayer and finance. The Servants of Love have already commissioned a team of eight to ten missionaries who serve among the Quechua of Cusco.

The Journey

Torturous, however, has been the path from the euphoria of a prayer retreat in the gentle hills of Pennsylvania to fruitful mission among a people who live ten thousand feet above sea level in the snow-capped Andes.

The investigation team linked up with the mission agency of their family of churches—Eastern Mennonite Missions. With the help and leadership of their mission agency, they researched Peru and the people groups of that land. They laid the foundation for trusting relationships with mission agencies and churches in Peru. They formed networks for counsel in determining the right location of their mission and were advised to consider the Cusco clan of Quechua.

Acquiring visas for missionaries was a major obstacle. For several years it was impossible to acquire Peruvian government registration status for the Servants of Love. The government also determined that there would be no new visa quotas for any missionaries. So the Servants of Love borrowed visas from other missions lacking enough missionaries to fill their assigned quotas.

The missionaries had to learn Spanish. In most cases that meant a full year of tedious language study in Costa Rica (Central America) before they arrived in Peru. They also had to learn the Quechua language. For the first several years, the team struggled to learn not only one but two unrelated languages.

The missionary team and their supporting churches pray that God's angels will protect them. The Shining Path Maoist guerrillas roam the mountains. Occasionally they have killed people doing humanitarian work among the Quechua.

The team has experienced gunpoint robberies. One of the missionaries, Howard Yoder, was abducted, tied to a tree, and threatened with death. After the robbers abandoned him, he managed to wriggle free of the ropes and walk six hours across the mountain passes, arriving home late that night. Twice vehicles have been stolen. The team has downgraded its autos to low-cost Volkswagen 'Bugs.' The missionaries keep in close contact with local friends who counsel them on safety.

The People

For the first five years, the team focused on learning the languages and developing relationships. They explored the culture and tried to enter into the Quechua worldview.

The Quechua people believe the town of Cusco forms the center of the earth. The term *cusco* means "navel." Cusco was also the center of the mighty Inca Empire, which stretched 2,500 miles along the western regions of South America during the last half of the fifteenth century and the early sixteenth century. Cusco is also the name of a prominent Quechua clan. By making their residence in Cusco, the missionaries were locating in the center of the Quechua universe.

In their traditional religion, the Quechua believed they were the descendants of the sun god. Their gods also included the moon, thunder, earth, mountains, or sacred animals. They built temples to their gods. They offered animal sacrifices to the gods of the mountains. Occasionally animal sacrifices for the fertility of the soil are still offered in the mountains. In ancient times they offered human sacrifices as well. The gods demanded the best they could offer.

Various animals were sacred and venerated, especially the mountain lion known as the puma. Above Cusco lie the ruins of an enormous temple complex devoted to the puma and sun god. Although today a large image of the Christ stands near the puma temple overlooking Cusco, the Quechua combine distorted biblical themes and traditional religion in a syncretistic fusion. They mix together and venerate divinities or beings such as saints, mountain gods, the sun god, the puma, and Mary.

The Quechua have a rich culture. Yet the sixteenth-century Spanish Christian conquest of the Inca empire has inflicted a wound on their spirit which has never vanished. The Quechua were closely associated with the Inca; their self-identity was entwined with the Inca empire. Ever since the destruction of that empire, they have felt destroyed.

Even Christ was introduced as the warrior who subdued by the sword all who did not bend to Spanish imperial rule. Because of these Christian imperial invaders, the Quechua have become and are treated as strangers within their own land. It is hard for them to conceive of Jesus as Savior.

Malaise afflicts the Quechua. Their mountains reveal evidence of ancient agricultural terraces and mountainside channels for bringing water from snow-capped peaks into their villages and fields. All this shows that five centuries ago they enjoyed a civilization which in many respects was more advanced than that of the Europeans who destroyed their culture and civilization.

But all their old monumental engineering accomplishments lie in ruins today. Instead of keeping terraced fields in repair, the Quechua farmers walk many miles into the high mountains where they scratch the earth on steep slopes for planting potatoes. Year by year the fertile soil erodes from those fields. Unless the terraces are reclaimed, someday the mountains will be desert.

The Missionaries

For five years the missionaries listened and learned from their Quechua hosts. Patiently they developed trust. They bonded with their hosts. The missionaries learned to love the Quechua people as they sat, ate, walked, worked, and learned with them.

The missionaries were also learning to work together. None had been friends before coming to Peru. They did not have a common background. Some were from long-established congregations and others from newly planted churches. Diversity is the characteristic of such churches, and the team mirrored those differences.

They invested much energy developing wholesome team relationships. Several times the Servants of Love sent resource people to Peru to guide the team in relationship-building skills. All were aware that strife in the team would block fruitfulness.

The Servants of Love to Peru are committed to wholistic mission. This means a mission to serve the whole person. The team includes a variety of skills—medical, agricultural, animal husbandry, business, community development, church planting, education, and theology. Each person on the team lives and witnesses evangelistically. They meet regularly for prayer and planning for fruitful mission among the Quechua.

They prayed that the Holy Spirit would lead them into relationships with those whom the Lord was preparing to receive the gospel. After several years of relationship building and witness, they experienced a surprise.

The Surprise

"Come, and teach us the Word of God," pleaded a messenger from the village of Lucre, twenty miles from Cusco.

With expectation, several missionaries visited Lucre. There a Quechua farmer, José, invited them into his home. They were amazed by his account of the Holy Spirit preparing the way for the missionaries. This is the story.

José Bombilla joined companions from Lucre for an adventure in gold panning in the distant jungle tributaries of the Amazon River. He was gone many months. It was a rough adventure. Leeches bit them. Huge vampire bats inhabited the area, and they could suck the blood from a sleeping man, killing him before morning. It was risky; not all such gold seeking adventurers returned home. The atmosphere in the camps was not conducive to good character. Debauchery was as dangerous an enemy as the vampire bats.

José met a surprise on this adventure. One gold panner from an area far from Cusco was a Quechua Christian. He told José about Jesus Christ. José was intrigued and astonished. He had never imagined such good news as the salvation offered by Jesus Christ. Before he returned home, his friend told him of a Christian radio broadcast in the Quechua language, including the shortwave band and the time of the broadcast.

Back home from his adventure, José gathered his family together and told them all he had learned about Jesus Christ. To learn more, they gathered around their radio again and again to listen to the Quechua language preaching. They invited neighbors to join them. Soon José's home was filled with eager listeners.

They needed help to understand the Christian faith more perfectly. They desired to network with other believers. They prayed about their need for a teacher of the Bible and fellowship with other Christians. They sent messengers to Cusco seeking for a Quechua-speaking Bible teacher. Friends introduced them to one of the Servants of Love missionaries.

The Opposition

The Bible-centered fellowship in José's home grew. Soon they began public worship in a small hall. The community as a whole was not happy about this growing group of Christians. They shut the church out of the hall. Even the young couple who arranged for the church to worship in the hall were turned out of their home. Villagers placed rocks and dead trees across the road to keep the missionary Bible teacher out of their hamlet.

The opposition reached a climax during the first baptisms, a public event in the broad stream that flowed through the town. Opponents of the church threw so many stones at the baptismal group that the church had to cancel the event. One stone came hurtling toward the head of the missionary pastor Joe Lockinger. He caught it just before it hit his head. Later they did have the baptism, but in an area remote from the village of Lucre.

A Prayer Meeting

I worshiped with the Lucre congregation six months after that baptism. They were back in their hall. No rocks or trees in the road prevented our entry into the town. Fifty were present for the Friday evening prayer meeting which I attended. It was a cold damp night, typical for an Andean village two miles above sea level. The floor of the hall was earthen and damp.

When prayers began, most of the congregation fell to their knees with their faces on the ground. Little children, older children, youth, adults, the elderly—all joined in prayer.

This will be a short prayer meeting, I thought. *The night is cold and the floor is damp.*

I was wrong. The event continued for three hours. Not only did they pray for one another and their community, they also fervently interceded for the North American church which had commissioned missionaries to share the gospel with the Quechua. People were converted that night and came forward for prayer with tears of repentance and joy. Others sought prayer for illnesses or difficult circumstances at home where family members opposed those who believed.

After the prayers I stepped outside; in those high mountains, the heavens were a canopy of stars more brilliant than I have ever seen.

A New Creation

"Why are you free now to worship in this hall?" I asked the young couple who had been thrown out of their home when they arranged for the church to meet in this very building.

"We are now free to worship in Lucre because everyone sees that the church is good," the couple said.

"For example, in our village most husbands beat their wives. Jesus

Christ is creating love in our homes. There is peace and no wife-beating in the homes of the Christians.

"So all the women in Lucre want all the men to become Christians. The whole village now knows that Jesus Christ gives new life, which is good for everyone."

In the darkness, I drank in the wonder of the stars as this young couple spoke. Then I noticed the Southern Cross perched above Lucre. That cross-like constellation can be seen only in the Southern Hemisphere.

The base of the Southern Cross pointed to where we had just experienced a remarkable prayer meeting. That night the Southern Cross was a poignant sign of the power of the gospel of Jesus Christ crucified. Here I had met a new creation. These people joyfully witnessed that the gospel is the power of God unto salvation for all who believe.

Quechua Missionaries

Already the Lucre congregation was reaching other hamlets with the gospel. In a nearby community I worshiped with a second fellowship, which was only a few months old. The believers gathered in the home of a carpenter. While we ate supper in the living room, the children gathered in the bedroom. In uninhibited gaiety they were singing Quechua gospel choruses as we ate.

I learned later that the children had surrendered some of their evening dinner of fish and potatoes so that we, their guests, would have ample food. Although their supper was skimpy, the children sang spontaneously of Jesus Christ as they danced around their bedroom.

A sad, middle-aged man was present that night. This was the first time he had ever been in a Christian meeting. He had come because he heard that missionary Gerald Miller was a doctor. Much later that evening he led us through a muddy track and then up a very steep ladder into a loft where his wife lay on a wooden bed. She was dying of cancer. The doctor promised to return the next day.

Development and Justice

Jesus said, "I have come that they may have life, and have it to the full" (John 10:10).

It is therefore not surprising that almost as soon as these new Quechua congregations formed, they created development committees. In a famine several months earlier, the Lucre congregation had organized a feeding program for all the hungry children in their community.

The program was a massive effort. It involved purchasing the food, cooking soup and potatoes, and organizing an orderly feeding program. Most of the money for food purchases came from congregations supporting the Servants of Love. The Lucre congregation's contribution was lots of hard work and organization.

The development committees were also planning other aspects of broad-based community development. The missionaries with business and development expertise were working with the congregations in planning for community uplift. Improved agricultural practices, better nutrition and hygiene, and some business infrastructure such as a grain grinding mill were possibilities.

As the church develops, these Christians will also be concerned about the justice issues which propel the Shining Path guerrillas. But the methods by which they strive for justice will be different from the violent tactics used by the communists. The Servants of Love missionary team will stand with the church as it works for justice, sometimes providing counsel and helping to empower these efforts.

One manner in which missionaries can help empower an oppressed people is through enabling their leaders to meet with leaders of other indigenous groups within the region. In 1992 during the five hundredth anniversary of Columbus's first navigation to the Western Hemisphere from Spain, indigenous Christian leaders from the Central American region met to consider what the Columbus event had meant for their own peoples. This experience of discovering one another within a region dominated by European and especially Spanish culture was immensely reassuring and empowering.

The Leaders

Authentic and capable leaders need to develop among the Quechua to carry their mission forward among their people, as well as to empower the churches for the development and justice concerns they are beginning to address. As we met with their emerging leaders, we heard their desire for Bible teaching and equipping for pastoral leadership. The missionary team is giving those requests high priority.

However, they all realize that equipping leaders is more than just learning facts about the Bible. They do need a thorough understanding of the biblical story, but equally important is in-service training.

Within weeks of the birth of this church, the first believers had begun to walk through the mountains in teams of two, preaching the gospel from hamlet to hamlet. Then the teams would return to their homes. Missionaries would meet these evangelists, hear their stories, and learn together from what they had experienced.

"Tonight there is trouble brewing in the village we shall be visiting," explained the Quechua evangelists to the two missionary men who were to accompany them by vehicle into a remote village for a Bible study. "These last few days there have been ambushes."

"Then we had better not go," conjectured the missionaries.

"Why not?" asked the astonished evangelists.

"We might get hurt or killed," responded the missionaries.

"You surprise us," reprimanded these evangelists, who had first believed in Jesus Christ only a few months before. "Surely you are not afraid to die for the sake of Christ?"

It is not just the missionaries who do the teaching! The Quechua disciples of Jesus possess gifts of grace, wisdom, and commitment to teach the missionaries.

The City

A quarter million people live in the city of Cusco. Nevertheless, the Servants of Love missionaries have focused on planting churches among the people of the hinterland. However, Cusco City is the crossroads of the entire province. It is the commercial and educational hub of the region. Therefore, the new congregations and the missionaries have decided to plant a thriving city church within the next two years. That church will be bilingual—Spanish and Quechua.

The decision to plant a thriving city church is right. Today our world is 50 percent urban. All serious efforts in world mission must also consider church planting and ministry within the cities of our world.

It has always been that way; Jesus himself commanded his disciples to begin their mission in Jerusalem, a huge city many miles from the rural homes of the disciples. They would have preferred a mission to their home communities of Galilee.

But Jesus commanded the disciples to begin in the city. Jesus knew that if the church was firmly planted in Jerusalem, it would easily spread from that crossroads metropolis to communities throughout the Middle East region. And Jesus was exactly right.

The same is true of Cusco. Quechua people move in and out of

Cusco. This is where the students study and learn modern ideas and insights. One finds wealth and tremendous poverty in Cusco. This is their Quechua Jerusalem, where thriving churches must be planted for Jesus Christ to influence the entire Cusco clan of the Quechua nation.

Other Missionaries

The Servants of Love to Peru are in conversation with the Amor Viviente church in Honduras about the possibility of sending a church planting missionary to Cusco.

The Honduras church has planted thriving city churches in more than half a dozen major urban centers in Honduras and in foreign countries as well. Their church planting strategy is based on the growth group principle. Amor Viviente has a lively interest in foreign missions and especially in planting thriving city churches.

There would be advantages in having missionaries on the team from regions other than North America—

1. Such missionaries help demonstrate that the gospel is not an expression of North American cultural imperialism.

2. They help bring fresh ideas into the team.

3. If they are from a country with a culture similar to Peru, these missionaries would help the team understand the local culture.

4. They would help to broaden the prayer commitment for the mission in Peru.

5. They would be a revelation that the church is truly a global missionary movement.

Missionary teams from several cultures and churches is the way mission will happen increasingly in the future.

* * *

As I stood in the cold night outside that shack in Lucre after the three-hour prayer meeting, I relived another prayer meeting in Liberty, Pennsylvania. There we had stood in a circle and prayed for the unreached people in our world. We knew as we prayed that Jesus Christ himself was standing in the center of our circle. And he had spoken: Go to Peru!

Now I stood at the conclusion of another prayer meeting six years later. I knew this prayer meeting would not have happened had we not heard and obeyed the Lord's command for mission in Peru that day at Liberty.

Tonight I had heard children on their faces on the cold damp ground interceding in fervent prayer for the people in North America. Six years earlier we had also prayed fervently for the people of Peru.

Although I was absorbing the beauty of the Southern Cross above us in the cold sky as I chatted, I was also listening carefully to the young couple who had been thrown out of their home when they first believed in Jesus Christ.

I heard them describe the power of the gospel in their own lives, in the newly created church, and within their village.

I was baptized with joy.

What a privilege, what a gift of grace to partner with the Holy Spirit in the mission of the Lord Jesus Christ.

Reflection

1. Who are the unreached people? What should your congregation or mission do concerning such people groups?

2. Reflect on the interaction between prayer and planning for the mission in Peru.

3. Why was it important for the missionaries to understand the Quechua culture and religion? Describe the culture and values of the people of your community.

4. Consider the advantages of having some missionaries from a country other than the United States on the missionary team.

5. Why is mission to cities such as Cusco so important in planning for fruitful mission in any region of the world? Consider the importance of cities upon your life and community. Why did Jesus command his disciples to begin the first Christian mission in the city of Jerusalem?

6. Comment on this statement: the Peru account in this chapter is a continuation of biblical Acts. Consider ways in which the mission of your own congregation is a continuation of Acts.

7. What do we mean by wholistic mission? In what ways is the Servants of Love Mission in Peru wholistic? To what extent is your congregation committed to wholistic local and global mission?

* * *

Suggested background Scriptures—Matthew 24:14; 28:16-20; Acts 1:1-8; 6:1-7; 13:1-3; Philippians 4:14-19; Revelation 5:9-10.

Appendix A

The Manila Manifesto

1. We affirm our continuing commitment to the Lausanne Covenant as the basis of our cooperation in the Lausanne movement.

2. We affirm that in the Scriptures of the Old and New Testaments God has given us an authoritative disclosure of his character and will, his redemptive acts and their meaning, and his mandate for mission.

3. We affirm that the biblical gospel is God's enduring message to our world, and we determine to defend, proclaim, and embody it.

4. We affirm that human beings, though created in the image of God, are sinful and guilty, and lost without Christ, and that this truth is a necessary preliminary to the gospel.

5. We affirm that the Jesus of history and the Christ of glory are the same person, and that this Jesus Christ is absolutely unique, for he alone is God incarnate, our sin-bearer, the conqueror of death, and the coming judge.

6. We affirm that on the cross Jesus Christ took our place, bore our sins, and died our death; and that for this reason alone God freely forgives those who are brought to repentance and faith.

7. We affirm that other religions and ideologies are not alternative paths to God, and that human spirituality, if unredeemed by Christ, leads not to God but to judgment, for Christ is the only way.

8. We affirm that we must demonstrate God's love visibly by caring for those who are deprived of justice, dignity, food, and shelter.

9. We affirm that the proclamation of God's kingdom of justice and peace demands the denunciation of all injustice and oppression, both personal and structural; we will not shrink from this prophetic witness.

10. We affirm that the Holy Spirit's witness to Christ is indispensable to evangelism, and that without his supernatural work, neither new birth nor new life is possible.

11. We affirm that spiritual warfare demands spiritual weapons, and that we must both preach the word in the power of the Spirit, and pray constantly that we may enter into Christ's victory over the principalities and powers of evil.

12. We affirm that God has committed to the whole church and every member of it the task of making Christ known throughout the world; we long to see all lay and ordained persons mobilized and trained for this task.

13. We affirm that we who claim to be members of the body of Christ must transcend within our fellowship the barriers of race, gender, and class.

14. We affirm that the gifts of the Spirit are distributed to all God's people, women and men, and that their partnership in evangelization must be welcomed for the common good.

15. We affirm that we who proclaim the gospel must exemplify it in a life of holiness and love; otherwise our testimony looses its credibility.

16. We affirm that every Christian congregation must turn itself outward to its local community in evangelistic witness and compassionate service.

17. We affirm the urgent need for churches, mission agencies, and other Christian organizations to cooperate in evangelism and social action, repudiating competition and avoiding duplication.

18. We affirm our duty to study the society in which we live, in order to understand its structures, values and, needs, and so develop an appropriate strategy of mission.

19. We affirm that world evangelization is urgent and that the reaching of unreached peoples is possible. So we resolve during the last decade of the twentieth century to give ourselves to these tasks with fresh determination.

20. We affirm our solidarity with those who suffer for the gospel, and will seek to prepare ourselves for the same possibility. We will also work for religious and political freedom everywhere.

21. We affirm that God is calling the whole church to take the whole gospel to the whole world. So we determine to proclaim it faithfully, urgently, and sacrificially, until Jesus comes.

Appendix B

God's Call to Mission

This is the outline of the statement, *God's Call to Mission:* Theological reflections, context, and principles guiding the mission strategy of Eastern Mennonite Board of Missions and Charities, which formed the basis for this book. The full 13-page booklet is available at EMM, Salunga, PA 17538.

Mission Statement
Theological Reflections on Mission

> God Creates and Calls a People for Mission
> God Lives Among This Called-out People
> God Sent Jesus, the Christ
> God's People Live Under the Rule of Christ
> God's Word Guides Us in Mission

The Context of Mission in the 1990s

> A Global Community
> A Worldwide Fellowship

Principles Guiding Our Mission Strategy
　　To Build on Jesus Christ
　　To Pray and Plan
　　To Work as Partners
　　To Develop Leaders
　　To Minister to the Whole Person
　　To Evangelize and Plant Churches
　　To Value Culture
　　To Channel Resources

Summary

Bibliography

Sources Cited in the Text

Barrett, David. *World Class Cities and World Evangelization*. Birmingham: New Hope, 1986.

Bloom, Allan. *Closing of the American Mind*. New York: Simon and Schuster, 1987.

Davies, Paul. *The Mind of God, The Scientific Basis for a Rational World*. New York: Simon and Schuster, 1992.

Engel, James F., and Norton, H. Wilbert. *What's Gone Wrong With the Harvest? A Communication Strategy for the Church and World Evangelism*. Grand Rapids: Zondervan, 1978.

Freud, Sigmund. *The Future of an Illusion*. Trans. W. D. Robson-Scott. London: The Hogarth Press, 1973.

Girard, René. *Violence and the Sacred*. Trans. Patrick Gregory, Baltimore: Johns Hopkins University Press, 1981.

Hick, John, and Paul F. Knitter, eds. *The Myth of Christian Uniqueness: Toward a Pluralistic Theology of Religions*. Maryknoll: Orbis, 1987.

Knitter, Paul F. *No Other Name? A Critical Survey of Christian Attitudes Toward the World Religions*. Maryknoll: Orbis, 1985.

Leeuwen, Arend Theodor van. *Christianity in World History: The Meet-

ing of the Faiths of East and West. Trans. H. H. Hoskins. New York: Charles Scribner's Sons, 1964.

Lindsey, Robert L. *A Hebrew Translation of the Gospel of Mark, Greek-Hebrew Diglot* (with foreword by David Flusser). Jerusalem: Dugith Publishers, 1973, and *The Jesus Sources: Understanding the Gospels.* Tulsa: Hakesher, 1990.

Newbigin, Lesslie. *Mission in Christ's Way.* New York: Friendship, 1987.

Pickthall, Muhammad M. *The Meaning of the Glorious Qur'an Text and Explanatory Translation.* New York: The Muslim World League, 1977.

Sanneh, Lamin. *Translating the Message: The Missionary Impact on Culture.* Maryknoll: Orbis, 1989.

Young, William G. *Handbook of Source Materials for Students of Church History, Up to 650 A.D.* The Christian Literature Society: Madras, 1969.

Selective Bibliography

Anderson, Gerald H., Philips, James M., Coote, Robert T., eds. *Mission in the Nineteen 90s.* Grand Rapids: Eerdmans, 1991.

Banks, Robert. *Paul's Idea of Community.* Grand Rapids: Eerdmans, 1980.

Bennis, Warren, and Nanus, Burt. *Leaders: The Strategies for Taking Charge.* New York: Harper & Row, 1985.

Bosch, David J. *Transforming Mission: Paradigm Shifts in Theology of Mission.* Maryknoll: Orbis, 1991.

Bright, John. *The Kingdom of God: The Biblical Concept and Its Meaning for the Church.* Nashville: Abingdon Press, 1983.

Carpenter, Joel A., and Wilbert R. Shenk, eds. *Earthen Vessels: American Evangelicals and Foreign Missions, 1880-1980.* Grand Rapids: Eerdmans, 1990.

Cassidy, Michael. *The Passing Summer: A South African Pilgrimage in the Politics of Love.* London: Hodder and Stoughton, 1989.

Chacour, Elias with David Hazard. *Blood Brothers.* Grand Rapids: Zondervan, 1984.

Chadwick, Henry. *The Early Church.* Baltimore: Penguin, 1975.

Chaney, Charles. *Church Planting at the End of the Twentieth Century.* Wheaton: Tyndale House Publishers, 1984.

Cho, Paul Y. *Prayer: Key to Revival.* Waco, Texas: Word Books, 1984.

Church, J. E. *Quest for the Highest: Diary of the East African Revival.* Exeter: Paternoster Press, 1981.

Claerbaut, David. *Urban Ministry.* Grand Rapids: Zondervan, 1983.

Conn, Harvie M. *Eternal Word and Changing Worlds: Theology, Anthropology, and Mission in Trialogue.* Grand Rapids: Zondervan, 1984.

Costas, Orlando E. *Christ Outside the Gate: Mission Beyond Christendom.* Maryknoll: Orbis, 1982.

Covell, Ralph R. *Confucius, the Buddha, and Christ: A History of the Gospel in Chinese.* Maryknoll: Orbis, 1986.

Cragg, Kenneth. *The Call of the Minaret.* New York: Oxford University Press, 1964.

_____. *Christianity in World Perspective.* London: Lutterworth, 1969.

_____. *To Meet and To Greet: Faith with Faith.* Westminster: Epworth Press, 1992.

Donovan, Vincent J. *Christianity Rediscovered: An Epistle from the Masai.* Notre Dame: Fides/Claretian, 1978.

Driver, John. *Kingdom Citizens.* Scottdale: Herald Press, 1980.

Ellul, Jacques. *The Presence of the Kingdom.* New York: Seabury Press, 1967.

_____. *The Subversion of Christianity.* Grand Rapids: Eerdmans, 1986.

Foster, John. *Church History: The First Advance.* London: SPCK, 1972.

Foyle, Marjory F. *Overcoming Missionary Stress,* Europe: MARC, 1984.

Global Prayer Digest. Available from U.S. Center for World Mission, 1605 Elizabeth Street, Pasadena, CA 91104.

Greenleaf, Robert K. *Servant Leadership.* New York: Paulist Press, 1977.

Greenway, Roger S., and Timothy M. Monsma. *Cities: Missions' New Frontier.* Grand Rapids: Baker House, 1989.

Hooft, W. A. Visser't. *The Fatherhood of God in an Age of Emancipation.* Geneva: WCC, 1982.

Hopler, Thom. *A World of Difference.* Downers Grove: InterVarsity Press, 1981.

Jacobs, Donald R. *Pilgrimage in Mission.* Scottdale: Herald Press, 1983.

Kateregga, Badru D., and David W. Shenk. *A Muslim and a Christian in Dialogue: Islam and Christianity.* Nairobi: Uzima, 1985.

Kealy, John P., and David W. Shenk. *The Early Church and Africa*. Nairobi: Oxford, 1973.

Koyama, Kosuke. *Mount Fuji and Mount Sinai: A Critique of Idols*. Maryknoll: Orbis, 1985.

Kraft, Charles H. *Communication Theory for Christian Witness*. Nashville: Abingdon Press, 1983.

————————. *Christianity and Culture*. Maryknoll: Orbis, 1979.

Krass, Alfred C. *Evangelizing Neopagan North America*. Scottdale: Herald Press, 1982.

Kraus, Norman C. *The Authentic Witness: Credibility and Authority*. Scottdale: Herald Press, 1979.

Kraybill, Donald B. *The Upside-Down Kingdom*. Scottdale: Herald Press, 1978, 1990.

Ladd, George Eldon. *The Gospel of the Kingdom*. Grand Rapids: Eerdmans, 1981.

Leaman, James R. *Faith Roots: Learning from and Sharing Witness with Jewish People*. Nappanee: Evangel Press, 1993.

Lind, Millard C. *Yahweh Is a Warrior*. Scottdale: Herald Press, 1980.

Mbiti, John S. *African Religions and Philosophies*. London: Heinemann, 1971.

McGavran, Donald A. *Effective Evangelism: A Theological Mandate*. Phillipsburg: Presbyterian and Reformed Publishing Co., 1988.

Meeks, Wayne. *The First Urban Christians*. New Haven: Yale University Press, 1983.

Nazir-Ali, Michael. *Islam: A Christian Perspective*. Exeter: Paternoster Press, 1983.

Neill, Stephen. *Christian Faith and Other Faiths*. London: Oxford University Press, 1970.

————————. *A History of Christian Missions*. Baltimore: Penguin, 1973.

Newbigin, Lesslie. *Foolishness to the Greeks: The Gospel and Western Culture*. Grand Rapids: Eerdmans, 1986.

————————. *The Gospel in a Pluralist Society*. Grand Rapids: Eerdmans, 1989.

————————. *Honest Religion for Secular Man*. London: SCM, 1966.

————————. *Mission in Christ's Way*. New York: Friendship Press, 1987.

Nida, Eugene A., and William D. Reyburn. *Meaning Across Cultures.* Maryknoll: Orbis, 1981.

Niebuhr, H. Richard. *Christ and Culture.* New York: Harper & Row, 1951.

Nielsen, Niels. *Revolutions in Eastern Europe: The Religious Roots.* Maryknoll: Orbis, 1991.

Operation World. Grand Rapids: Zondervan, 1993.

Parshall, Phil. *Beyond the Mosque: Christians Within Muslim Community.* Grand Rapids: Baker House, 1985.

Peck, M. Scott. *People of the Lie.* New York: Simon and Schuster, 1983.

Peters, George W. *A Biblical Theology of Missions.* Chicago: Moody Press, 1979.

Phillips, James M., and Robert T. Coote. *Toward the 21st Century in Christian Mission.* Grand Rapids: Eerdmans, 1993.

Pippert, Rebecca Manley. *Out of the Saltshaker and into the World.* Downers Grove: InterVarsity Press, 1979.

Richard, Lawrence O., and Clyde Hoeldtke. *A Theology of Church Leadership.* Grand Rapids: Zondervan.

Richardson, Don. *Eternity in Their Hearts.* Ventura, California: Regal Books, 1981.

Schaller, Lyle. *Looking in the Mirror: Self-Appraisal in the Local Church.* Nashville: Abingdon, 1984.

Schreck, Harley, and David Barrett, eds. *Unreached Peoples: Clarifying the Task.* Pasadena: MARC/World Vision, 1987.

Scott, Waldron. *Bring Forth Justice: A Contemporary Perspective on Mission.* Grand Rapids: Eerdmans, 1980.

Senior, Donald, C.P., and Carroll Stuhlmueller, C.P. *The Biblical Foundations for Mission.* Maryknoll: Orbis, 1983.

Shenk, David W., and Ervin R. Stutzman. *Creating Communities of the Kingdom: New Testament Models of Church Planting.* Scottdale: Herald Press, 1988.

Shenk, David W. *Mennonite Safari.* Scottdale: Herald Press, 1974.

───────────, *Peace and Reconciliation in Africa.* Nairobi: Uzima, 1983.

Shenk, Joseph C. *Kisare, A Mennonite of Kiseru: An Autobiography as Told to Joseph C. Shenk.* Salunga: EMBMC, 1984.

Shenk, Wilbert R., ed. *Exploring Chruch Growth.* Grand Rapids: Eerdmans, 1983.

Shenk, Wilbert R., ed. *The Transfiguration of Mission, Biblical, Theological, and Historical Foundations.* Scottdale and Waterloo: Herald Press, 1993.

Sider, Richard. *Rich Christians in an Age of Hunger.* Downers Grove: InterVarsity Press, 1982.

Stott, John R. W. *The Art of Preaching in the Twentieth Century.* Between Two Worlds, Grand Rapids: Eerdmans, 1982.

Stutzman, Ervin R. *Welcome: A Biblical and Practical Guide to Receiving New Members.* Scottdale: Herald Press, 1990.

Stutzman, Linford. *With Jesus in the World: Mission in Modern, Affluent Societies.* Scottdale: Herald Press, 1992.

Theissen, Gerd. *The Social Setting of Pauline Christianity.* Philadelphia: Fortress Press, 1982.

Tillapaugh, Frank R. *Unleashing the Church.* Ventura, California: Regal Books, 1983.

Trueblood, Elton. *The Incendiary Fellowship.* New York: Harper & Row, n.d.

_____. *The Validity of the Christian Mission.* New York: Harper & Row, 1972.

Wagner, Peter. *Your Spiritual Gifts Can Help Your Church Grow.* Ventura, California: Regal Books, 1979.

Wallis, Jim. *The Call to Conversion.* San Francisco: Harper & Row, 1981.

Yoder, John Howard. *The Original Revolution.* Scottdale: Herald Press, 1972.

Yohannan, K. P. *The Coming Revolution in World Missions.* Altamonte Springs: Creation House, 1986.

Wagner, C. Peter. *Strategies for Church Growth.* Ventura: Regal Books, 1987.

Wink, Walter. *Unmasking the Powers: The Invisible Forces that Determine Human Existence.* Philadelphia: Fortress Press, 1986.

Winter, Ralph D., and Steven C. Hawthorne, eds. *Perspectives on the World Christian Movement: A Reader.* Pasadena: William Carey Library, 1981.

The Author

David W. Shenk grew up in Tanzania, in the home of pioneer missionaries, where he was influenced by the East Africa revival. Recognizing the reality of God's grace in these mission efforts helped form his mission vision. David continues to have a deep desire to reach lost people with the gospel of salvation.

An Eastern Mennonite College graduate in biblical and social studies, David has also studied at New York University, where he earned a doctorate in anthropology and religious studies education. He has authored a half-dozen books related to church history in Africa, the gospel and culture, and the gospel and world religions.

Although David has taught elementary through graduate school (both in the U.S. and Africa), his first calling and commitment is to pastoring, especially on the frontiers of evangelism. He and his wife, K. Grace Witmer, have always served on the frontiers of church planting and formation—in mountain congregations during college years in Virginia, during two years of voluntary service in New York City as an alternative to military conscription, during their ten years in a Muslim country in Africa, and throughout six years in Nairobi.

Now in suburban Lancaster, Pennsylvania, they have also helped to pastor a congregation which experienced good growth through evangelistic outreach. Their four children—Karen, Doris, Jonathan, and Timothy—have always supported their parents in ministry.

During the 1980s and 1990s, David has been serving as director of home missions, then of overseas missions, with a Mennonite mission board. This involvement has placed him in intimate contact with scores of church formation efforts, both in North America and all the other five world continents. He lives in the experience of cross-cultural church planting.

David and Grace are members of Mountville Mennonite Church in Mountville, Pennsylvania.

LINCOLN CHRISTIAN COLLEGE AND SEMINARY

266.001
SH546G

LINCOLN CHRISTIAN COLLEGE AND SEMINARY

90807

266.01 SH546G
Shenk, David W., 1937-
God's call to mission

DEMCO

3 4711 00086 2112